W9-ATG-444

South Africa into the 1980s

WITHDRAWN

Other Titles in This Series

Apartheid and International Organizations, Richard E. Bissell

Ethnicity in Modern Africa, edited by Brian M. du Toit

Botswana: An African Growth Economy, Penelope Hartland-Thunberg

Zambia's Foreign Policy: Studies in Diplomacy and Dependence, Douglas G. Anglin and Timothy Shaw

Crisis in Zimbabwe, edited by Boniface Obichere

Westview Special Studies on Africa

South Africa into the 1980s
edited by Richard E. Bissell and Chester A. Crocker

The question of South Africa's future has become a paramount issue in global politics. This book examines the position of South Africa as it faces the 1980s—its strengths, its weaknesses, and the probable influences of other states on South Africa in the years to come.

The authors share a common interest in an analytical approach to a topic often argued with more emotion than rationality. They discuss South Africa's internal situation, with particular emphasis on the interests and aspirations of the political parties competing for power; then they focus on external realities, looking at the country's ability to project influence abroad as well as the power of others to affect events within it. In sum, they highlight crucial trends shaping South Africa's current and future development.

Richard E. Bissell is managing editor of *ORBIS* and research associate at the Foreign Policy Research Institute.

Chester A. Crocker is director of African studies at Georgetown University's Center for Strategic and International Studies and associate professor of international relations at the university's School of Foreign Service.

South Africa into the 1980s

edited by Richard E. Bissell
and Chester A. Crocker

Westview Press / Boulder, Colorado

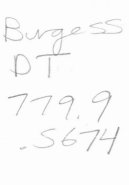

Burgess
DT
779.9
.S674

c. 1

Westview Special Studies on Africa

All rights reserved. No part of this publication may be reproduced or transmitted in any form or by any means, electronic or mechanical, including photocopy, recording, or any information storage and retrieval system, without permission in writing from the publisher.

Copyright © 1979 by Westview Press, Inc.

Published in 1979 in the United States of America by
    Westview Press, Inc.
    5500 Central Avenue
    Boulder, Colorado 80301
    Frederick A. Praeger, Publisher

Library of Congress Cataloging in Publication Data
Main entry under title:
South Africa into the 1980s.
    (Westview special studies on Africa)
    Bibliography: p.
    Includes index.
    1. South Africa—Politics and government—1961- 2. South Africa—Race rela-
tions. 3. South Africa—Foreign relations. 4. Africa, Southern—Politics and govern-
ment—1975- I. Bissell, Richard E. II. Crocker, Chester A.
DT779.9.S674   320.9'68'06   79-14152
ISBN 0-89158-373-4

Printed and bound in the United States of America

For Suzanne

and

For Saône

80-11-11 mks

Contents

Introduction

The explosion of news coverage with South African date-
lines since the April 1974 Portuguese coup d'etat has strained
the absorptive capacity of informed Americans. Lacking a historical basis of familiarity with the region or a generally accepted understanding of U.S. interest there, our society is in the
midst of an almost breathless "catch-up" operation concerning
southern Africa, and Africa more generally. News of discrete
events in this most troubled of regions is interpreted by and for
persons who have only the most limited context against which
to judge them. As a result, it seems likely that another great
debate lies ahead over the nature of the conflicts in southern
Africa, the issues at stake for the United States, and the alternatives available to policymakers and citizens. The Republic of
South Africa is the centerpiece of this debate. To date, there is
disturbing evidence that it may be shaped in substantial measure
by ignorance of that country's complexities and by the polarized emotions that South Africa so readily generates. Given the
absence of consensus on basic foreign policy premises in the
United States, the South Africa debate in the 1980s could
develop into a major testing ground of American purposes more
broadly.

The purpose of this book is to explore critical trends,
patterns, and underlying relationships that are sufficiently
durable to provide a basis for considering South Africa's development as we enter the 1980s. The volume is not intended to
be a definitive or comprehensive contemporary analysis of the
South African system. Its scope is far from encyclopedic in that

the emphasis lies on the political dimension of South African development. At the same time, it ranges well beyond the primarily domestic focus of a one-country study to address the complex external environment in which the republic's white and black elites will have to function. In planning the volume, the editors envisaged a need for analytic thinking about the realities of power, influence, bargaining, and conflict that appear most likely to shape the actual course of events in and around South Africa in the coming period. Accordingly, the contributors were not selected in order to achieve homogeneity of ideological orientation, nor were they asked to draw conclusions for policymakers in their chapters.

South Africa into the 1980s seeks to move away from current headlines in order to establish some elements of the bigger picture. Long-time observers of African affairs are only too well aware of the pitfalls of casual or speculative prediction. Moreover, the methodological and conceptual obstacles to rigorous forecasting in this arena are awesome to contemplate. With hindsight, one can point to a number of foolhardy assessments of South Africa's imminent violent transformation in the wake of the Sharpeville tragedy, in which some seventy-two unarmed Africans were killed by police gunfire nearly two decades ago. Today, voices are again being raised suggesting that the white-dominated system will collapse within a few years under the onslaught of African nationalist pressures. Set against these prophecies of apocalypse is the conventional wisdom of the late 1960s and early 1970s that so readily dismissed the prospects of revolutionary change in the former Portuguese territories and Rhodesia just a few short years before such change came to a head. Other assessments—about the capacity of Afrikanerdom to redirect or crush the majoritarian ("one man–one vote") ideal or, alternatively, about the inherent illegitimacy of black leadership in the government-sponsored Bantu homelands (Bantustans)—stand as testimony to the risks of prediction.

The essays in this book provide background material, analysis of contemporary factors deemed most salient for each topic, and a modest forward projection. Our intent is to shed light on factors influencing the policies and perceptions of various actors as South Africa enters the 1980s. We make no pretense—and it would surely have to be pretense—of offering a prediction of South African developments ten years hence. In the case of several chapters, the author's task was to evaluate alternative sets of conclusions about recent events and to derive implications for the years immediately ahead.

In organizing the volume, the editors were painfully aware of the artificiality of devising neat and crisp divisions between the various factors shaping South African reality. The momentum of the conflict for power in South Africa points to continued and perhaps increased linkage between domestic, subregional, African, and international influences. The time has surely passed when the action of any local or external party could effectively buffer the republic from broader rivalries and conflicts. On the other hand, it is premature to conclude that any one racial or political group, state, or group of states will be capable of seizing decisive initiative from the others. To take but one example, the process and direction of change in the Rhodesia/Zimbabwe conflict has been monopolized by no single actor. Yet South African interests and options are certain to be influenced in significant measure by what transpires just across its borders.

The first part of the book focuses on internal South African dynamics and local views of relationships in the immediate southern African region as change unfolds in Namibia and Rhodesia/Zimbabwe. The second part focuses on the regional military balance and linkages between South Africa and the "external" context of African states, the Communist powers, and the Western industrial powers. The reader is exhorted not to attach great importance to the sequence of chapters, except to note the growing impossibility of precise conceptual distinctions between internal, regional, and external dimensions of South Africa's future development.

The book ends with an essay on the nature of the "South African issue" in the 1980s in which the editors discuss aspects of the domestic, global, and African climate that are likely to shape our thinking about South Africa in the coming period. Like the other chapters in this book, the conclusion is designed to provide provocative, future-oriented thinking about South Africa. However tentative the conclusions and projections offered in these pages, the book will have served its purpose if it encourages others to join us in addressing the underlying forces at work in the republic.

The Contributors

John Seiler is associate research fellow at the Center for Strategic and International Studies, Georgetown University, and is conducting research on the South African response to external pressure. He has published in numerous journals on South African political development and taught political science at Rhodes University, Grahamstown, from 1972 to 1977.

Steven F. McDonald, educated in Missouri and at the University of London, served until recently as a Foreign Service officer, having held posts in Pretoria and Kampala.

Roy Godson is associate professor of government and director of the International Labor Program at Georgetown University. He is the author of *American Labor and European Politics, The Kremlin and Labor*, and other works focusing on the interrelationship between government and nongovernment forces across state boundaries.

Chester A. Crocker is director of African studies at the Center for Strategic and International Studies, as well as associate professor at the School of Foreign Service, Georgetown University. He is the author of numerous articles and monographs on southern African politics and African military and international issues.

I. William Zartman is professor of politics and former department head at New York University. He is the author of *Interna-*

tional Politics in the New Africa, as well as other books and articles on Africa.

W. Scott Thompson is associate professor of politics at the Fletcher School of Law and Diplomacy, Tufts University. He is the author of *Ghana's Foreign Policy, 1957-1966*, and the editor of *The Third World: Myths and Realities*, as well as other books.

Brett Silvers received his B.A. from Yale and is completing his Ph.D. at the Fletcher School of Law and Diplomacy.

Bruce J. Oudes is an independent journalist specializing in African affairs and widely published in the United States and Britain. He is the author of *Small Countries Are a Nuisance*, a study of U.S. policy in Africa.

Lawrence G. Franko, currently coholder of the U.S. Professorship of the Corporation and Society, Center for Education in International Management (CEI), Geneva, is former director of the Project on American Policy and European Economic Interests at the Carnegie Endowment for International Peace.

Richard E. Bissell is managing editor of *ORBIS* and visiting professor of political science at Temple University. He is the author of *Apartheid and International Organizations*, as well as numerous articles on African international politics.

Part 1
Internal Dynamics
and Sources of Change

1
The Afrikaner
Nationalist Perspective

John Seiler

For the foreseeable future, the central fact of South African political life will be the effective domination of all political institutions by Afrikaner nationalism. Since the November 1977 parliamentary elections, the standing and prospects of white opposition parties have reached a historical low point. As external and internal pressures increase, South African whites are likely to become even more supportive of the National party (NP) government and more willing to accept repression of black and white dissent at home and assertive military steps in the region.

Whatever change comes in South Africa—short of a prolonged civil war augmented by external invasion—will be defined by Afrikaner nationalist perceptions, shaped by Afrikaner nationalist interests, and processed by institutions monopolized by Afrikaner nationalists. Thus any effort to measure the likelihood and character of change emanating from white South Africans must be, in the final analysis, an assessment of Afrikaner nationalist perceptions, interests, and institutional behavior.

The Role of White Perspectives and Attitudes

The ruling National party does not function in a vacuum. To the contrary, it is remarkably sensitive to Afrikaner political and economic interests, most especially the overriding preoccupation of many Afrikaners (too often associated only and over-narrowly with *verkrampte,* or very conservative, individuals) that

Afrikaner communal identity or even its survival will be at risk if too many concessions are made to pressures for change initiated outside Afrikaner nationalist circles. National party interest in non-Afrikaner support is another matter altogether. Only intermittently, but clearly more often since the 1974 Portuguese coup with its repercussions for increased regional instability, the South African government has actively sought support from non-Afrikaner whites (and even from Coloureds, Indians, and blacks). At a rhetorical and conceptual level, the term "Anglo-Afrikaner nation" is used to suggest a coherent group distinct from and functioning vis-à-vis the other officially sanctioned "nations" within South Africa: Coloureds, Indians, Zulu, Xhosa, Tswana, Sotho, Shangaan, Vemda, et al. In practice, the government still does very little—except coincidentally via shared training and active service requirements in the South African Defense Force—to carry out the implications of a single white community. Only one English-speaking white holds a cabinet post—Senator Owen Horwood, minister of finance. Most top-level civil service posts are held by Afrikaners. Non-Afrikaner whites (including a substantial Jewish community and relatively small numbers of Portuguese, Greek, and other groups) are asked to support government policies, but because Afrikaner nationalist distrust of non-Afrikaners remains very strong, they can only hope for a passive, supportive role. Whether by calculation or instinct, the government will probably succeed in this policy, since most whites find government policy—especially its foreign and security policies—increasingly attractive and seem likely to continue their support.

Because the perceived attitudes of its Afrikaner nationalist constituents are the key to South African government policy-making, clues to the direction and limits of policy change lie in shifts in the strikingly narrow range of these attitudes. To be fair, this range (as measured by opinion surveys) encompasses a growing willingness to accept Coloureds as full members of the Afrikaner political community and to make major concessions in social-economic (but not political) matters to blacks. The "gamut" of views held by National party leadership runs from the "accommodationist" position held by Piet Koornhof and

R. F. (Pik) Botha to the "dogmatic" position espoused by Andries Treurnicht. Koornhof and Botha, along with some number of their cabinet colleagues, seem willing to consider major adaptations in existent policies in order to reduce or at least to mitigate international and domestic pressure bearing on the government. At the other extreme, Treurnicht represents a growing sector that believes that even marginal policy changes —the opening of the Nico Malan Theatre to nonwhites, extensive interracial athletic competition—will lead inevitably to a profound dilution of the central elements of separate development policy and, in time, to the dissolution of Afrikaner integrity. Despite these significant differences, aired often vehemently in the Afrikaans press and apparently growing in intensity, both the "accommodationists" and the "dogmatists" share a profound commitment to the dual causes of Afrikaner communal identity and ethnically based political development. Given this commitment, their differences remain tactical and should not be interpreted as symptomatic of polarization or even disintegration of Afrikanerdom.

To buttress their own underlying commitments, Afrikaner nationalist leaders share a peculiar political myth: they construe their constituents to be far more conservative than themselves, what is sometimes called *verkrampte* (inwardturning, stubbornly resistant to change), in polar opposition to *verligte* (enlightened, open to change). Frequent opinion polls belie this conviction, but it remains the dominant constraint to policy change among both cabinet members and National party parliamentarians. For those leaders with *verligte* instincts, their efforts to adjust policies require persuasion of their own colleagues, then the NP parliamentary caucus, and finally prominent Afrikaner nationalists outside of government so that this mythical Afrikaner constituency will not somehow rise in wrath and disown the government. As a reflection of this unrealistic appraisal, those few Afrikaner institutions with genuinely *verkrampte* attitudes —especially the white miners union—get far more attention than their numbers justify. In any case, even if the government were willing to take into account the implications of opinion surveys, its members are profoundly committed to separate development, certainly in the political realm, almost as clearly in the social realm, and more ambiguously (given the interdependent nature of the South African economy) in the economic realm.

The Concept of Change in Afrikaner Nationalist Politics

Anglo-American political thought gives centrality to the articulation of political differences through political parties and to their resolution in peaceful electoral competition. Thus, conflicting values are at least accepted as inescapable, with emphasis put instead on the processes by which they are resolved or mitigated. Very few white South Africans hold to this faith. Afrikaner nationalists were prepared to use democratic electoral processes to achieve political power, but since 1948, despite a strong lingering regard for the independence of the judiciary, the press, and the universities, they have responded bluntly to repress any opposition to their continued domination. In the decade or so after World War II, liberal democratic values were relatively widespread among English-speaking whites, but the rapid decline of effective political opposition after the NP victory in 1948 shrunk their ranks and left the few survivors embittered and apolitical. Now, most South African English-speaking whites, without referring to any cogent political philosophy, prefer a benign politics wherein conflict is resolved by executive mandate and their own interests are protected. Their institutions—family, schools, churches—all support deference to and respect for established authority. Neither social nor political conflict is encouraged. Each is seen as distasteful, lacking in civility, when not actually a threat to social and civil order.

For most Afrikaners, this pattern of deference and loyalty to established authority takes on a more rigorous (and, some observers would say, ideological) form. Despite its antidemocratic implications, it is justified as democratic, because it provides distinct realms for independent activity for family, school, church, and government, under the overarching rubric of religious and ethnic loyalty. In practice, since 1948 and even before, the National party has most often defined and effectively constrained the range of freedom available to each of these social realms. Although public criticism of government policy has become increasingly acceptable—in Afrikaans newspapers, but not in the English-language papers more critical of the government—and stringent, although imprecise limits still exist on the extent and maintenance of such criticism. The professional and social ostracism heaped on Professor Willem Kleynhans and Rev. Beyers Naudé are classic cases from two decades ago. The very recent instances involving Gerhard Tötemeyer at Stellenbosch University and Professor J. D. van der Vyver at Potchefstroom University demonstrate that the pressures toward conformity are as strong as ever.

In any case, for most Afrikaners the widespread international discussion about what might serve as acceptable change in South Africa has neither significance nor relevance. For them, the policy of separate development is the only acceptable platform for change, a process that most of them believe has been occurring in a sustained way at least since Dr. Hendrik Verwoerd announced twenty years ago the eventual independence of black homelands. The 1961 declaration of the republic was another crucial step in this evolving process. Whatever differences they may have among themselves about particular points in the process, they have faith that the basic changes implied in separate development will continue for the foreseeable future. Pressure from outside Afrikanerdom is either not acknowledged at all or (a newer trend) interpreted as misinformed or even evil in intent, and hence not to be taken into account. "Conflict" has no constructive role in this change process, although its existence even among Afrikaners becomes increasingly difficult to deny. When it becomes necessary to note basic changes in policy, the impact of present or potential pressure is not acknowledged and often not perceived. Instead, the government and the media (even the opposition newspapers) talk blithely of new "dispensations," without any awareness of the authoritarian history of the term.

Proposals for Basic Change from Non-Afrikaners

Against this background, the continued Afrikaner nationalist negative attitude about proposals for basic change emanating from non-Afrikaner sources should be more comprehensible. It is true that some immeasurable shift has taken place since the National party's confidence about its political primacy increased from the early 1950s to the peak of confidence achieved toward the end of the 1960s. It may even be that the massive electoral victory of November 1977 has given P. W. Botha's new government confidence enough not only to assess more dispassionately such proposals, but even to acknowledge their import for subsequent policy changes. Nonetheless, long-term evidence to the contrary cannot be ignored.

There has been a plethora of recommendations for basic social change from non-Afrikaner sources, including opposition political parties, English-language newspapers, academicians at English-language universities, businessmen and business organizations, church leaders and church organizations, and (most conspicuously) the South African Institute for Race Relations, the Christian Institute of South Africa, and the National Union of South African Students.

Although generally unenthusiastic about all such recommendations, the government has always given at least modest attention to the moderate opposition parties—first, the United party, and now its successor fragment, the New Republic party. At the same time, proposals from the Progressive party and its successors—the Progressive Reform party and the current Progressive Federal party—get scathing public comment. More than anything else, this probably reflects NP sentiment that moderate opposition can be converted to NP support, something borne out by the November 1977 elections, whereas "liberal" opposition (South African liberals are usually considerably to the right of their U.S. counterparts) represents a latent threat to the survival of Afrikanerdom.

Business interests get attention on relatively narrow matters affecting their own well-being and profitability. Their public criticisms of underlying government policies are usually muted, and on one of the rare occasions when a predominantly English business group entertained a discussion generally critical of the government, Prime Minister Vorster himself bluntly warned its conferees that they took a grave risk in going beyond the boundaries of acceptable discourse.

Proposals from other non-Afrikaner sources get even less consideration, because the government sees the organizations involved as influential with blacks and potentially disruptive of racial harmony. The *Rand Daily Mail* and to a lesser extent the *Star* (Johannesburg) are national newspapers with substantial black readership. Some churches have black members and even in a few instances black leadership. The South African Institute for Race Relations has in its long history consistently endorsed a liberal approach to racial policy and actively encouraged black participation and leadership. More recently, the Christian Institute of South Africa (proscribed from further operation in October 1977), led by Beyers Naudé, took an even stronger position in opposition to racial policies. The government has often rebuked these organizations, sometimes warned them of unspecified greater hazards, and finally resorted to banning individual leaders and staff. In understandable response to the debilitating impact of this government attitude, most English-speaking critics have become extraordinarily cautious about both their criticism of present policy and their advocacy of alternative policies.

The irony is that almost all proposals originating from non-Afrikaner sources in the past fifteen years have been strikingly moderate, even conservative, in their assumptions, goals, and timetables. In addition, perhaps to ease an expected negative reaction from the government, most have been narrowly focused rather than all-inclusive in nature. Throughout this entire period, only the National Union of South African Students called for the rapid dismantling of separate development, a position that never gained support either among university students or the wider white population. For the rest, the most "radical" position was adopted by the Liberal party in its call for a qualified nonracial franchise. After the dissolution of the Liberal party under the terms of the Interference in Politics Act of 1964, because it had both white and black members, its successor, the Progressive party, adopted the same position. The general posture was distinctly ameliorative, in the hope that gradual political change would satisfy blacks while at the same time protecting established white political and economic interests.

A very good example of inherent moderation and disproportionate official reaction lies in the report of the Study Project
on Christianity in Apartheid Society (Spro-cas), sponsored by
the Christian Institute of South Africa. Its political commission,
composed of thirteen distinguished members, some nonnation-
alist Afrikaners and others English-speaking, met occasionally
from August 1969 until February 1971. Its report was drafted
during 1972 and published in 1973.[1]

With strikingly lucid organization and style, the report
attacked the ethical and functional underpinnings of separate
development policy as actually implemented by the South
African government. Then, it examined the implications of
South Africa's "divided plural society" and concluded that
alternatives to the Westminster system—including consociational
models utilized in some smaller Western European countries—
deserved more attention. Without forcing specific political
preferences onto its readers, the commission argued for a
number of transitional steps that it believed took into account
both the demands of justice and the complexities of South
African society.[2]

The government's reaction was frosty. In turn, the Christian
Institute of South Africa felt impelled to take a more aggressive
approach in the encouragement of social change. In its next
project, Spro-cas II, it sharply and often wildly attacked the
government, characterizing it as fascist and evil. It was an
approach unlikely to win support even from critics of government policy, so there was relatively little public sympathy to
the institute when the government first cut off its access to
foreign financial contributions and then in October 1977 ended
its activities and banned Beyers Naudé.

Recently, the report of the first project has become ironically
relevant to the burgeoning public discussion of political alternatives to the Westminster system. In 1974 and 1975, consoci-
ationalism was taken up with more enthusiasm than insight by a
number of Afrikaner scholars. It was then given wider credence
by a cabinet committee headed by P. W. Botha, which recommended as one beginning step the Council of Cabinets—linking
white, Coloured, and Indian executive bodies—whose full implementation is not yet completed. By the end of 1978, con-

sociationalism was the rubric for most discussion in Afrikaner media and scholarly circles about South Africa's political future. Abstruse and increasingly accurate references are made to the detailed operations of Swiss cantons, to cultural accommodation in the Netherlands, and other such examples.[3] In all this current enthusiasm, which is unlikely to fade, no retrospective thanks have been extended to Spro-cas for initially raising the prospective relevance of this political approach.

The same intrinsic moderation dominates the 1978 constitutional plan offered to the white electorate and to any interested blacks by the Progressive Federal party (PFP). Drafted by a committee chaired by PFP parliamentarian Frederic van Zyl Slabbert, a former sociology professor, the PFP plan does move away from the concept of a qualified franchise, at least by implication accepting the fait accompli of universal adult suffrage now common in black homelands. It holds to the long-honored liberal South African call for a national convention to adopt a basic constitutional framework, but even here it is cautious in its insistence that participation would be denied groups "which advocate or use violence or subversion." Reflecting a growing abhorrence among whites of the black nationalist resort to violence, what whites inevitably see as "terrorism," the PFP plan is ambiguous about the status of the South African National Congress and the Pan-Africanist Congress, which are presently committed to the use of force. In any case, the National party has repeatedly dismissed the argument for a national convention, arguing that sufficient consultative mechanisms already exist to resolve any important problems and that under no circumstances will the political future of the Afrikaner community be determined in any context other than that of Afrikaner institutions.[4]

Given this profound disparity in perspective, it is unlikely the NP would even focus attentively on the specific proposals that the PFP would make to a national convention, once called. Among other things, these would entail strong regional states and a weak central government within a federal structure. Although not explicitly acknowledged, it seems apparent that the PFP proposals would take into account ethnicity in the determination of state boundaries, although rationalization for enhanced effectiveness would be a high priority. Still another feature would be proportional representation in the federal executive, reflecting the distribution of seats in the federal legislature, and a blocking veto of 10 to 15 percent in both the federal cabinet and legislature (except on appropriations for existing programs). On the whole, these steps would make major social-economic change exceptionally difficult, while simultaneously providing considerable political devolution. In addition, the judiciary would be responsible for the protection of both individual and state rights, a feature carried over from the U.S. Constitution, but often denounced by Afrikaner scholars and jurists as irrelevant to the Dutch-Roman legal tradition on which much of South African law is founded.

Over the next decade, some of these proposals will probably become more attractive to Afrikaner nationalists, although they are unlikely to acknowledge the PFP initiative in presenting them. P. W. Botha has already suggested that homeland consolidation may be appropriate. That process might entail a dilution of the principle of ethnic-based homelands, in a way approaching the PFP model for states. The idea of a blocking veto in multiracial political settings is one already discussed for South-West Africa/Namibia by the Democratic Turnhalle Alliance (DTA). It might become useful for a functionally expanded Council of Cabinets. But the notion of a weak central government runs against the grain of Afrikaner institutional development, and it is very difficult to imagine its being endorsed, except in circumstances of very harsh international and domestic pressures.

The Parameters of Change
As Seen by Afrikaner Nationalists

The centrality of ethnicity is the common element in all the proposals for policy evolution and change that emanate from Afrikaner nationalist sources. Nowadays, disagreement occurs often about specific details and the pace of policy development, but the underlying commitment to Afrikaner communal identity and to ethnicity as the basis for South African politics remains constant.

Government policy toward both rural and urban blacks reflects this commitment. The ethnic connection between rural and urban blacks gets great attention, whereas the growing community of class-based interests among urban blacks—cutting across ethnic lines—has been until very recently largely ignored. The long-term political future of blacks lies either in or (for those urban blacks whose labor services to whites make them indispensable) vis-à-vis their ethnic homelands. They must be homeland citizens, whether or not their homelands accept the South African offer of political independence.

For that minority of South African blacks actually resident in homelands, some marginal compensations have emerged. Homeland administrations led by black ministers (although often staffed largely by Afrikaner civil servants seconded from Pretoria) have ended some of the oppressive features of life under direct South African governance. Legal segregation has often ended, although de facto segregation usually continues in housing, schooling, and social life. Education in Afrikaans, a hated symbolic feature of Bantu education, has ended in some homelands, with some combination of the local language and English used instead. Substantial South African budgetary subsidies and capital development programs have provided employment and built an embryonic civil servant–teacher middle class. On the other hand, the political style of the new black leaders is often harsh and authoritarian.

For urban blacks, homeland development has given no benefits. Only since the urban riots that began in Soweto in June 1976 has the government slowly reexamined the situation of urban blacks. Modest but significant changes have taken place. Efforts will be made to improve the quality of teaching in black schools, although the government's insistence that these schools be staffed almost entirely by black teachers even now when too few black teachers have adequate training reflects a stubborn commitment to ethnicity over priorities of quality education. Black businessmen have been encouraged by various changes in legislation to make larger and more diversified financial commitments, although in practice few have the capital to do so. Finally, long leases are being made available to black house owners to provide them with effective stability, despite the continued implacable refusal of the government to permit black land ownership in white South Africa. There are even hints from official circles that concern about building a black middle class will lead the government to make further concessions to urban black community councils set up under recent legislation but given only limited administrative authority. Whatever the nature of these potential concessions, it seems likely that their political range will be narrow and in some way linked to homeland political systems.

The circumstances of black industrial labor also gets considerable attention from the government. Now acknowledging finally that reliance on black labor cannot be ended (it was once popular in conservative Afrikaner circles to talk of ending all use of black labor by some combination of sophisticated machinery and primitive self-reliance), the government searches for ways to assure both supply stability and labor's social stability. Although the government believes influx control to be essential, it dislikes the stigma its administration of pass laws gives it internationally, and it has apparently persuaded some homelands to adminster travel documents that would effectively serve to constrain the movement of blacks from rural areas to industrial centers. Opposition concern with Crossroads and other settlements where black workers illegally keep their families gets only grudging response from the government, which, by and large, prefers the course of having most black workers reside in conveniently demarcated homelands so that they can commute daily to work in major urban centers. This works well for Pretoria, Durban, and East London, although it forces on the homeland governments the multiplicity of social problems that would otherwise be the direct responsibility of the South African government. The quirks of geography make such a solution infeasible for Johannesburg, Port Elizabeth, and Cape Town, as well as for a larger number of smaller black townships situated adjacent to white towns throughout white South Africa.

Involvement of black workers in industry-wide collective bargaining is not desired by either government or most businesses. If it comes, either voluntarily by government acceptance of a recommendation from the pending Wiehahn Commission on black labor or later in tacit response to pressure from Western governments, it almost certainly will contain two basic constraints. First, no overarching national organizations of black workers will be permitted to engage in collective bargaining. At the industry-wide level, limits on legal strikes and the overwhelming leverage employers have over workers (because of the large numbers of unemployed blacks and the absence of required union membership) will be influenced by black labor. Second, in some way, black unions will be tied to homeland governments, thus diffusing their potential power and, when necessary, providing a mechanism for playing off homelands against one another.

Finally, as the immediate result of Prime Minister Botha's January 1979 announcement about reexamination of homeland consolidation, a commission will begin an analysis of that underlying determinant of homeland viability and attractiveness. Although the government initiative is encouraging, it is unlikely that any early steps will result.

Official policy toward the Coloured and Indian communities has taken a very different channel, but the same Afrikaner preoccupation with Afrikaner survival and ethnicity dominates. First, in regard to the Coloureds, the government made abundantly clear in its reaction to the report of the Theron Commission that it would not accept the eventual political integration proferred by the commission. At the same time, less explicitly, it finally rejected the demand often made by both *verligte* and *verkrampte* Afrikaners for a Coloured homeland. The Coloureds would continue to be cast as close, but junior relations, sharing language and religion, deeply imbedded in Cape Province's economy, but not permitted to share common political institutions.

In 1977, P. W. Botha's special cabinet committee on South Africa's constitutional future recommended that a Council of Cabinets be established including the white, Coloured, and Indian executive bodies to deal with matters of common concern. In theory, the council would rest on the legislative actions taken by the House of Assembly, the Coloured Representative Council (CRC), and the Indian Representative Council (IRC). Its collective executive role would be controlled by the appointment of an executive president whose powers would be considerably greater than those of the present state president, the House of Assembly having 50 percent of the votes toward his election.

This approach still faces several basic barriers. First, it does not have general approval from the CRC and the IRC, much less from the broader Coloured and Indian communities, which tend to see the two councils as ineffective instruments of National party policy. Second, no apparent progress has been made in defining the functional responsibilities of the proposed council in a way that would make it powerful (and hence attractive to Coloureds and Indians) without seeming threatening to South African whites. Third, and probably most important at this present stage in nationalist politics, statutory provisions for a strengthened executive president do not have much chance of being presented to the House of Assembly, because the incumbent state president, John Vorster, has lost considerable support among NP parliamentarians and rank-and-file NP members for his ambiguous role in the still unfolding Information Department scandal.

Long-Term Plan or Ad Hoc Reactions?

The overall pattern of policy evolution poses a perplexing contradiction. On the one hand, Afrikaner nationalists share a general view of the political future toward which their policies aim. Southern Africa would be composed of a number of fully independent states, of which white South Africa would be one, the independent homelands—Botswana, Lesotho, and Swaziland, and now Namibia—among the others. White South Africa's economic preponderance in this region would ensure economic and political stability, providing of course that other regional governments shared the same view of self- and regional interests put forth by South Africa. Consultations among these governments would be necessary. These could be ad hoc, or at most they might be structured formally into a confederal arrangement, with very limited functions and powers at the center—mostly of an economic-scientific/technical-cultural sort.

How to move toward this eventual goal produces basic disagreement among Afrikaner nationalists. The pragmatists, more attentive to the maintenance of present power and perhaps less optimistic about the feasibility of the long-term goal, monopolize official decision making. They proceed in paths that zig and zag, for the most part firmly attached to principles of separate development (although in the peripheral area of sports policy, it might be argued that the language of "inter-national" competition disguises the reality of desegregated, if not altogether integrated, competition), making policy aloof from public or media scrutiny (at least until they wish to announce new "dispensations" or to suggest the possibility of them, in order to placate foreign critics or more often nowadays black moderates within South Africa).

On the other hand, the dogmatists paradoxically address themselves more coherently to the longer-term implications of separate development policy. Blacks must be removed from squatter communities in white South Africa. Homeland political development and even consolidation must be facilitated, despite obvious financial burdens to the white electorate. Their time frame is shorter and their sense of urgency greater than those of the pragmatists.

To further complicate the pattern of policy implementation, bureaucratic inertia, especially in the Department of Plural Relations, which deals with blacks, remains strikingly resistant to ministerial control—assuming, of course, that efforts at control are made. To cite just two recent important examples: reform of urban black education, a burning issue in the June 1976 Soweto riots, had been reviewed in a nominal way within the Department of Bantu Education since at least early 1975; electrification of Soweto, accepted in principle by the government as a useful step to ease household pressures after those same riots, had not yet begun in early 1979, despite the offer of major lending facilities by four South African banks as early as the first months of 1977.

There are some embryonic signs that more coherent planning may be imposed on government policies. In regard to urban blacks, a cabinet committee chaired by the minister of plural relations was set up early in 1978 to better articulate and co-ordinate policy that inevitably involves a number of ministerial areas of responsibility. That committee may find itself seeking connections between its policy domain and that for Coloureds and Indians. From a very different official vantage point, the South African Defense Force is already and will become an even more potent focal point for "functional moderation" in policies that affect, directly or indirectly, its growing dependence on nonwhite soldiers and on nonwhite industrial workers to sustain military equipment requirements. Much less important, although of some value when in consonance with governmental inclinations, South African corporations, working individually and via the Urban Foundation and various business groups, will probably give marginally greater attention to ameliorative steps that they can carry out themselves. They are unlikely to have much impact on the broad lines of government policy.

Some basic directions are highly improbable. Liberalization of domestic policies is most improbable. Power sharing in a unitary government for all of South Africa has no prospect of achievement by peaceful means. Partition, as defined in international discussions of South Africa's future, with its central implication that the residual white state would forsake all its political-economic influence over its black neighbors, is implausible. Neither white South Africa nor the nascent black states on its periphery would want this. Put another way, neither believe that Western governments would provide the alternative economic support required to sustain even that minimal level of development now possible by way of South African public aid and private investment.

Thus, barring a major international intervention, by way of sustained full-scale economic sanctions or conventional invasion, the South African government will continue its present pattern of policy. The rhetoric of international opposition and the low-level military challenges it now faces at its borders and sporadically in its cities have so far only hardened its commitment to separate development as the best road to both its own communal survival and reasonable regional stability. Assuming only that Afrikaner nationalism can hold together as the implications of the Information Department scandal become more clear in 1979, there is no other reason to doubt the loyalty of

Afrikaner nationalists to their present policy and to their present political leadership and institutions.

Notes

1. *South Africa's Political Alternatives*, Report of the Political Commission of the Study Project on Christianity in Apartheid Society, Sprocas Publication no. 10 (Johannesburg: Ravan Press, 1973).

2. Ibid., especially chapters 9-13.

3. *Financial Mail*, August 18, 1978, p. 596.

4. *Financial Mail*, October 27, 1978, pp. 298-99; and Ken Owen, in *Sunday Times*, October 29, 1978.

2
The Black Community

Steven F. McDonald

It takes a cheeky person—to use a term that is in popular use in South Africa, particularly as it relates to a black person who seeks to maintain his dignity in face of the dehumanizing system that he faces day to day—to attempt to deal academically with the subject of a society to which he or she does not belong. There is little doubt that a white person writing about blacks, their aspirations, desires, and frustrations, is presumptuous. More importantly that person generally makes the mistake of addressing a world whose nucleus must escape him. The author's vision may be clear, his intentions good, and his experience significant, but of necessity he knows only a periphery and the glimpses he has of that vibrant center are brief and ephemeral. I accept this limitation and valid criticism. Yet, I have agreed to attempt to give some insight into the black South African community. This is because I feel that the story of black South Africa is given little exposure overseas by objective observers. Furthermore, this story is vitally necessary to the understanding of the South African situation, just as the history and motivation of the Afrikaner are necessary. Therefore, any attempt, however limited, to add to the historiography and to first-hand testimony cannot but be valuable to the struggle of black South Africa. Black consciousness spokespersons have disparaged whites who patronizingly presume to speak for blacks. I agree; however, I do not claim to speak for blacks, only to reflect what I have seen and learned from my associations in southern Africa. I hope it adds something to world understanding of this volatile situation.

Black South Africa, although it doesn't often like to admit it, is a disunified and unhomogeneous whole. By way of explanation, this reference is not to the well-known and often overdrawn divisions between blacks (Africans), Coloureds, and Indians as defined by South African law. These three communities often have different and even conflicting perspectives, interests, and goals. The differences are to a great extent created by the system and are certainly reinforced by it. They are real, however. The Coloured and Indian communities, particularly the former, often feel closer to the white than black. They have a privileged position compared to blacks that they would like to maintain. Indians may look at Africa and despair at the often brutal treatment of Indian communities elsewhere. These differences are well documented academically and are the basis of much of the South African government policy toward the communities. I believe, however, in the long run these communities will find, for the most part, a coincidence of interests as outcast groups from the political power structure. Many young persons in their ranks seem to have already realized this and will probably not seek to create major divisions within black South Africa. Also, one of the tenets of recent black consciousness philosophy is that "black" represents all those peoples who have been oppressed by the white authority of South Africa.

Whatever the truth of this logic, the fact is that the Coloured and Indian communities are periphery groups to the drama of South Africa being played out between African and white. Therefore, these two groups will be forced to choose their future alliances one day. Although the temptation to move toward the white structure, made more tantalizing by the new constitutional proposals scheduled to be brought before the white Parliament in 1979, is great, the trend amongst the young and politicized Coloured and Indian is to side against the nonblack minority that still wraps itself in a closed political system. Whichever allegiance they choose, however, the Coloured and Indian will not be major players on the stage of South African history. For these reasons, "black," when used in this essay, will refer to members of all three groups, although the black African is the dominant player. Where interests deviate enough for special mention, the division by ethnic group will be identified.

Therefore, the divisions and disunity mentioned above refer to the entire black community. They are based on regional, educational, cultural, sociological, and generational factors. Although there are certain similarities in outlook and experience throughout black South Africa and certain eventual goals that are often universally agreed upon, the thoughtful observer must always keep in mind the differences.

Why? The view of an eighteen-year-old urban student who over the last two years has spent fourteen months in detention, without charge or trial and often under brutal conditions, is going to differ radically from an uneducated tenant or traditional homeland farmer whose most pressing problem is the care and feeding of his three wives and ten children. Not so obvious will be the difference in views between the student and government-accepted black leadership figures, such as homeland leaders, township Community Council members, or prominent businessmen, all of whom may purport to share the student's goals and outwardly seem in sympathy and agreement. Still less obvious, but just as real, will be the difference between the student's feelings and the generally nonviolent, but certainly radical views of genuine black community leadership, epitomized by crusading journalists, active community figures like doctors, church and labor leaders, social workers, and some of the moderate Black Consciousness Movement leaders. After all of this, however, we will find that the student does not represent the leftmost point of our political spectrum. There are underground groups and/or groups leaning toward violence, some flowing from the now banned black consciousness organizations and some based on or involved with the known black liberation groups based externally, the African National Congress (ANC) and the Pan African Congress (PAC).

In the course of this essay, these differences in outlook will be reiterated and often expanded. However, this introductory caution is deemed necessary because too often the interested observer is bombarded by black "spokespersons" from South Africa and, depending upon who these people are and by whom they are sponsored, the observer can come away believing that "the revolution" is imminent or, by way of contrast, that the

South African government is addressing the most pressing grievances of blacks and time is all that is needed. Neither of these extremes represents the whole picture, but together they account for the confusion often felt by concerned observers. Noting the divisions within the black community explains why this confusing situation can occur when the same system is praised on the one hand and condemned on the other by members of the race group who are supposedly oppressed by it. Emphasizing these differences, as I have done, leads one to the logical and correct conclusion that there has been no great unity of action throughout the history of black nationalism in South Africa. Organizational efforts have been relatively easy to nip in the bud not only due to South Africa's massive and effective security machinery, but also to the crosscurrents that run through black aspirations and goals. These crosscurrents and the black attempts to deal with them constitute the theme of this essay.

Background

Much has been written on separate development as an ideology and functioning political system. The premises of it are simple. Blacks are members of various "national" groups, each one analogous to the white "nation." These various nations desire self-determination and self-rule, without which it can only be expected that they will compete for dominance over and subjugation of each other. To avoid embroiling South Africa in such a bitter struggle, it is necessary to demarcate geographic areas in which each group will reside and to give that group political hegemony there and no political rights elsewhere. Although blacks must be excluded politically from white areas, it is their "right" to seek employment, and temporary residence, in white areas. Of course, these premises are challengeable and this essay will seek to do that. This brief background, however, must be kept in mind for it is through the mechanisms that enforce this political system that the lives of black people are defined and controlled. Therefore, black strategy, when and where it has been articulated and employed, is based on a black conception of South African ruling policies.

Certain black consciousness spokespersons may take objection to this statement. Many, like the late Steve Biko, view their struggle as one in which blacks must remove themselves from concern for white opinions and solutions and look within themselves for their own answers. This inherently means a concentration on blacks to the exclusion of whites, raising black pride and confidence as the first necessary step in the struggle. Biko appealed to blacks to "talk more about ourselves and our struggle and less about whites."[1] Most adherents of black consciousness and student leaders, Biko included, are quick to put forward traditional values and lifestyles, i.e., to return to "mother Africa," and to reject racial integration as a goal or ideal upon which their perceived struggle is based. Many observers, and probably National party policymakers, might well conclude that these blacks give unknowing but solid support to separate development as a policy based on traditional ethnic divisions and segregation.

Black attitudes, however, seem to be governed by the need to withdraw from whites as the paternalistic, controlling factor of their lives, but, at the same time, by the fact that white policy concepts do indeed control their situation and pervade their lives. Black strategies and attitudes are reactive, even if not so conceived, to white policy. Yet, the black rejects the white policy as contrived. Even if separate development meant a division of land and resources that was fair, the white has dictated it and the black has not been consulted. To the black, it is a white conception of traditional and ethnic differences and economic imperatives upon which policy is based and for which they see little basis in reality. This rejection of white rationale permeates the black community, even amongst those who have chosen to work within the white system.

The above paragraphs concentrated on black consciousness attitudes, which, in reality are not new concepts but go back to well before the turn of the century. These concepts have been growing more activist and radical as time has passed and they will shortly be discussed at greater length. But, coinciding with the growth of black consciousness has been the building of the framework of the National party policy based on Bantustan or homeland concepts. This development is absolutely necessary to the ideology of separate development, and many blacks have accepted the concept of separate homelands. The following discussion will try to address each facet of the black community separately, those who accept and those who reject government policy, and then try to reach some meaningful conclusions from the evidence presented.

The Demographic Challenge

According to the South African Department of Statistics, as of mid-year 1976, South Africa's population, including the Transkei, which was then soon to become "independent," was estimated at 26.1 million persons. Whites represented 4.3 million or 16.4 percent of the population. Of the remainder, black Africans composed 18.6 million or 71.2 percent of the population, Coloureds accounted for 2.4 million persons, and Indians numbered 0.7 million. Urban/rural divisions are almost impossible to get at present for the black population. The 1970 census shows 53.6 percent of blacks, or over 10 million persons at present population projections, as living in "white" areas. This means those outside the homelands and includes blacks who are legal tenant farmers in white farming areas. The 1970 census showed the division of this 53.6 percent to be 29.6 in urban areas and 24 in rural. This comes out to be approximately 6 million blacks living in urban areas legally. Black observers, however, as well as predominantly white groups who keep statistics on a current basis, such as the South African Institute of Race Relations (SAIRR) and the South African Council of Churches (SACC), have estimated that the urban black population may be as great as 10 million. Certainly, considering the illegal "squatter" populations, as well as the numerous migrant laborers who would be present at any given time in urban areas, it seems improbable that urban populations are much less than the 10 million given in this projection. Urban blacks, therefore, represent over a half of South Africa's black population.

Homelands

There are nine major tribal groups in South Africa, although many of them have a shared linguistic root. These nine are the Xhosa, Zulu, Tswana, Pedi (north Sotho), South Sotho, Venda Ndebele, Swazi, and Shangaan. South African policy has given each of these major groups a "homeland," with the exception of the Xhosa people who have two, the Transkei and Ciskei. Two of these homelands, the Transkei and Bophuthatswana, are now declared independent and the logical extension of the South African government policy is to bring the other homelands to a sort of independence. In at least one or two other cases, this independence will emulate the statehood given to the Transkei and Bophuthatswana. In other cases, it will never reach this point, either due to unwillingness on the part of the homeland leaders or to the unviability of the geographic entities involved. It will, however, still amount to an autonomy that will allow Pretoria to rationalize the exclusion of any black citizenship in white South Africa by having provided political dispensation to all blacks in some homeland.

The motivation and the history of this homeland policy are an important aspect of understanding black frustrations. The original architects of the policy saw it as a means by which white political dominance could be protected but, at the same time, white economic privilege maintained. The use of cheap and controlled black labor and the exploitation of black purchase power, combined with the denial of black political aspirations, were the keys to the system. That is not to say that the concept is new. It grew from a long and complex history of racial separation that began formally over one hundred years ago with the establishment of African reserves in Natal. A newly elected National party in 1948 would have had a hard time implementing a policy of separate development had not white South Africa already been conditioned to think that separate homelands were relevant parts of the flow of their history. Originally, black reserves grew out of a physical fear of the black military threat, as well as a perceived need to control the labor supply in rural areas, control tax revenues from Africans, and provide a subsistence base for Africans both to obviate their need to be permanently in white areas and to create a class of African producers. As decades passed and the mining industry grew, separation by the reserve, township, and later homeland concept, became a specific mechanism for guaranteeing a cheap and controlled labor force that theoretically could demand no political rights. The framework for homelands originally reflected the reserve systems of Shepstone, but with the 1913 and 1936 land acts, these areas began to take their present form. During the 1950s and early 1960s, officials of the South African government chose to redefine the concept in a more "positive" sense, to use Verwoerd's own words, and thus they began to articulate the eventual independence of these entities. The variety of legislation, from the Bantu Authorities Act of 1951 right through the Bantu Homelands Constitution Act of 1971 and finally the independence legislation for the Transkei in 1976 and Bophuthatswana in 1977, has put this concept into practice.

The motivation, however, has always been clear. Verwoerd, speaking on behalf of the Bantu Self-Government Act of 1959, the law that became the cornerstone of subsequent homeland legislation, said that the bill was necessary to insure "white survival."[2] It was intended that all blacks would eventually be resident in a homeland, de jure, if not de facto, and they would be "temporary sojourners" in a white South Africa, there to sell their labor on a short-term basis. Ideally, blacks would administer and govern themselves in the homeland and, with white assistance, see to homeland development. This concept has certain grave drawbacks just from a physical point of view when one looks at the amount of land allotted homelands, i.e., 13 percent of the total land mass for over 71 percent of the population; the lack of industrial, mineral, or commercial centers in most of the homelands; and the general underdeveloped nature of the land. These problems are exacerbated by the close proximity of most homelands to developed white areas, which ensures continued black labor movement into the white areas and discourages outside investment in the homelands. This leaves the homeland in a predestined state of perpetual underdevelopment. Even a pro-policy entity like the government appointed Tomlinson Commission of 1950-1954, which advocated "ultimate, complete separation between Europeans and Bantu,"[3] still predicted that the homelands, if developed along the commission's recommended lines, could accommodate only

60 percent of the estimated African population by 1981 and 70 percent by the end of the century. By the commission's own estimates—which have proven to be very low on black population figures—this would still leave more blacks in white areas than whites in the year 2000.[4]

Apparently, government policy, in cognizance of these realities, has changed in its philosophical approach in recent years. Recognition has been given to the permanency of the urban black. This is reflected in certain recent government policy pronouncements. In brief, one can cite the new ninety-nine-year leasehold scheme for urban resident blacks; the allowance of urban township community councils to have some autonomy in such areas as housing and education; the stated intention to electrify, beautify, and generally to improve the townships; the easing of restrictions on black businesses in townships to allow expansion in size and type of business; the rise in the education budget and the announced extension of compulsory education to blacks as well as greater teacher training facilities; and some moves to ease the color bar and wage restrictions and to increase skills training for blacks.

These attempts to alleviate the black living conditions are welcome but represent no change in the basic premise of separate development policy. Whatever their standard of living, blacks will have no political say in South African affairs.[5] This was emphatically reiterated by the former minister of plural affairs, Connie Mulder, on August 15, 1978, when he told a National Party Congress in Natal that "the decision making power of whites will remain in white hands . . . [there will be no] politically mixed system of government." Mulder said all reforms for black living conditions would be carried out in "the framework of government policy," and that means every black is regarded as a homeland citizen.[6] Despite some optimism garnered by the recent appointment to the cabinet of two comparatively liberal men on race issues, Piet Koornhof as minister of plural affairs and Punt Janson as minister of education and training, it seems very unlikely they will herald any new look at basic policy, although their style of dealing with blacks may vary significantly from past ministers. This lack of potential change is brought home by the concurrent and offsetting appointment of arch-conservative Andries Treurnicht as the Transvaal National party leader, a position of traditional power and in the past a stepping-stone to the premiership. In short, under present government policy, political aspirations for blacks can only be met in the homelands.

This, then, is the institutional and legal framework in which blacks find themselves. As mentioned earlier, many blacks have chosen to fight the system, but many have decided to work within this framework. The political platforms, regional sources of strength, and the mechanisms utilized in the pursuit of power or goal attainment, vary for each of those leaders who have chosen to stay in the system, as well as the motivation for this commitment. There are often conflicting signals from individual leaders on their attitudes toward the system. One sequence of events best exemplifies this tendency. In January 1975, all homeland leaders jointly and publicly pledged to reject independence unless commonly agreed to. Subsequently, of course, Matanzima and Mangope broke the pledge and now there are indications that Mphephu of Venda will soon follow.

In light of these inconsistencies, it is often difficult to arrive at a satisfactory explanation of why so many homeland leaders play the game as they do. Among the ingredients of an explanation are these factors: a desire to maintain an established power position, varying degrees of personal self-interest, and a sincere conviction that the black man should take such opportunities as present themselves to pursue his economic and political aspirations. Some leaders profess to see the homeland as a "Trojan horse" by which they can work from the inside to gain some greater element of freedom to serve their people and, at the same time, work in their own way to make South Africa a shared entity, generally through a federation concept. Many observers feel that Bophuthatswana is exhibiting this motivation with the establishment of a constitutional bill of rights, and its attempts to repeal, albeit selectively, security and apartheid legislation.

Each homeland leader has unique problems and an individual approach to the system of homeland independence. As mentioned, Matanzima, Mangope, and Mphephu have readily accepted independence. Others like Phatudi of Lebowa, Ntsanwisi of Gazankulu, and Sebe of Ciskei accept the principle of independence with prerequisites, most notably land consolidation, development, and land expansion. Others, particularly Buthelezi of Kwazulu and Mopeli of Basotho QwaQwa, reject independence outright but accept work as homeland representatives because of the platform and security it provides.

Motivations of the leadership are not as important, however, to the overall black struggle in South Africa as the acceptance, or lack of it, by the general black community of the decision these leaders have made to work within the homeland concept. This, too, presents the observer with a mixed picture. Most urban blacks reject the homeland principle. In the homelands themselves, the policy has also met with significant opposition from politically aware segments of the community. It is important in this context to reiterate that blacks were never consulted during the evolution of the policy. During the debates on the Bantu Self-Government Act in 1959, Verwoerd dismissed the need to consult, saying that he knew the "type of native" who was for the act and the type against and that the mass of Africans were "not able to decide on a matter of this nature."[7]

Even though certain of the homelands, in particular the Transkei and Kwazulu, have some claim to a historical base, there have been strong black voices of disagreement from within throughout the development of homeland theory and legislation. Articulate opponents can be traced at least as far back as the institution of self-government in the Transkei, where Chief Poto and his followers opposed Matanzima and the policy in the early 1960s. Most homelands have or have had active and vocal opposition parties, who for the most part base their opposition on a rejection of independence. Active and strong opposition in the Transkei came from the Democratic party of Hector Ncokazi. Matanzima's reaction was to jail and harass this opposition and to pass draconian security laws that were "more South African than the South Africans." Strong opposition showings elsewhere have met with oppression, as was the case when the Bophuthatswana National Seoposengwe party rallies were broken up by Security Police prior to the August 1977 elections and the party leader, Herman Masoloane, expelled from the legislative assembly. In Venda, Baldwin Madau's

Venda Independence party won the majority of elected legislative assembly seats in July 1978, only to have most of the elected members subsequently detained before the vote on a new chief minister. The Ciskei has also passed ominous security legislation, as has Venda and the Transkei, and has not hesitated to detain opposition members.

Despite this significant opposition at the level of politically aware persons, it is probable that the majority of the homeland dwellers living a subsistence rural existence or filling the ranks of migrant labor view separate development apathetically. This may reflect the fact that they have, as a group, never been called upon to think of the implications for them of such a policy. When the reality of the policy is brought home, such as at the time of independence, many of these apathetic masses may reassess their positions on very pragmatic if not theoretical grounds. A trip through Bophuthatswana prior to the August 1977 elections and independence in December of that year revealed a surprising concern amongst low income workers and subsistence farmers. These concerns revolved around potential travel difficulties—many who live in Bophuthatswana work daily in the "white" areas of the Pretoria-Vereeniging-Krugersdorp triangle—and administrative corruption or inefficiency. There was a particular concern expressed by pensioners and persons receiving unemployment aid over possible loss of benefits due to the change of administration. Since independence the unemployment problems facing homeland dwellers have been exacerbated. According to the Black Sash, a group that works daily with persons victimized by Influx Control laws, recruitment of labor in the homelands has been severely restricted, and persons with no Section 10 rights of residence under the Group Areas Act have little hope of being registered for work. With increased penalties for employers who hire unregistered workers, homeland dwellers are finding it difficult to locate jobs when they leave their areas illegally, which is the only method available to them.[8]

It might be prudent here to deviate somewhat to a brief but separate discussion of Chief Minister Buthelezi. Buthelezi and his primary political organization, the Zulu cultural movement Inkatha, must be looked at in a separate light from other homeland leaders. Buthelezi sees himself very much as a part of the black struggle and likes to associate himself with the ANC and PAC. He also, as mentioned before, rejects independence and professes a concept of South Africa not at all dissimilar from that of the black consciousness advocates. He defends his use of the homeland leadership as a necessary evil to give him the platform by which he can serve the Zulu people, promote his ideas of wider black unity—exemplified by his abortive Black Unity Front in 1976 and the still active South African Black Alliance—and seek to dismantle the separate development system from within.

Yet, Buthelezi is constantly drawn out for special ire from black consciousness and student groups. It is hard to exaggerate the depth of feeling against him, and not just by the young radicals. Both Steve Biko and Robert Sobukwe told me that Buthelezi represented the most dangerous element to black unity and, therefore, to their eventual goal of majority rule. No matter how Buthelezi puts his case, these and other similar spokespersons for black consciousness feel he has fallen into Pretoria's trap by using the ethnic, homeland base. The unity of the Zulu behind him and the very fact that he is independent enough to reject territorial independence, they say, just proves the ethnic identity argument that lies behind the policy of separate development. Some blacks see Buthelezi as a personally ambitious man and doubt his sincerity. They feel he is just trying to launch himself into an eventual moderate leadership role to which the South Africans will have to turn, as has been seen to happen in Rhodesia with the internal settlement there. Other critics do not question his motives, but feel that because of his widespread appeal, ability, and charisma, he diverts the attention and energies of his own people and outsiders away from the unity needed to confront the white system and join the "real struggle." With all of these events, however, Buthelezi is a big cog in the wheel of black dynamics in South Africa and will be an important figure in the black struggle for a share in their land of birth, even though critics might feel him to be a negative factor.

Black Consciousness and Nationalism

Modern black nationalism has its roots in the efforts of African individuals and groups, sometimes in league with liberal-minded whites, who in the latter part of the nineteenth century began the fight against segregationist policies of the dominant white authority. Through these individuals and groups, African political journalists, and separatist churches, the long process of attempting to weld a unified front in face of growing white domination and oppression was carried out. Thomas Karis, in an unpublished paper,[9] lists seven "all-in" efforts to forge this unity in the form of a variety of conferences from 1909 into the 1970s through which black nationalism has flourished. These are the South African Native Convention of 1909, the All African Convention in 1935 and 1936, the Atlantic Charter Committee in 1943, the Interdenominational African Ministers' Federation (IDAMF) in 1956, the IDAMF Consultative Conference in 1960 called after the bannings of the ANC and PAC, the organization conferences of the Black People's Convention in 1971, and the Black Renaissance Convention of 1974.

The themes of these conferences broadly represent the progression of black nationalism, from the South African Native Convention in 1909 asking for "equitable justice" and expansion of franchise rights for Africans in the Cape to the Black Renaissance Convention demanding "a society in which all people participate fully in the government of the country through the medium of one man one vote." This history of black nationalism and consciousness is one of increasing radicalism, as represented simply by the major leaders of the ANC. One by one these leaders and spokespersons have stepped aside, thought to be too moderate, as a new militancy has come to the fore. So it was with Jabavu, Duma, and Msimang, replaced by Xuma, then Moroka, to be followed by Gumede, then Luthuli, and now Mandela and Tambo. At present the student generation sees Mandela as respected but outdated, Subokwe as moderate, and Tambo as "exiled and irrelevant."

Historically, this leftward movement has been due to many factors. Externally, an important factor was the movement of the world toward more liberal policies, exemplified by the Atlantic Charter, the "winds of change," and the emergence of an independent Africa. Combined with this has been the emergence of the great socialist nations and the assertion of Marxism as a world force, both economically and socially. Internally,

South African whites have moved steadily and unwaveringly away from a nonracial common society. The hopes of Africans after the Boer War that English liberalism would hold sway were dashed by the union government. Not only was the franchise not extended, but the color bar was introduced, by 1936 Cape Africans were removed from the roll, and by 1959 even indirect African representation in government was ended. The year 1948, following the somewhat euphoric postwar months when the principles of the Atlantic Charter excited black hopes, saw the final victory of Afrikanerdom and the coming to power of the National party. The next decade saw the plethora of laws that was to bring apartheid and separate development in as the legal framework of the country. In concert with this legal metamorphosis has been the growing oppressive security machinery that has been established to deal with black discontent and replace constructive communication.

Old-line black nationalism had its last fling in the 1950s with the Defiance of Unjust Laws campaign and the Pass Marches, the long-running Treason Trial from 1956 to 1961, and the Sharpeville confrontation of 1960. The ANC and PAC were then banned and the leadership either imprisoned or exiled. Black nationalism still exists, of course, and many of its leaders, Sobukwe and Mandela particularly, have places of reverence wherever black activists meet. As a matter of fact, despite the hiatus in any nationalistic activity during the decade subsequent to their bannings and the fairly common attitude current among students and black consciousness leaders that they have lost relevance, the ANC and, to a much lesser extent, the PAC, seem to have been growing recently both in efficiency and organization. The last year and a half has seen dramatic evidence of this fact in both urban terrorist incidents at a heretofore unknown level in white South Africa and significant guerrilla activities in border areas. Even Justice Minister Kruger and former Security Police Chief Brigadier Zietsman have made public admissions of concern about guerrilla activity. On November 19, 1978, Kruger announced the capture of twenty-three armed PAC "terrorists," saying they were conducting "psychological warfare" against the government.[10] Since that time there have been several encounters with ANC guerrillas in the north and western Transvaal

near the Botswana border. Their activity has obviously
increased and the black community grown more acquiescent to
their efforts. The ANC in particular has increased its recruitment efforts among student exiles and has broadened its contacts with internal leaders, both those publicly recognized and
those underground. It also continues to demand world attention
as the "legitimate representative" of black South Africa. Depending on the course of events, therefore, and the legitimacy
accorded the external groups by African, Eastern, and other
third world nations, they could play an increasingly critical role
in the next decade. At present, however, they are seen as historically important but mostly irrelevant to internal developments by students and black consciousness leaders. It is instruc-
tive here to point out that their recent rise in prestige and effectiveness was due to the reintroduction of open radical black
politics—to be discussed later—and the attention-gathering
confrontations between black students, black consciousness
organizations, and authorities in recent years. The external
groups were not involved directly in these incidents, despite
South African government claims to the contrary.

The continued rejection of the ANC and PAC as "the" spokespersons for black South Africa has several explanations, not the
least of which is a feeling that they are riding the coattails of
the students and the activities of internal nationalists. Also,
there is a suspicion of their sincerity. External officials are often
perceived as living lives of luxury, courted by liberal and leftist
circles abroad. There is some distaste, as well, for the open
affiliation with European Communist nations. An often expressed sentiment is that blacks in South Africa do not want to
be anybody's pawn, neither of the West nor the East. Further, in
this sophisticated philosophical atmosphere, black leaders see
ANC and PAC exiles as often simplistic and naive in their approaches to solutions. They are, as some say, "out of touch."
This does not mean that time and world opinion may not one
day place these exiles in an important, if not predominant, role.
At present, however, they do not play such a role in mainstream
black nationalist thinking.

To return to the historical development of black nationalism,
however, there had been a lull in ANC/PAC activity since the

early 1960s. The ANC and PAC were forced to become externally based liberation groups, supported mainly by outside powers, with a limited operational base inside the country and a decreased influence on the flow of events. The international outcry at the time of Sharpeville was weathered by the government with little serious repercussions and the nation embarked on its most economically prosperous decade, with booming growth rates and world recognition as a good investment risk. For almost a decade black ferment was kept from the public eye. Leo Kuper cites this as a periodic "recoil from radicalism" that has always haunted effective liberation action. He mentions what he sees as a basic conservatism in African political life exemplified by the reaction against the Communist party in the Industrial and Commercial Workers' Union in 1926 and the conservative period of the ANC under the presidency of Gumede.[11] By way of explanation of this conservatism one must take into account the self-censoring and modifying effect that the formidable security forces of the country have had on black radicalism as well as the inherent divisions that have contributed to a lack of unity. Still, there has been a continual, albeit understandable, ebb and flow of radical, national liberation politics. The 1960s were to be one of the most significant ebbs. It was not until the growth of black consciousness in the late 1960s that the tide began to flow again.

Despite the historical role they have played and the potential for a greater future role, particularly if the course of events takes South Africa toward the precipice of racial confrontation, the nationalists of the ANC and PAC generation have been replaced by the Black Consciousness Movement, itself now effectively banned through its organizations. The first of the black consciousness movements, and probably most important as a parent organization, was the South African Students Organization (SASO), formed in 1969. It came out of a reaction against the claim of the white National Union of South African Students (NUSAS) to represent blacks. This dissatisfaction had earlier outcroppings in the formation of the Non-European Unity Movement, the African Students' Association, and the African Students Union of South Africa in the early 1960s. With the collapse of these organizations by the mid-1960s,

NUSAS again claimed to speak for black universities through the University Christian Movement. As a reaction, SASO was formed. Its manifesto defines the concept of black consciousness. It reads:

> Black consciousness is an attitude of mind, a way of life.
>
> The basic tenet of Black Consciousness is that the Black man must reject all value systems that seek to make him a foreigner in the country of his birth and reduce his basic human dignity.
>
> The Black man must build up his own value systems, see himself as self-defined and not defined by others.
>
> The concept of Black Consciousness implies the awareness by the black people of the power they wield as a group, both economically and politically, and hence group cohesion and solidarity are important facets of Black Consciousness.
>
> Black Consciousness will always be enhanced by the totality of involvement of the oppressed people; hence the message of Black Consciousness has to be spread to reach all sections of the Black community.

SASO was not formed as an overtly political group, but it, and its seed organizations, became just that. It was a self-examination, self-help group seeking to instill black pride and self-reliance. By the early 1970s, however, black consciousness was indeed becoming a movement whose aim was to bring a unity of political purpose and strategy to the diverse groups it had spawned as well as the old-line black nationalism and liberation groups. From the root of SASO came the South African Students Movement (SASM), the Black People's Convention (BPC), the Black Community Programmes (BCP), and various other regional bodies. SASO was always a student organization at the university level, although the definition of student was stretched considerably. SASM was more or less the secondary school equivalent of SASO. The BCP was the realization of the practical side of self-help and, although only in its infancy at the time of its banning, it had already accounted for at least three community centers around the country, complete with libraries and record and reading rooms; at least one complete rural clinic in the eastern Cape; a mobile clinic in Soweto; and a budding attempt at educational assistance funds. The BPC was overtly a black political party. When it officially came into being in July 1972, its founding charter stated that its mission was to provide "a political home for all Black people who could not reconcile themselves to working within the framework of separate development, and to promote Black solidarity." It was by policy a blacks-only party. Its charter showed its close connection with black consciousness as it pledged "to preach, popularize, and implement the philosophy of Black Consciousness and Black solidarity . . . [and] to implement the principles and philosophy of Black communalism—the philosophy of sharing."

The platform of black consciousness as a political movement represented by these different groups was never fully defined before its effective banning. It was generally for a black-ruled state, but not necessarily to the exclusion of whites. Spokespersons often reflected socialist ideals—or "black communalism"—for their envisioned future state, but there was little dogmatism and a general rejection of outside dominance, particularly white, including rejection of Soviet or Cuban control. It was primarily for self-reliance and, the one point agreed by all, against the system of separate development. It was, therefore, on a collision course with all blacks who accepted homeland concepts, whatever their motivation. Its appeal was primarily urban where the meaning of ethnic affiliation could still evoke cultural pride but not political loyalty. Black consciousness adherents were growing in number, but it was only after the events between June 1976 and October 1977 that the broad mass of urban blacks began to look to it as their guiding philosophy and to its organizational ramifications as the heirs to the ANC and PAC.

Going back to the earlier discussion about the ebb and flow of radicalism in the black community, some observers have predicted and even detected another ebb since the brutal reaction to student street politics and the security crackdown on black consciousness in the last two years. There is no doubt that the government has succeeded in taking the sting out of radical politics by brutalizing many of its adherents, banning its organizations, and detaining, exiling, or killing its leaders. Black consciousness activities have either been compromised, moderated, or forced underground. The movement is momentarily without a program of action and is in a "holding pattern," waiting for the next logical opportunity. Many individuals are using this time to return to school, to study and write, to increase their qualifications and abilities. However, since the events of and subsequent to June 16, 1976, things have changed. There will never be an ebb in the same sense as occurred in the 1960s and previously. Urban sensitivities have been changed and, to use an overworked phrase, the consciousness and awareness of the black community have been raised. This applies countrywide and probably explains the fact that even homeland leaders, Buthelezi particularly but others as well, feel the need to articulate the rationale for their positions in black consciousness terminology.

The confrontation of June 16 and the many deaths that followed, even though the scale was far beyond that of Sharpeville, would not by itself have insured the reaction that has taken place and that so vividly contrasts with the years after Sharpeville. It was a combination of many factors, a coincidence of historical fact, that so deeply affected black attitudes. First, the June disturbances occurred as South Africa was seeing the encroachment of black-ruled Africa, mostly socialist, on its borders and looking to further encroachment as Zimbabwe and Namibia joined the now independent former Portuguese territories. The white buffer was going, and to South African blacks this was far more meaningful than those distant "winds of change" that had been blowing up north for the last twenty years. Blacks were conscious of this trend, as the pro-FRE-LIMO rallies in Natal in 1974 showed. An additional factor was the grave economic crisis in which South Africa found itself after over a decade of unprecedented growth. Although this crisis was exacerbated by political instability due to the 1976 disturbances, it was mainly a result of worldwide inflation, gold price fluctuations, and dropping investor confidence, which caused adverse balance of payments problems and a sharp drop in the economic growth rate. The situation not only deflated that illusory cushion upon which many white South Africans rested but exacerbated black economic discomfort, mainly by critically increasing unemployment. Also, during this period, the first homelands, Transkei and Bophuthatswana, became independent.

The general, radicalizing effect of these events cannot be overstated. For the first time, the apathetic masses were being affected by homeland policy. Some blacks have actually been "repatriated" to their homelands for various reasons, and that threat remains over all other Xhosa or Tswana speakers. As mentioned above, employment has become more difficult as homeland blacks are viewed with caution by prospective employers. More important, however, is the psychological effect. The reclassification from Xhosa to Transkei citizen, from Tswana to Bophuthatswana citizen, whenever a passbook has been presented at an administrative board office, and the nullification of Section 10 rights have brought home to the average working-class urban dweller that even the modicum of security that he or she depended on is no longer there. These events, combined with the preliminary brutal reaction of the police to student demonstrations and subsequent tightening of security measures, a plethora of Security Act and Terrorism Act trials, and at first a refusal to communicate with moderate community spokespersons, topped by the bannings and detentions of many of those moderates on October 19, 1977, have instilled a new mood in urban black South Africa.

I can testify from several personal associations that members of the parental group, who in June of 1976, although sympathetic to students' grievances, had little sympathy for their confrontational methods, were, by the end of that year and certainly by October 19, 1977, in despair at the chances for accommodation with the white authorities. As one elderly lady pledged, the next time she would be in the streets with her children. It must be noted here, also, that a serious generational difference came into existence that was unprecedented and reflected on the new consciousness of black South Africa. The parental group could remember the days before the Group Areas Act, Homelands Constitution Act, Suppression of Communism and Terrorism Acts, and other influx control, apartheid legislation. It was a time when total separation from whites was not legislated. Respected nationalists like Robert Sobukwe could speak with understanding of white fears and motivations, and could draw hope from past associations with whites on a human basis. Even the black consciousness advocates in their early and mid-thirties could harken back to their days of association with NUSAS and the Afrikaans Studentbond and see whites on a human level. But the students in the street in June 1976 had a different perspective toward whites, who represented only authority figures and exhibited no humanness with which they could relate. A white was either a policeman or an administrative board official. The students' world was closed and the only humanity to which they could relate was black. Isolation, alienation, radicalization, and hostility created and are still creating the mood of the day.

This new view within student ranks, as well as their perceptions of a need for greater organizational impetus, led after the first disturbances in Soweto to the formations of student representative councils (SRCs). By 1977 most major urban townships had fledgling SRCs. Although separate in organization and often in tactics from black consciousness adherents, these SRCs must be considered in the same category. Many of them were made up of SASM members and most had direct ties, sometimes organizational advice, from SASO and BPC. Certainly their guiding philosophy was that of black consciousness. The SRCs, particularly in Soweto and the Pretoria townships of Atteridgeville and Mamelodi, took the lead in organizing effective boycotts for the 1976-1977 school year as the next stage in their protest against separate development personified to them in the Bantu education system. After the first round of direct street confrontations with the authorities, during which many students died, they decided on this less violent course. Casualties this time took the form of detentions, and hundreds of student leaders around the country spent long periods in jail with no charges against them. Like the mainstream black consciousness groups, the students were to find their leadership decimated and the Soweto SRC itself banned by the end of 1977. Outwardly, the ebb has again occurred and students are back in school. But the attitudes are permanently changed.

Where these changed attitudes take the new black leadership in the 1980s is hard to envision. The climate in which they are going to seek to organize is undoubtedly going to grow more

oppressive, both legally and politically. Financing may become
one of the most difficult problems as external sources are cut off
by government fiat. Mass bannings and detentions, as in October 1977, do not seem the present preferred method of control by the government, although they cannot be ruled out in
the next decade. More likely will be continued selective bannings and detentions to keep the movement always off-guard.
Organization for the near term, then, will probably remain
mostly an underground activity and black leadership will
become increasingly unidentifiable.

Moderate Community Leaders

Brief attention must be given to the individuals and groups
who fall between the extremes of militant and radical activists
for black consciousness goals and those blacks who accept, for
whatever reason, to work within the system. Ironically, those
persons generally play a role themselves in the system. They are
doctors, journalists, clergymen, labor leaders, academics,
businessmen, social workers, etc. But, because they are not seen
to be furthering the aims of the system, they are given the
courtesy of a hearing by black consciousness adherents and can
still rightfully claim some credibility. The government appears
willing to let certain organizations, particularly churches, ethnic
or cultural groups—Inkatha is a good example—and unions,
operate up to a point. Along with individuals, such as doctors
and social workers, these groups have considerable potential for
meeting day-to-day needs in the black community. Recent private
sector attempts at addressing housing shortages and unfair labor
and wage practices are examples. These groups and individuals
find themselves serving a needed and welcome role in the community. They also find themselves often in a position of serving
as the bridge to and even the voice of more radical elements in
the society. They, too, have helped bear the brunt of bannings
and detentions meted out to black leadership. They will also
face suspicion and some harassment from South African authorities in the coming years.

Even so, this class of leader is generally found to be more
concerned about dialogue between the race groups and is, at

least in principle, against any racist overtones that may appear in black consciousness concepts. For this reason, members of the moderate leadership often find themselves caught in the middle of the opposing forces. The Black Parents Association, led by Soweto leaders Dr. Manas Buthelezi and Sally Motlana, was just such a group, trying to seek a hearing with government ministers to present student grievances in 1976, only to be turned away by the government and then rejected by the students as irrelevant. Other groups such as the Housewives' League and the Soweto Committee of Ten have faced similar dilemmas of seeking short-term objectives and thereby spawning doubts in the more militant elements of the community about their credibility. These moderate elements, generally the persons best known to outsiders for the simple reason that they are willing to talk to foreign representatives, generally share the same reservations about separate development and aspirations for a future South Africa as the black consciousness members. They are also accurate observers of their own society and reflect it well. But, due to their inherent "fairness," these members of the black community generally will not serve as key players in directing the movement to attain black goals. The impetus for this will come from their Left and may well leave its mark on them as it passes. As one well-known journalist privately told me, "We shall be the victims of the revolution because we've insisted on talking to both sides." Although their community services are needed and welcome, these groups and individuals seem to be following rather than leading the cause of black nationalist ideology and strategy.

Conclusion

Blacks are seriously divided in their approaches to the oppressive situation they face in South Africa. Those who advocate either pursuing the homelands concept as the best way of giving blacks a political voice, or who work from within that concept as a platform from which to pursue other stated aims, seem to be working against the grain of the younger and increasingly militant segment of the community to whom the leadership mantle will soon fall. Even those moderates who reject separate development but advocate dialogue between black and white are coming dangerously close to being discredited in the eyes of the young black consciousness adherents as radicalization increases. Black consciousness, then, is the mood of the day and the overall trend is leftward amongst the politicized, generally educated faction who will become the opinion leaders of tomorrow for the greater but more apathetic masses. Their vision of the future, however, is still uncertain. All see a black-ruled state, although seldom to the exclusion of whites. In these intellectually elite ranks, socialism as the economic mode—or "black communalism" as the BPC would have said—seems to be the favored direction. Ironically, the very thing that many whites fear, the destruction of their capitalist way of life and cultural values, seems to have significant defense in a black community that is more educated, industrialized, and modernized than any other on the continent. Therefore, at some future date, in the course of the black struggle, the ideological conflict of socialism versus capitalism may rear its head.

At present, the black movement is in an organizational calm with, again ironically, the Zulu-based Inkatha as the most significant functioning group. Since October 19, 1977, many attempts have been made to produce the next echelon of leadership and to give it an organizational base. The Soweto Student League followed the Soweto SRC and the Azania People's Organization (AZAPO) attempted to fill the void left by the BPC's banning. Each in its turn has been subjected to harassment and detention of leadership and has been, for all practical purposes, stillborn. But black South Africa seems determined not to acquiesce in its struggle to seek a full share of the human dignity and self-determination within the geographical boundaries that are its birthright.

The imponderables, then, are the modalities for carrying out this struggle. Undoubtedly new organizations will rise in the future to carry the mantle of black nationalism and consciousness. A return to the old ANC tactics of civil disobedience and labor or consumer boycott may well be the next step. Direct confrontational tactics, like Soweto 1976, are probably out for the immediate future, although there is little doubt that sporadic flare-ups, possibly of major proportions, will occur.

Old organizations may also reemerge in importance, particularly if the ANC carries on with its avowed guerrilla campaign and if the propensity grows in the black community to accept violence as a legitimate and necessary means to meet their objectives. It is unlikely that urban terrorism or guerrilla warfare will make significant headway in seriously challenging the regime in the next decade. However, they may well serve as increasing pressure points on the government as domestic and international opinion reacts to such incidents. Certainly this type of action seems on the increase, although it is still in the formative and amateurish stage when compared to the level of terrorism evident even in Western Europe.

Whatever the tactics employed, it seems clear that, at the least, South Africa's blacks are demanding a shared political system and that, despite "recoils of radicalism," this demand will not be voluntarily stilled and can only be suppressed for the short term. With the seeming determination of the current nationalist government to stick with separate development as the foundation of its policy, even with the fulfillment of the promised amelioration of black living conditions in urban areas, the potential for confrontation between the race groups is growing. Unless men of goodwill on both sides begin to seek areas of accommodation in the near future, their ability to influence the increasingly radical black youth will be lost, and that confrontation will become inevitable. South Africa is on a collision course and its greatest luxury is time—time that must not be wasted.

Notes

1. Steve Biko, "Black Consciousness and the Quest for a True Humanity," in Mokgethi Motlhabi, ed., *Essays on Black Theology* (Johannesburg: University Christian Movement, 1972), p. 27.

2. Gwendolen Carter, Thomas Karis, and Newell Stultz, *South Africa's Transkei: The Politics of Domestic Colonialism* (Evanston, Ill.: Northwestern University Press, 1967), p. 65.

3. *Commission for the Socio-Economic Development of the Bantu Areas*, Summary of the report (Pretoria: Government Printer, 1956), p. 106.

4. Ibid., p. 184.

5. Note should be taken of the three-tier constitution proposal that is due to come before Parliament in 1979. This proposal brings the Coloured and Indian communities into the decision-making process to the exclusion of Africans. Although they are still subordinate to white domination, many Coloureds and Indians see some attraction in the proposals, as they have in the representative councils previously.

6. *Rand Daily Mail*, August 16, 1978.

7. Carter, Karis, and Stultz, *Transkei*, p. 65.

8. "Interim Report, February to August 1978," Black Sash Johannesburg Advice Office, September 13, 1978.

9. Thomas Karis, "South African Black Organizations and Their Demands and Aims" (Paper delivered at the Conference on Urban Conflict and Change in South Africa, Department of State, Washington, D.C., April 28-29, 1977), pp. 4-6.

10. South African Broadcasting Corporation television interview, Johannesburg, November 19, 1978.

11. Leo Kuper, in Monica Wilson and Leonard Thompson, eds., *The Oxford History of South Africa, 1870-1966*, vol. 2 (London: Oxford University Press, 1975), p. 471.

3

Black Labor as a Swing Factor in South Africa's Evolution

Roy Godson

There are two perspectives on the sorts of changes that would give all South Africans, black and white, control of the government and resources of the country. There are those, particularly the South African exiles, who believe thoroughgoing peaceful change is impossible. There are others, however, who speculate about less violent, less tragic methods of change. They also inquire into the possibility of using democratic, if not necessarily parliamentary, means to bring about the emergence of a racially integrated democratic system. They ask, above all, whether black (and white) leaders can emerge and bring about major shifts in the system of government through democratic procedures and in ways that will extend the democratic system to all races.

The answer to this question is a cautious yes. This essay will argue that although there may be other paths to democratic change, the development of strong trade unions for black workers would create the potential not only for the emergence of black leaders committed to the democratic process, but also for institutions sufficiently strong to coalesce with others and bring about and maintain democratic change.

To some extent this thesis is at variance with both liberal developmental theorists who foresee the breakdown of the apartheid system as South Africa modernizes, and also the "revisionist" scholars who have attacked the liberal theorists, maintaining that the apartheid system can adjust to modernization and remain basically intact.[1] Indeed the argument here is that both sets of theories underestimate the necessity for and significance of *specific types of institutions* such as organized labor that are in a position to take advantage of the contradictions of modernizing society to bring about change.

Those concerned with the development of a racially integrated democratic society should not despair; but neither should they assume that it will evolve automatically. Instead it will be necessary to take advantage of the opportunities presenting themselves in the 1980s to build institutions that can emerge in the 1990s as a swing factor in the evolution of South African politics. This may appear to be a long-term strategy, but even those who emphasize violent methods cannot expect to bring about major change much earlier.

Organized Labor as a School for Democracy

If there is to be lasting democratic change in South Africa, a necessary condition will be skilled black leaders committed to democracy. Indeed, the most potent argument used by white South Africans against sharing power with blacks—even urban blacks—is that they are not committed to and they do not understand the nontribal, democratic system. It is pointed out that they have been denied almost any experience with democratic institutions; that traditional beliefs and behavior can hardly lead to the expectation that if they had power they would respect each other's rights, let alone the rights of the white minority; and that the experience in the rest of Africa does not lead to sanguine expectations about the maintenance of democracy in a postapartheid environment.

These, of course, are serious arguments and those concerned with democratic institutions cannot ignore them. But the proponents of these arguments go further and conclude that it is impossible for a democratically oriented black leadership to emerge, and therefore, understandably, they are reluctant to share power with leaders who have not demonstrated their commitment to the democratic process.

However, there is already a potential vehicle for developing skilled democratic leaders—even in advance of sharing control of the government. The development of a democratic trade union movement, genuinely open to blacks, could provide such a vehicle.

To begin with, a democratic trade union movement would bring workers, blue- and white-collar, together on a nonracial, nontribal basis. This of course is not to say that racial and tribal barriers, stereotypes, and discrimination would be overcome completely, anymore than they have been in the United States, the United Kingdom, or other developed countries. Nevertheless, were all the workers represented by the organization, both leaders and workers would have to strive together to promote its aims. If they were to secure the support in trade union elections of a significant proportion of workers in any given factory, railroad, office, or school, the leaders in each union would have to submerge their tribal and ethnic differences.

Second, the democratic process within the unions could enable thousands of blacks to learn the rudiments of democracy. They would learn to compete for power through the electoral process, to propagandize, to build coalitions, to run electoral campaigns, to operate through parliamentary procedures, and to respect the rights of minorities. They would also have to learn to be responsive to their constituents or lose power. It is one thing for a leader to be elected once, particularly if he founds an organization (or country). It is quite another if he has to learn to compete for power and appeal to his constituency on a regular basis. Finally, the democratic process in the labor movement would enable blacks to learn that if they are unsuccessful at the ballot box, they will lose power, but they will have another chance to regain it—something that has happened only rarely in Africa.

Third, through experiences in the trade union movement, union leaders would appreciate that they have an extraordinary stake in the maintenance of the democratic system. Usually, only democratic systems allow workers to organize, bargain collectively, and strike to protect their own interests. Trade unionists throughout the world are very conscious of this. This is the major reason union leaders in Europe and America were amongst the first to oppose all forms of totalitarianism. Even when leaders in business, government, and the intellectual community were reluctant to oppose Lenin, Stalin, Hitler, and Mussolini, trade union leaders spoke out and organized to protect themselves. Sometimes they failed, but they were almost always in the vanguard of the antidictatorial and human rights movements of the day.

Similarly, if black leaders in South Africa developed a stake in a democratic system, a system that through the power of the labor movement propelled them into positions of power and prestige, they would not want to see it undermined. They might not, on their own, be able to maintain a democratic system, but like the labor movements in the United States, West Germany, Israel, and Britain, etc., they would be likely to become firm proponents of it, and anchors in a sea of instability. Not only would the labor movement provide blacks with the opportunity to gain experience with the democratic process, it would give them a stake in its maintenance in a postapartheid environment.

Finally, through running large, financially independent organizations and participating in national and even international decision making, scores of blacks would have the opportunity to become experienced and skillful leaders. At present, few blacks ever gain such experience, and even fewer have the chance to become experienced elected leaders. The tensions of running large institutions and competing for electoral power have frequently overcome leaders of new states. This perhaps could be avoided in South Africa.

It is true that neither the trade union movement nor the democratic system itself is always a perfect school for democracy. Union leaders, like democratic politicians and others who wield power, can develop corrupt practices and authoritarian traits. Moreover, the trade union movement frequently has been the target of Communists and assorted extreme leftists who want to use this strategic institution to propel themselves into political power. To some extent these characteristics may become obstacles to the development of democratic black trade union leaders.

However, with some skill and care they should not prove insurmountable. The majority of unions are not corrupt. Indeed, in industrialized countries outside North America, instances of union involvement in financial scandals are rare.[2] Antidemocratic practices, however, are and have been a problem in all democratic organizations, but by carefully regulating trade union elector procedures as is done in the United States and other countries (e.g., financial disclosure, mail ballots, limited terms of office, and frequent elections), it should prove relatively easy to ensure that the democratic process works in the South African labor movement.

Finally, through regulation of the trade union electoral process to ensure that there is no interference with the democratic process and the immediate development of black unions, the Communists and other extremists probably could be prevented from taking over the unions at a later point. In very few countries where the trade union movements were organized by strong democratic forces have the Communists been able to gain control of them. When they have dominated unions the Communists have typically gained control by filling a vacuum left by the elimination of democratic forces during a war or a dictatorship—when the democrats were imprisoned, dead, preoccupied, apathetic, or without resources. The history of postwar Europe and most recently Portugal are excellent examples of this phenomenon.[3] The organization of strong democratic trade unions at an early stage is the best defense against the Communists' efforts to appear to be the champions of the working man.

In addition, when one examines the specific South African context, it is unlikely that the obstacles of corruption, Communism, and bossism would prove insurmountable. Corruption in the approximately 200 unions that make up the South African labor movement is practically nil—almost certainly less than that which prevails among South African politicians and financiers. The white unions also appear to have been models of democracy—indeed some have claimed that they are too democratic and reflect too much the conservative instincts of the membership. And finally, Communist efforts to gain control of labor generally have failed.[4]

Indeed when one looks at the few black unions and particularly the only major black union in South Africa, the National Union of Clothing Workers (NUCW), the model of what could be is quite apparent. There are now approximately twenty-two black unions in South Africa with a membership of about 60,000 (as against 40,000 four years ago). Almost half of these workers (23,000), however, are paid-up members of the NUCW, located in the Transvaal.

The NUCW originated in the decision of the leadership of the Garment Workers Union of South Africa, a mixed union of white, Coloured, and Indian clothing workers, to organize black women in the clothing industry, who, because of a loophole in the law (the Industrial Conciliation Act), were allowed to belong to recognized trade unions. When this loophole was closed, with the passing of the Bantu Labor (Settlement of Disputes) Act in 1953, black members set up a garment workers union for black women. In 1962, this new union, the Garment Workers Union of African Women, merged with the South African Clothing Workers Union, a smaller male counterpart, to form the NUCW.

The NUCW cannot be "registered" (legally recognized) in terms of the Industrial Conciliation Act and thus may not participate in the official decision-making process of the Industrial Council for the clothing industry in the Transvaal. Nevertheless, employers accord a degree of recognition to the work of the NUCW and bargain with the leadership and the approximately 350 shop stewards who are elected by the workers. The union also is able to help members resolve grievances and find work, to assist them with such matters as unemployment benefit applications and to administer a death burial fund. Difficulties in the ways of collecting dues (the checkoff is illegal for black unions) have been partially overcome by charging an administration fee for the burial fund.

Although the union is constrained by its unofficial status and by the cautious approach that its officers and stewards are obliged to assume, its demonstrated success in improving the material conditions of the membership and in giving them some sort of voice in industrial society is something that, as will be discussed later, many South Africans from the *verkrampte* right to the racially exclusivist and Communist left prefer to forget. Here we have a clear example of multitribal, democratic, experienced, skillful, honest, and decent leadership—leadership committed to democracy, multiracialism, and internationalism.

Another twenty unions with several thousand leaders, representing even perhaps only 2 million workers out of a projected black work force of 10-13 million and controlling significant financial resources, would give South Africa something only a few other black African countries have—strong black leaders emerging from the democratic process with a stake in its continuation, who could coalesce with whites and blacks from other sectors. At a minimum they would be able to prevent the labor movement being used to destroy the vestiges of the white democratic system and perhaps they could provide the leadership for its extension to other sectors of society.

The Potential of the Black Labor Movement

To what extent could these democratic black leaders, were they to emerge, bring about significant change? There is, of course, no clear-cut answer. A great deal would depend on the quality of the leadership and its ability to take advantage of the opportunities that presented themselves. Nevertheless, based on assumptions about the major political and economic forces operating into the 1980s and 1990s,[5] the projection of trends in South Africa, and what is known about the strength of organized labor in industrial society, it is not unreasonable to conclude that black union leaders would be able to influence the evolution of South African society.

Based on current projections, it seems likely that urban blacks as workers and consumers will be a very important sector in South African society. By the end of the century most estimates indicate that the South African population will double. Blacks will constitute about 75 percent of the population and whites 13 percent (currently blacks are 70 percent and whites are 17 percent).[6] By the year 2000, there will be 13.5 million males of working age (about two and a half times the 1970s figure) and most will be black. To keep unemployment or underemployment from rising as a proportion of the total male work force (currently 1.5 million out of a total work force of 7 million), another 8 million jobs or approximately 1500 jobs per day will be needed—and again most will be for black workers.[7]

In addition to the absolute and relative increase of blacks in the population as a whole and the absolute and relative increase of blacks as a percentage of the work force, the numbers of blacks in urban areas also will increase dramatically. Even under the conditions of petty apartheid, at any given time approximately 30 percent of blacks live in cities and 20 to 30 percent in white farming areas (the rest live in the homelands). Also at any given time about 2 of the approximately 7 million blacks in white areas are migratory workers living away from their families.[8]

By the year 2000, assuming that the economy finances a rate of growth of about 5 percent per annum, which allows new entrants to the labor market to find employment, the effect will be a huge growth in the black urban population. It is probably a reasonable assessment to state that the total population in the cities will be well over double what it is now (probably 20 million compared to the current 7 million) and that the population in the cities will be over 50 percent black (as opposed to the 30 percent at present). In other words, the majority of people in the cities will be black and the advanced sectors of South African society will be manned by blacks to a much greater extent than at present.[9]

Moreover, it is likely that there will be a need for many more skilled black workers and hence more blacks can be expected to become permanent residents in urban areas. For example, in 1970 there were 1.3 million white-collar workers in South Africa of whom 875,000 were white and 425,000 of other races. It is estimated that by 1990 the demand for workers in this category will increase to 2.8 million, of whom at the very most 1.3 million will be white. Also, there is already a need for additional skilled black workers in manufacturing and construction, so much so that jobs reserved for whites have almost completely been abolished. Without increasing the numbers of skilled blacks, most observers believe the economy is doomed to stagnation.[10]

In addition to the importance of black labor as the population and the economy grows, particularly in urban areas, blacks are becoming an increasingly important economic force as consumers. During the period from 1970 to 1976 real black earnings in the cities (excluding private service) rose by approximately 50 percent per employee; white rose by only 4 percent. Taking into account the higher direct tax payment of whites vis-à-vis blacks, the real disposable income of whites has probably declined.[11]

Although the abysmally low level of black income has increased, it is unlikely that the rate of black earnings over the next few years will match the rate of increases between 1970 and 1975. However, it is anticipated that real per capita income of blacks could grow at a rate of 2.25 percent during the next twenty years. White per capita income is expected to grow at a considerably lower rate, bringing about a relative redistribution of income. If, in addition, increases in white wages are eroded by higher tax rates for defense, etc., the percentage of disposable income accruing to blacks may be even higher. One major estimate predicts that black disposable income, which was only 35 percent of the disposable income of the country in 1975, could go as high as 60 percent in the year 2000.[12]

Based on calculations by the business community, the Reserve Bank suggests that a 100 percent increase in disposable income will be accompanied by almost an 88 percent increase in consumption and expenditure. It can be anticipated that over the next twenty years there will be a vast increase in internal demand—and most of this demand will come from black workers, usually in or near urban areas.[13]

Thus, barring unforeseen circumstances, it seems likely that urban blacks as workers, consumers, or even unemployed urban residents will play an increasingly important role in South African society. If there is economic and political stability and these blacks are productively employed consumers, the economy is likely to flourish. Moreover, blacks as skilled workers and managers in advanced positions and in most, if not all, major sectors of the economy will be in a position to decisively affect the functioning of the economy. In addition, as consumers they will hold another lever of power. If they decided to use this strength they would be able to affect the power of major institutions—just as consumers' boycotts and preferences have affected the workings of other societies in the past, most notably the American south in the 1950s and 1960s.

Similarly, even if the economy falters and urban blacks are unemployed in vast numbers or discontented, alienated, unproductive, and disruptive, they also will have great potential for

influencing the society. In this latter case, they will of course be
able to affect not only the economy, but also the very security
of the state. Indeed, former Prime Minister Vorster warned that
massive urban black unemployment was one of the greatest
threats to South African security. In sum, whichever way South
Africa turns, the urban black labor force will have a major
impact. The more dependent the economy becomes on this
labor force, the greater the potential.

How can this potential be realized? Will the state be able to
offset it, mold it, and shape it to adapt to the apartheid structure? Certainly this has been the case until now. As a number of
revisionist attacks on the liberal developmental theorists have
put it, "racial particularism" has successfully resisted the
demands of "universalistic industrialization."[14] On the other
hand, there has been little, if any, analysis of the potential
power of a mobilized black work force. Assuming even the partial organization of this work force by black (and white) union
leaders, the shift in the balance of internal forces could be considerable.

Union leaders in industrial society usually are powerful
figures. Their power is derived partially from personal skill, but
mostly from the institutions they control. These institutions are
powerful because they control significant organizations in key
sectors of society and because they have special access to millions of people.

Union power is based first and foremost on organization—the
large staffs and financial resources that many unions possess.
The larger and better coordinated the staff, the more powerful
the institution. In industrial societies it can be expected that
individual unions and national confederations will each have a
loose, but hierarchically organized large staff of elected and appointed full-time, part-time, and volunteer officials on the local,
regional, and national levels. These individuals will not always
agree on all major issues, and there will be varying degrees of
efficiency; but once a consensus has been reached by the leadership, the hierarchical nature of the organization usually ensures
a high degree of movement in the specified direction.

In the United States, for example, the typical major union
will have one part-time or volunteer elected official for every

150 to 200 members, a full-time professional or clerical staff person for every 1,000 members, and a full-time elected or appointed professional for every 2,000 members. This means that there is almost a small army of hierarchically related volunteer and paid officials in the United States—over 500,000 persons or 2.5 percent of the 20 million members of organized labor (one-fifth of the work force) working together, with varying degrees of efficiency, on the local, regional, and national levels.

The same is true in many developed countries, so it can be expected that a similar pattern could exist in South Africa. If only 20 percent of the black work force was organized—or approximately 2 million out of a projected 10 million—then there would be approximately 10,000 paid and volunteer officials working together in major urban centers. Blacks, of course, have never had such an organization.

The second characteristic that gives the organization power in Western nations is independently controlled financial resources. Although it may take outside pump priming to start an organization, once it starts to deliver services to the members (e.g., handling grievances, bargaining collectively, providing sick and death benefits, and offering education) and once the checkoff becomes legal, it can be expected that the membership will pay regular dues. The amount, of course, will vary according to the industry, working conditions, and services provided. But if 1 to 2 million workers pay 1 percent of their income to the union— not an unusual phenomenon in developed countries—the union over a five- to ten-year period will begin to amass considerable resources, and if in addition it is able to acquire control of health insurance and pension funds, it will begin to become a force in the economy of the country. Again, no black organization in the urban areas has had this kind of opportunity.

A third characteristic of organized labor is that usually it is very influential in key strategic centers of the economy. These sectors—transportation, communications, energy, and government—are strategic because if any one of them stops for even short periods of time, the whole society is thrown into turmoil and usually will grind to a halt within a few weeks, if not days. Again, blacks never have been able even to threaten, let alone use, this kind of power.

Finally, the union leadership has access to hundreds of thousands if not millions of people on a daily basis. There are few organizations in modern society that can reach anywhere from 20 percent to 50 percent, depending on the degree of affiliation and family size, of their population on a regular basis. There are two major ways this is done—through the labor media and through personal contact with full- and part-time officials.

Trade union media and particularly the labor press are little known outside the labor movement, but they are an important communications link, reaching literally millions of workers in both the developed and developing worlds. In the United States alone there are well over 550 publications put out by national unions, city central bodies, state federations, and major local unions, reaching approximately 20 million workers each year. In addition to monthly national papers mailed to each member, there are weekly and monthly local and regional papers circulated to the 20 to 30 percent of the membership that is active. These papers cover a wide range of human concerns in addition to parochial union issues, ranging from health care and recreation to domestic and international politics. In Europe and elsewhere a similar pattern can be observed. In addition to the labor press, unions reach their membership through specially prepared films and programs on radio and television.

Finally the unions have the ability to reach their membership through the contact their staff has with the membership on a daily basis. Although some unions have more officials than others, of necessity, they are in contact with the membership regularly, if not daily. In conversations on docks, ships, planes, and loading platforms, and in factories, schools, and offices, they reinforce or diminish the message in the labor and regular media. They explain the bad times and the good times; they identify the workers' "friends," and they point to the workers' "enemies." Perhaps only the church has as much persistent contact with the people as organized labor.

A similar pattern already exists in South Africa, of course. The current trade unions, white and Coloured, reach several hundred thousand workers. However, with the major exception of the black garment workers in the Transvaal, there is no major labor publication for black workers. The pattern of contact and the high quality and broad interests to be found in the garment workers' paper could become the model for a nontribal, multiracial communications pattern that has not yet been seen in South Africa.

If black union leaders were to have extensive organizations in key sectors and access to millions of workers on a daily basis, it must be expected that they would be able to exercise unprecedented influence over the evolution of South African society. If in addition they were to be democratically elected and even somewhat responsible to the membership, they would give urban blacks a democratic voice not only in setting the conditions of work (industrial democracy), but also in the evolution of the South African economy and, as economics affects politics, the future of the political system.

At present and in the foreseeable future, there are and will be few ways in which the white establishment can ascertain the views of urban blacks about the desired direction of change. Although the government can take polls and consult a few blacks, it has no reliable way of anticipating black feelings, aspirations, and likely reactions. The repeated and usually unanticipated outbursts and violence are indications of this. Indeed, it would be remarkable if the government could do this—it would fly in the face of the democratic experience that has shown the necessity of periodic elections to determine the true will of the people.

But not only would the organization and democratic election of black trade union leaders provide blacks with a voice in the evolution of their society and provide whites with a genuine measure of the feelings of blacks, it would, as was discussed, provide the society with a black leadership committed to democracy as an end and not just a means. This leadership would have a stake in the maintenance and extension of democracy. It would be a bulwark against Communists or black extremists who would seek to use the workers in strategic sectors of the economy to destroy any hope of peaceful and democratic methods of change. In large part because this leadership would provide such a powerful vehicle for peaceful democratic change and a strong institution with a stake in the emergence of a democratic system, there are those in South Africa and elsewhere who would prefer not to see the emergence of a strong democratic labor movement encompassing blacks.

There are several major groupings opposed to the development of democratic black unions—the *verkrampte* right, the Communists, and the racially exclusive left. The *verkrampte* right has ensured that blacks find it very difficult, though legally possible, to organize. Apart from the country's racial and labor laws, which impose a number of major restrictions on black labor,[15] many individuals seeking to organize black unions have been harassed or banned. It has been estimated, for example, that more than thirty key union officials working in the labor field have been banned during the past few years alone. Indeed, that black unions have been able to survive, let alone grow to the point that they represent about 1 percent of the black industrial work force, is remarkable.[16]

Another group opposed to the development of strong democratic unions is composed of Moscow-oriented Communists. In the 1940s and 1950s, the Communists were able to gain major influence in the African National Congress and in the main co-ordinating body of black unions, the South African Congress of Trade Unions (SACTU). By 1961, SACTU claimed to have forty-six affiliated unions and 53,000 members, but the same year also marked increased harassment by the South African government. A number of organizers were jailed on charges of sabotage and 3 members in Port Elizabeth were hanged in 1964.

By 1967, SACTU could no longer operate legally and since then it has continued to work, as it puts it, "underground." Although it does not claim to be the sole representative of South Africa's black workers, SACTU maintains that only those trade unions that work illegally are genuinely working for the "liberation" of black people.[17] SACTU works with the Soviet government and is affiliated to and receives material support from the Prague-based World Federation of Trade Unions.[18] It is also the beneficiary of Soviet efforts to discredit the black unions operating in South Africa.[19]

Finally, there is a racially exclusivist group of blacks who are unhappy at the prospect of a democratic, racially integrated society and of course unhappy with black and white trade union leaders striving together to bring about such a society.

Black opponents of an integrated democracy can be found in the more extreme parts of the Black Consciousness Movement that came to the fore in the early 1970s and particularly in the South African Students Organization (SASO). In conversations with this writer and an American group of black and white young political leaders in Johannesburg and Durban in 1972 and 1973 and in their analysis of world politics, SASO and some other leaders of the Black Consciousness Movement have expressed their hatred of all whites, South African or not. They also have been contemptuous of Western-style democracy and expressed their preference for the Mozambiquan and Chinese brands of "socialism." Although it is possible to sympathize with the frustrations of young blacks who have been raised in contemporary South Africa's cities, it is also easy to understand that they detest and seek to discredit as "Uncle Toms" those black trade union leaders with an interest in bringing about an integrated labor movement.[20]

However, there are now other major groups pressing for the development of genuine democratic black unions. Many industrialists, some white and even Afrikaans, union leaders, and church and intellectual figures now believe that if South Africa is to have stable industrial relations, as well as political stability, it is necessary to organize black workers. They argue that without trade unions industrial peace is not possible, without industrial peace there will be little investment, particularly from abroad, without investment there will be no growth, and without growth there will be massive black unemployment, disruption, and ultimately chaos and violence. Coalescing with those South Africans that seek the approval and support of the West (and particularly Western trade unions), there are growing pressures on the government to reverse its opposition to the growth of black trade unions. To resolve the dilemma, the government has appointed Professor Nic Wiehahn to chair a Commission of Inquiry into Labor Legislation. Wiehahn, who as a professor at the University of South Africa was inclined to favor the development of black unions, is expected to report to the minister of labor in 1979.

Should government policy change, there will be unprecedented opportunities to provide for the democratic evolution of

the country. Even if government policy does not change officially (and the South African government has been skillful in
changing even when there appears to be no official change in
policy), there is considerable opportunity for the black labor
movement to come into being so long as it is clear that the government does not actively oppose it. In contrast perhaps with
the situation in the United States many South African employers want to recognize unions and bargain with them. As
the Association of the Chambers of Commerce put it, "Trade
unions should be free to represent all ethnic groups. . . . Failing
all race groups being represented in one trade union, then black
trade unions should be registered and recognized."[21] So long as
the government lets it be known that it does not oppose black
unions, the employers will gradually begin to recognize and deal
with them, and over a period of time, the courts will enforce
the collective agreements.

Even without changes in legislation, union leaders can be
trained at labor education centers in universities, or by existing
unions and labor-oriented organizations such as the Urban
Training Project. Financial pump priming to train and equip
organizers in the field is available from existing unions, founda-
tions, and churches.

So long as the South African government does not interfere
with the process, one of the few major factors that could
impede the development of black trade unions is the attitude of
both internal and external trade unions and labor-oriented
organizations. If these organizations and groups conclude that
democratic black leaders can emerge and bring about change
through dialogue, discussion, persuasion, and communication,
then probably it can be done. Certainly, the prospects are sufficiently good to warrant the diversion of serious attention and
resources to this effort. On the other hand, if trade unions and
labor-oriented organizations both inside and outside the country conclude that the black movement cannot be an effective
force in bringing about democratic change, then they will be
creating a self-fulfilling prophecy that leaves South Africa and
the rest of the world facing the unacceptable and tragic choice
between violence and the status quo.

Notes

1. For a summary of both the liberal position (exemplified in the writing of Leo Marquard, Ralph Horwitz, and W. H. Hutt) and the revisionist attack (in the writings of Herbert Blumer, Stanley Trapido, and A. Asheron), see David Yudelman, "Industrialization, Race Relations and Change in South Africa," *African Affairs*, January 1975, pp. 82-96.

2. This is not to say that unions in the United States are any more corrupt than other segments of American society. As two leading students of American labor, John Dunlop and Derek Bok, argue, despite public perceptions to the contrary, a comparison of criminal prosecutions in various sectors including business and banking "yields no evidence that union officials are more prone to corrupt practices than other segments of society." Nevertheless, they continue, "despite these comparisons, the fact remains that corruption and abuses of democratic procedures seemed to occur more often in America than in the labor movements of Western Europe." Dunlop and Bok, *Labor and the American Community* (New York: Simon and Schuster, 1970), p. 67.

3. For a discussion of how the Communists, who controlled relatively small sections of the labor movement prior to World War II, emerged as the dominant force in postwar Italy and especially France, see Roy Godson, *American Labor and European Politics* (New York: Crane, Russak, 1976).

There is as yet no published study of how the Communists within a few years of the revolution in 1974 managed to gain control of two thirds of the approximately 360 unions of Portugal, especially when they can obtain only about 16 percent of the popular vote—and a great number of the Communist voters are to be found in the Alentejo, an agricultural region where there are few trade unions. For some additional details, see this writer's *"Eurocommunism": Implications for East and West* (New York: St. Martin's Press, 1978).

4. For a history and analysis of the labor and industrial relations in South Africa see J. A. Grey Coetzee, *Industrial Relations in South Africa* (Capetown: Juta and Co., 1976).

5. The following analysis assumes no major global war or major conventional wars involving South Africa or massive military buildups by South Africa. It assumes also that at this time there is no global depression nor major global economic changes and that economic sanctions have not been imposed on South Africa or, if they have, they are not "working." Finally, it assumes that the South African political system remains essentially the same, grand if not petty apartheid is in effect, the tribal areas

have changed little, and there is no major guerilla war although the tempo of domestic violence (terrorism, secret cell structures, etc.) has increased.

6. There appears to be a consensus in projections about South Africa's population and demographic cycle. Most analysts assume that white immigration and emigration will not add substantially to the white population and that the white birthrate is tapering off. Blacks on the other hand are expected to have a high though declining fertility rate, but also a continuing reduction in the mortality rate. Trends in the growth rates of the Asian and Coloured populations fall somewhere between these two poles. The most frequently cited calculations are those prepared by Professor J. L. Sadie, *Projections of the South African Population 1970-2020*, published in 1973 by the Industrial Development Corporation, Pretoria. See for example M. B. Dagut, *South Africa: An Appraisal* (Johannesburg: Nedbank Group Economic Unit, July 1977); and *Economist,* July 10, 1978, pp. 101-02.

7. See, for example, Harry F. Oppenheimer, "Apartheid Could Not Survive South Africa's Economic Growth," *Financier,* July 1978, pp. 24-28; *Economist,* June 10, 1978, pp. 101-06; *To the Point,* August 25, 1978, p. 13. For more detailed calculations see "Manpower and Unemployment in South Africa," 10th Annual Economic Cong., International Association of Commerce and Economic Students, Johannesburg, South Africa, July 4-5, 1977.

8. Oppenheimer, "Apartheid."

9. Ibid.

10. J. A. Parsons, "Manpower Needs for the Future—Projections, Issues and Strategies," *South African Journal of African Affairs,* no. 2 (1977), pp. 121-33. Also, Oppenheimer, "Apartheid."

11. See the interview with Professor Piet Nel, director of the Market Research Bureau, University of South Africa, in *To the Point,* August 25, 1978, p. 24. For more detailed calculations see "Survey of the Black Consumer Market and the Inherent Investment Opportunities," Max, Pollack, and Freemantle (private market research analysts), Johannesburg, November 1977.

12. Ibid.

13. Ibid.

14. See, for example, Randall Stokes and Anthony Harris, "South African Development and the Paradox of Racial Particularism," *Economic Development and Cultural Change,* January 1978, pp. 245-69.

15. See Coetzee, *Industrial Relations;* and "Infringements of Trade Union Rights in Southern Africa," Report submitted to the Economic and Social Council by the Ad Hoc Working Group of Experts appointed by the Commission on Human Rights, United Nations, New York, 1970.

York, 1970.

16. *Financial Mail,* July 28, 1978.

17. See, for example, the SACTU's monthly organ, *Workers' Unity,* September 1977. On the history of SACTU see Edward Feit, *Workers without Weapons* (Hamden, Conn.: Archon, 1975).

18. *Flashes,* October 11, 1978, pp. 4-5. *Flashes* is the biweekly newsletter of the WFTU.

19. For example, the U.S. Communist party and its youth arm, the Young Workers Liberation League, argued at a major antiapartheid conference on disinvestment in New York that only SACTU genuinely represented South African workers and that all other black unions should be regarded as State Department "sponsored." *Daily World,* November 18, 1978.

20. On the evolution of the black consciousness movement, see Gail M. Gerhart, *Black Power in South Africa: The Evolution of an Ideology* (Berkeley: University of California Press, 1978).

21. *Star* (Johannesburg), September 1, 1978.

Part 2
External Linkages and Pressures

4
Current and Projected Military Balances in Southern Africa

Chester A. Crocker

The Setting

By almost any conventional index of national military power, the Republic of South Africa continues to tower over any current or foreseeable African opponent or coalition. Its list of military assets and advantages is awesome in regional terms. During the 1970s, identified South African arms imports approached 50 percent of the imports into all the other countries of sub-Saharan Africa combined, though Egypt and Libya outspent the republic on imported arms.[1] In 1976, the last year for which comparative data is available, South African defense spending accounted for one-third of all African military expenditures (excluding only Egypt).[2] In terms of indigenous manufacture of licensed or locally designed defense equipment, it ranks along with such states as Brazil, Argentina, India, Israel, and Taiwan as a leading "third world" arms producer, far outdistancing the only other Organization of African Unity (OAU) member, Egypt, with the capacity to assemble or manufacture major weapons.[3] To be sure, the active duty armed forces of South Africa are comparable in size to, or smaller than, those of several African states—Algeria, Egypt, Ethiopia, Morocco, Nigeria, Somalia, and Sudan. But only Egypt can field a force comparable to the republic's trained, readily mobilized strength (including reservists) of some 404,500.[4] Standing behind South Africa's military establishment is the continent's strongest and most diversified economy, its leading steel and motor vehicle industries, a developed financial and communications system and transport infrastructure, and an unequaled pool of mana-

71

gerial and technological expertise.

This brief sketch only suggests the broad outlines of a South African regional military ascendency that few dispute. Debate centers largely on the extent and durability of the imbalance. Gervasi, for example, argues that to compare the republic with Nigeria militarily is inappropriate since it is "obviously far stronger than Brazil" and should be ranked alongside Iran, Egypt, or Japan.[5] Baker, on the other hand, questions the "citadel assumption" of South Africa's invulnerability:

> The fact of the matter is that the ferocious pace and revolutionary direction of change in southern Africa have overturned many of the most fundamental assumptions that have guided expert political analysis and American foreign policy since World War II. Conventional ways of thinking about southern Africa must therefore be reconsidered in light of these transformations, in particular, traditional evaluations of the strategic balance of power in the region.[6]

At first glance, a debate about the extent of South African military superiority could be dismissed as of only marginal interest provided that all observers have the same basic reading of the facts. But matters are not so simple, for three reasons. First, depending upon one's perspective, the military and internal security strength developed by Pretoria over the past fifteen years can be variously interpreted—as a threat to peace and security in Africa, an element of what little stability still remains on the continent, an invitation to outside intervention to support the cause of African liberation, a deterrent to such intervention, a form of insurance that will give the whites time to find a basis of accommodation with blacks and with neighboring black-ruled states, or a crutch that will enable whites indefinitely to postpone hard choices and real concessions. Thus, the prevailing balance of military power is inherently controversial and its policy implications for outside powers even more so. The extent of the imbalance, as perceived by both the local parties and outsiders, could have significant policy consequences.

A second reason for the debate's importance is that, as Baker points out, the situation is so dynamic. The *extent* of the imbalance may be less important than its *durability* once the guerrilla conflicts in Angola, Rhodesia/Zimbabwe, and Namibia are somehow resolved and strife comes ever closer to the republic itself, with unknown consequences for its own domestic tranquillity. Consequently, to project today's balance forward into, say, the mid-1980s, makes little sense unless alternative assumptions about intervening change are also considered. A future-oriented analysis of the southern African military balance requires discussion of conflict scenarios under varying assumptions about factors beyond Pretoria's direct control: external military intervention, external arms supplies and training for African guerrillas and government forces, the willingness and ability of its Western trading partners to bring substantial influence to bear, the pattern of political change in adjoining African countries, and the occurrence of conflict or crisis in other regions that may or may not thrust southern Africa into the leading place as a conflict zone of the 1980s. In sum, although the facts of military power today are of great importance, they do not speak for themselves.

Thirdly, consideration of South African military power is increasingly devoted to an analysis of how the republic acquired regional superiority. Some analysts conclude that Pretoria could not have become the military giant of Africa without the tacit or clandestine complicity of key Western countries that have provided arms, technology, and scarce skills for the buildup despite UN arms embargoes and official pronouncements.[7] Implicit in such charges of "conspiracy" is the notion that South Africa would be far less powerful (and less "threatening") in the absence of such ill-considered or malevolent assistance. There is the further implication that the republic can be significantly weakened by a strictly observed boycott of the trade in arms and defense-related equipment and technology. The importance of this line of reasoning is that it suggests a covert Western "commitment" to South Africa and implies a high degree of South African dependence on external supplies.

This chapter addresses each of the above aspects of the evolving military balance in southern Africa. Because of its current salience and its ability to shape one's vision of the future, the analysis begins with a discussion of the "conspiracy" theory of

the South African preponderance. Next, the historical development of the regional military balance is examined, and the near-
term significance of the current balance is assessed. The final
section looks at a range of changes, alternative assumptions, and
"gaps," or blindspots, in South African defense preparedness
that could alter the balance into the mid-1980s.

The "Conspiracy" Theory of South African Strength

Explanations of the southern African military balance hinge
in large measure on perceptions of history and the dynamics of
South Africa's growing international isolation over the past two
decades. Adherents of the conspiracy viewpoint argue that
(1) the white-dominated system is the embodiment of an evil
whose eradication should constitute a dominant priority in
Western diplomacy; (2) that system survives primarily because it
is supported by outside Western partners; (3) external "support" is based on a combination of racism, misguided preoccupation with maintaining regional stability against Communist
encroachments, and economic ("capitalist") interests; and
(4) external arms supplies have been kept tacit or covert
because they signify a "secret commitment" to South Africa.
As Gervasi puts it:

> The United States, then, has sold large quantities of relatively
> modern weapons systems to South Africa in recent years. And it has
> done so secretly. It has helped the apartheid regime to build a
> formidable military machine at the very time when a military chal-
> lenge is being mounted against it. . . . U.S. arms sales to South
> Africa represent a military commitment, a commitment to assist
> indirectly in the military effort which the apartheid regime is mount-
> ing to preserve the status quo, not only in South Africa but in the
> whole Southern African region.[8]

Finally, it is claimed that the "secret arsenal" acquired by the
republic from its Western partners disproves suggestions of its
military self-sufficiency. Although the country is indeed a major
regional power, that power depends directly on the decisions of
others.[9] From these arguments, it is a relatively simple matter
to suggest that the southern African "problem" could be satis-

factorily resolved if only the Western powers ceased buttressing Pretoria.

Like most conspiracy theories, this one is not without some factual basis. It can be argued that Pretoria has enjoyed much of the substance, but little of the political symbolism, of an institutionalized Western defense relationship. From 1945 up to the adoption of the voluntary UN arms embargo in 1963, Britain, the United States, and other sources openly sold military hardware to South Africa. During this period, the only significant constraint was the level of South African demand. From 1963 up to November 1977 (when the UN mandatory arms embargo was adopted), France and Italy assumed the leading role as arms sources, though there was little secrecy about these transactions. Gradually, concern over South African racial policies—and concern over being overtly associated with them—fostered greater discretion and camouflage: unreported third-party transfers, loopholes in embargo procedures, and the import of "dual" (civilian or military) use equipment or equipment readily converted to potential military use. Though the French and Italian roles were predominant—51 percent and 19 percent of reported weapons transfers in the period 1970-1976[10]—Jordan and Israel also sold defense equipment. The United States and United Kingdom continued to provide spares for earlier sales, dual use equipment, and components. Several hundred licensing and coproduction agreements were signed with various Western countries, giving South Africa an impressive base for self-sufficiency in armament production. Equally significant, formal controls on arms exports (where these existed) were not extended to a large array of items of obvious military value: communications, electronics, and radar systems; information processing equipment; civilian aircraft; and sophisticated engineering technology.

It is not yet clear how the export control and licensing procedures of major industrial countries will operate in practice as a result of the 1977 mandatory arms embargo against South Africa. However, the workings of U.S. embargo observance prior to 1977 have been fairly well documented.[11] It can be safely assumed that the procedures of Germany and Britain (and, of course, France and Italy) have been far less stringent.

In sum, until very recently South Africa has had little difficulty in acquiring via one means or another the imported hardware and technology to become a major regional military power. That much of this commerce has been conducted discretely (or "secretly," if one prefers) fuels the conspiracy charges and lends credence to the suspicion that something immoral, perhaps illegal, and certainly abnormal has occurred.

But the conspiratorial view of South Africa's regional preponderance has substantial flaws, and the implications of Western military commitment and South African military dependence are both misleading and inaccurate. These flaws are both factual and contextual.

In evaluating the southern African balance it is essential to recognize the extent of South Africa's ostracism and isolation, as well as its continuing Western ties. More important still, the basic direction has been one of steady erosion in the *political* basis of the Western relationship with South Africa during the postwar years. South Africa emerged from World War II as a member of the victorious Allied coalition and a close Western defense partner through the British connection. Until the 1960s, this military relationship rested on a reasonably firm basis of mutual interest, expressed both regionally and globally. South African leaders explored all available avenues to demonstrate the country's utility as a strategic-military partner of the West. In the 1940s and 1950s, this effort took the form of participation in Western collective defense efforts (e.g., Korea), the acquisition of defense articles oriented toward "allied" missions in the Middle East and the South Atlantic, and pressure for the creation of a Western security organization for Africa. Western arms exports were an integral element of this pattern, as reflected in the provisions of the 1955 Simonstown Agreement between Pretoria and London that formalized long-standing imperial cooperation for South Atlantic naval defense.[12] If this constitutes a Western conspiracy to build up South African armed strength, it is surely one of the most overtly conducted and publicly accessible conspiracies in modern history.

Over the course of the 1960s and 1970s, Pretoria assiduously cultivated Western military and political leaders, emphasizing a familiar litany of arguments: common anti-Communist policies, domestic stability, rich resource endowment, defensive strength, and Soviet naval and political ambitions centering on the maritime trade route around the Cape. Such overtures were echoed in sporadic proposals in Western military journals calling for a South Atlantic treaty or a southwards extension of NATO.[13] The Franco-South African military and intelligence tie grew in intensity, while interested Western defense establishments enjoyed the fruits of communications and intelligence cooperation, space tracking facilities, port access, and overflight rights. In the early 1970s, several NATO members showed rekindled interest in Indian Ocean strategic questions, as reflected in an increase in joint naval exercises with South African forces. During these same years, Pretoria achieved a growing level of Western engagement in its economy; and, as noted earlier, the arms supply nexus flourished despite the voluntary UN embargo.

But the political basis of the tie has eroded steadily. The republic's few gains in its effort to become a legitimate Western defense partner have proved to be remarkably ephemeral. The level of military cooperation has fallen far short of both Pretoria's aspirations and those of Western decision makers who would have preferred to act on straightforward "defense" criteria.[14] The most dramatic examples of this erosion—the 1977 UN mandatory embargo, Britain's unilateral termination of the Simonstown Agreement in 1975, and the political-diplomatic isolation of South Africa during the Angolan civil war of 1975-1976—only serve to confirm the underlying trend. Its exclusion from all formal alliance systems, political-cultural groupings such as the Commonwealth, numerous UN-affiliated organs, and international sporting competitions could not have occurred if South Africa's key Western partners were prepared to pay the political price of continued public association with it.

As a result, surviving forms of cooperation have been by necessity, sub rosa, vulnerable to hostile exposure; the very sensitivity of the subject limits the world view of Western decision makers who gradually internalize taboos and redefine threats to conform with political constraints. In South African eyes, the Western relationship is today a subject of the most profound ambivalence. On the one hand, Western (and especially American) actions over the past four years are viewed as a mixture of treachery, hypocrisy, and cowardice. Unless they are prepared to act and speak on the basis of a shared outlook concerning the "threats" facing southern Africa, Western capitals cannot be counted on. This interpretation is reflected in remarks by Foreign Minister Pik Botha as it became clear that Chapter 7 (mandatory sanctions) would be applied against Pretoria's arms imports in 1977: "Maybe it's just as well that it has started, because we can now unite our people and get our people to work harder in order to ensure our survival. . . . We now know where we stand, we clearly see we are alone. All this means is that we are on our own. We expected this. . . . We love our country. We are going to stay here."[15]

On the other hand, the emphasis in some South African discussions of Western policy suggests that current tensions in the relationship may last no longer than the current British and American governments.[16] But it would be a serious distortion to confuse the wishful thinking of some white South Africans with the underlying pressures shaping South Africa's future. Barring a major change in South African racial policies or a grotesque miscalculation by the Soviet Union and its allies in the region's conflicts or elsewhere, a South African military rapprochement with its former Western partners appears unlikely.

In sum, the historical sweep of South Africa's external relations points toward a far more complex picture than is conveyed by conspiratorial analyses. Despite the still expanding web of economic ties between the republic and its industrial trading partners, the momentum toward political and military disengagement is unmistakable, especially in the years since 1975. Strategic and economic incentives for continued arms supplies to South Africa have gradually become counterbalanced by the pressures of political embarassment and domestic controversy when arms deals are exposed. The "secrecy" discussed by conspiracy theorists is, in historical terms, the stepping-stone to an eventual termination of direct Western participation in the republic's defense effort.

Similar distortions are evident in other aspects of the conspiracy charge. The argument that Western arms embargoes have been narrowly confined to combat-related items and lethal hardware is, in reality, a veiled plea for selective (or, perhaps, not so selective) *economic* sanctions. In the postwar period South Africa has become a full participant in the world economic system dominated by the Western industrial nations; their trade and investment relationships permeate most sectors of its economy. To restrict the transfer of any end item, component, or technology of possible military application—engines, communications equipment, metal fabrication devices, chemical processes and systems, compressors, or electronic gear—would require joint (Western) enforcement procedures and machinery. The distinction between such an embargo and trade sanctions would be as difficult to define as that between a "civilian" or a "military" truck.

The concept of South African dependence on Western military support also raises important analytical issues. If some 55 percent of South Africa's 1977 military procurement was imported, 45 percent must have been indigenously produced. The ratio indicates that although the republic is not fully self-sufficient, it is by far the least militarily dependent of any country in Africa and one of the least dependent in the third world.[17] Moreover, the local armaments industries have acquired depth, breadth, and sophistication precisely during the past decade as it became increasingly clear that the days of easy access to Western arms might be numbered. Officials in Pretoria have accelerated the pace of planned acquisitions as the threat of isolation has increased, thereby cutting further the potential for external leverage on their actions. Nor would it be surprising if the net result of the 1977 UN embargo were to accelerate further the development and diversification of South African arms production, both for local consumption and export.[18]

A further problem with the notion of dependence, as South Africa enters the postembargo era, is the assumption that a nation imports items because it *cannot* produce them domestically. In fact, the principal obstacle to self-sufficiency is financial: given the scale of the market and the high initial investment required to increase the local content of arms manufactures, it is normally more cost-effective to import. But today, cost-effectiveness is only one of several competing priorities facing South African Defense Force (SADF) planners. Like other third world arms producers, the republic has security incentives for investing in self-sufficiency even at the expense of efficiency.[19] To assess the dependence issue properly, therefore, requires that one look beyond the ratio of imported versus local content in arms purchases to the more intricate question of *potential* technological self-sufficiency. This, as will be seen below, necessitates a review of the technological environment that the SADF must face, today and in the 1980s.

There is little doubt, as the critics of Western arms export policy charge, that substantial amounts of hardware and related technology have been purchased by Pretoria through various channels. Some of the claims made, however, have yet to be adequately documented; efforts by others to obtain verification are not known to have been successful. One wonders, moreover, why Pretoria would recently have resorted to purchases of such used and/or reconditioned items as F-104G fighter aircraft or U.S. armored vehicles.[20] Not only are these items lacking compatibility with comparable hardware already in the SADF inventory, but they would expose the SADF to the risk of parts or replacement scarcity at a time when security of the support pipeline is of increasing importance. Pretoria's armed forces are not known to be this desperate for basic combat equipment.

Finally, the conspiracy theory misconstrues South African dependence and Western responsibility in a more basic way by focusing attention exclusively on technological and arms transfer issues. South African military preponderance rests on far more than the arms inventory of the SADF. Other factors include the skill with which hardware is used, the military doctrine and training of the armed forces, the ability to mobilize disciplined and motivated manpower, and the logistics and communications available to support forces in combat situations. Relative to its African neighbors, South Africa possesses an abundance of these ingredients of military power, and they cannot be readily attributed to Western support. These advantages reflect the emergence in South Africa of a modern industrial society, however racially polarized and potentially explosive, whose governing white elite has major nontechnological assets to draw upon in seeking to retain power. The contrasts between the socioeconomic structure of this society and those beyond its borders are mirrored in the military balance.

Western involvement in South Africa has a 300-year history spanning all spheres of human activity. In this historical sense, the southern African balance is of Western origin, just as South Africa's literature, medicine, mining technology, and economic achievements have Western roots. Over time, however, the republic's possession of superior military technology may prove to be the least durable of its advantages, further weakening the view that white rule depends on external props.

The Evolution of the Southern
African Military Balance to 1979

There is nothing mysterious about the forces driving the South African military buildup. The whites face a mounting challenge to their political and economic position, amounting in their view to a threat to their physical and political security; and, they have the will and the resources to resist that challenge militarily. However, it is important to recognize how recently the South African security establishment has come to grips with the nature of the long-term pressures operating against the republic. Had it been otherwise, South Africa today would be far stronger militarily than it is. It would have spent larger sums on defense, recruited and trained a larger standing force and a deeper pool of technically competent civilian and military personnel, and acquired a far stronger basis for military self-sufficiency when the era of the mandatory embargo finally arrived. Instead, the republic has passed through two periods of what must be termed "relative complacency"—complacency, that is, relative to the ultimate threat.

In the years prior to 1960, South African defense expenditure remained under 1 percent of GNP and less than 7 percent of total government expenditure. Arms purchases were limited to modest amounts of U.K.- and U.S.-originated equipment (two squadrons of F-86 Sabre jets, several hundred T-6 jet trainers, up to 200 Centurion and Sherman (M-4) tanks, various types of armored cars), all of which together by the standards of the 1960s could accurately be described as "a practically obsolete Defence Force."[21] Little emphasis was placed on local arms manufacture owing to the ready availability of cheaper imported hardware. This is all the more striking in light of the significant level of armament production achieved by South Africa in World War II—including such items as bombs and ammunition, bomb sights, armored cars, howitzers and antitank guns, radios and naval instruments, vehicles, and small arms.[22] Interestingly, the South African Navy was the one relatively up-to-date service, though organized on a small scale. This reflected Anglo–South African naval integration and procurement decisions emphasizing maritime reconnaissance, high seas patrols, and an antisubmarine warfare (ASW) orientation.

By 1960, the SADF was an accurate mirror of conventional defense assessments of the late 1940s and 1950s. For political reasons, the prospects of future joint operations with Western forces beyond sub-Saharan Africa were minimal. At the same time, the level of threat from Africa itself was correctly perceived to be nonexistent, whereas Western predominance in the Indian Ocean and South Atlantic remained an apparently abiding reality. Together with the internally oriented police establishment, the SADF was fully able to cope with the threat of African nationalist uprisings or sabotage, and there was no imminent prospect of cross-border guerrilla actions.

Nonetheless, the first period of relative complacency came to an abrupt end with the advent of the 1960s. Between 1960 and 1966, SADF expenditure increased fivefold before leveling off for another seven years of relative spending stability up to 1972.[23] Key factors in South Africa's revised assessment included the Sharpeville tragedy and subsequent international reactions, as well as further evidence of the sacrifices Africans were willing to make, however futile, to challenge white power through political and terrorist organization. The independence of most sub-Saharan African states between the years 1960 and 1966 also played a role in Pretoria's decision to spend more on defense. A further significant jolt was the loss of direct access to traditional arms sources for most major weapons systems after the United Kingdom and United States adhered to the voluntary UN arms embargo of 1963.

Reading these signals, South African decision makers undertook a major increase in the defense effort. During the 1960s, the republic spent 2 to 3 percent of GNP and 15 to 20 percent of the national budget on defense; about $1 billion was allocated to arms procurement in the eight years up to 1969. New generations of armored vehicles, jet aircraft, transports, naval vessels, helicopters, and missiles were acquired, principally from the French and Italians. The SADF's miniscule Permanent Force (professional regulars serving as a command and control cadre and a training and maintenance establishment) rose 65 percent, while the Citizen Force conscripts and reservists rose nearly sixfold and the Commando reserves rose 18 percent.[24] Pretoria moved to resurrect its substantial local arms production capacity with the formation in 1966 of the Armaments Development Corporation of South Africa (Armscor) operating under the wing of the statutory Armaments Board to implement the drive for increased self-sufficiency. A salient feature of this period was Pretoria's emphasis on increasing local assembly and the local content of equipment produced under license agreements negotiated with external powers; thus, in the 1960s, South Africa embarked on the first of several stages required to achieve any important degree of military self-sufficiency.[25]

By the early 1970s, the SADF was a vastly stronger force than its predecessor of a decade ago, and the rate of increase in defense spending had leveled off. In the naval field, South Africa continued to be torn between the traditional ASW and maritime patrol missions associated with the Simonstown–United Kingdom connection and the development of a more defensive posture aimed at threats toward South Africa itself. Thus, it continued to seek modernization of its ASW units (naval and air), while ordering submarines and fast patrol boats. Despite this apparent uncertainty on naval matters, an estimated 80 percent of the military budget was oriented to the "landward threat."[26] There was little doubt that Pretoria's attention was focused principally on the possibility of unconventional guerrilla or terrorist activity from within or without and, to a lesser extent, of conventional attack from the north supported by a major power. By the same token, there was little debate among informed analysts—writing in 1964, 1970, or 1972—on the judgment that the guerrilla threat to white power in South Africa remained remote. Direct African intervention by OAU member states was considered "probably impracticable without the generous backing of a superpower."[27] The prevailing imbalance of power, when seen in the context of African nationalist goals, could "eventually embroil the great powers," as Brown and Gutteridge warned in 1964.[28] But such intervention was not seen to be imminent, and the sequence of events that might alter the prospects for a military challenge to white power in southern Africa remained obscure.[29]

The second period of relative complacency ended in the mid-1970s, as suddenly as the previous one fifteen years earlier. However well prepared Pretoria was for the threats of the recent past, its defense planners quickly concluded that a wholly new situation had emerged with the events of 1974-1977. Table 1 reflects the rise of South African concern:

TABLE 1

SOUTH AFRICAN DEFENSE SPENDING 1965-1978

(millions of current $)

1965 -- 296	1972 -- 581
1966 -- 347	1973 -- 773
1967 -- 398	1974 -- 1070
1968 -- 424	1975 -- 1450
1969 -- 509	1976 -- 1950
1970 -- 489	1977 -- 2231
1971 -- 575	1978 -- 2622

Sources: World Military Expenditures and Arms Transfers (ACDA), data for 1965-74 and 1967-76; data for 1977 and 1978 drawn from The Military Balance, 1978-79 (IISS).

In addition to sharp budget increases, a number of other trends are clearly visible in the republic's defense effort since 1974. The recruitment, combat training, and operational deployment of Africans, Coloureds, and Indians have burgeoned since the early 1970s. Given the sensitivity of this issue in white domestic politics, it is striking to note the speed with which Pretoria has overcome its past reluctance to take strides in this direction and, in particular, to discuss the matter publicly.[30] Estimates of the current nonwhite manpower contribution to the SADF Permanent Force (active duty regular soldiers, sailors, and airmen) point to about 2,000 men or some 12 percent,[31] excluding the embryonic homeland units and the tribally based and multiethnic units recently raised in Namibia. Nearly half of the active duty police are African, many of them armed.

These developments must be viewed in the context of the country's long-standing, postwar tradition of maintaining only a skeletal force of white regulars, the Permanent Force. Their function is to train and lead a larger pool of draftees (national servicemen) and to serve as a base for the mobilization of the Citizen Force and Commando reserves. (Only whites are subject to the draft and reserve obligations.) This cadre concept is particularly pronounced in the army, which maintains only 7,000 to 8,000 regulars or 2.9 percent of total ground forces (active duty and reserves).[32] As official pronouncements from Pretoria have recognized, a manpower structure whose professional component constitutes only 6 percent and whose trained, full-time ranks constitute but 17 percent of the overall SADF establishment is not adequate. In the words of the 1977 Defence White Paper:

> The full-time component cannot cope with the situation, and should already have been expanded to meet present requirements. The number of members of the Permanent Force and the national service component must indeed be doubled, and the civilians (in the S.A.D.F.) must be supplemented to some extent. In view of the strains put on the system of providing manpower, an investigation is under way into the most practical ways by which the necessary expansion can be effected.[33]

Accordingly, measures have recently been taken to (1) increase the recruitment and utilization of white women, (2) extend the national service obligation from twelve to twenty-four months, (3) improve the retention ratio of both professionals and national servicemen on short-term contracts through enhanced pay and benefits, and (4) expand the absolute size of the Permanent Force. Overall, the active duty armed forces rose 18 percent to 65,500 by 1978.[34]

Thus, the increased use of African, Coloured, and Indian manpower comes at a time of increased mobilization of white draftees and volunteers. The issue facing the SADF is *not* a shortage of potential military manpower—or, even, a shortage of potential *white* manpower. Rather, South Africa is only now coming to grips with the need for a larger standing force, especially in the army, and for a larger pool of professionals, training cadres, and technical personnel in all services. The republic has just begun to tap its substantial manpower resources. In doing so, it is confronting problems found in many military establishments, e.g., retention of officers, noncommissioned officers (NCOs), and technicians, as well as problems that are more specific to South Africa. Many factors enter into the South African manpower equation: white morale, the manpower needs of the civilian economy, a relative scarcity of professional cadres and especially instructors, the perceived "reliability" of African, Coloured, and Indian units, and financial and military trade-offs between expanding white versus black forces. To date, the evidence points to a cautious expansion of African, Coloured, and Indian manpower while primary attention is given to making the most efficient possible combination of white professionals, conscripts, and reservists for an environment of continued, low-level warfare.

The basic trend in South African policy in the 1974-1978 period has been a marked concentration of effort toward the operational defense problems the republic actually faces. This overall focusing of effort is seen in manpower increases, in expansion of local hardware procurement, in new procurement priorities, and in shifts in defense doctrine and organization. For the first time in its post-1945 history, the republic must deal with day-to-day military requirements, and it can no longer afford to diffuse its efforts over a multiplicity of hypothetical defense roles and force structures.[35]

Thus, for example, greater weight is now placed on maritime defense of the republic itself and far less attention is given to long-range maritime patrol (ASW). The refusal of the Western powers to supply modern maritime patrol aircraft and France's termination of contracts for two submarines and two corvettes after the adoption of the mandatory UN embargo have simplified SADF naval planning. Apart from the need to have a presence in South Africa's 200-mile exclusive economic zone (EEZ), the navy's main mission is coastal patrol against the threat of insurgent landing or interference with shipping in

South African waters. Longer-range ASW patrol is a Western, not South African, requirement. Accordingly, new procurement stresses fast patrol boats, minesweepers, and related missile armament.[36]

Similarly, the SADF is now organized to give priority to counterinsurgency efforts in Namibia and the northern and eastern Transvaal and semiconventional operations to strike at guerrilla concentrations across the republic's borders. While secondary attention is given to large unit conventional training, the SADF's regulars, national servicemen, paramilitary police, and reservists are gaining firsthand experience in counterinsurgency operations with associated air support. It must be remembered that South Africa's involvement in the Namibian and Angolan conflicts in recent years represents the first operational combat experience of the SADF since the Korean War, and this experience is decisively shaping what had previously been a skeletal peacetime defense force.

Weapons procurement policy reflects the new environment. In 1976-1977, Armscor and the Armaments Board were consolidated in a new structure aimed at streamlining the designing, ordering, and acquisition process. New resources have been made available to private subcontractors to enable priority to be given to local self-sufficiency in such items as telecommunications equipment, armored vehicles, missiles, and patrol boats. An indication of the involvement of local industry in SADF procurement is provided by the fact that some 1,000 firms are reported to have received 80 percent of locally spent procurement funds.[37] It is unlikely that Pretoria anticipated a mandatory arms embargo coming as early as it did, but there was ample warning of increased restrictions on its access to external hardware. Accordingly, the republic had several years to identify gaps, stockpile critical imported components, and expand production facilities. The new situation in southern Africa presents concrete current threats, as well as longer-range hypothetical possibilities. Thus, one would expect that Pretoria has given special attention to building up an adequate stockpile of "consumable" items for which there is a need now or will be in the near-term future—ammunition and bombs, missiles, howitzers and mortars, utility and light strike aircraft, helicopters, antitank weapons, mine-clearing equipment, radios, sensors, and other electronic detection devices.

Given past experience, a basic question must be asked about the South African response to the events of 1974-1978. One wonders whether the conventional judgment concerning South African military superiority remains valid over the next one or two years. Is there a possibility of a third phase of relative complacency in which Pretoria initially upgrades its effort and then "coasts" without adequate regard to "worst case" scenarios of politico-military change to the north? What type of scenario would be required to challenge seriously the South African defense and internal security apparatus, and what is the likelihood of such a challenge?

The expanded defense effort of recent years may be only the first stage in a process of escalation that could ultimately oblige South Africa to dig far more deeply into its potential resources. Its potential for further military expansion is beyond question. Current defense spending accounts for about 20 percent of the budget and slightly over 5 percent of the GNP. Some 1.3 percent of overall manpower between the ages of eighteen and forty-five is on active duty; if only whites are considered, the figure would be 7 to 8 percent. In financial terms, the South African defense effort is now greater than that of such countries as Poland, Turkey, Spain, and Brazil. It approximates the effort of South Korea and Sweden, and is closing the gap with Canada, India, and Israel. Yet, a signficant number of countries, facing less severe potential security problems, dedicate as much or more of their manpower, financial, and industrial resources to defense.[38] Consequently, the real issue is the possibility of near-term surprises, miscalculations, or hidden vulnerabilities as a result of complacency or a further transformation of the external environment.

The Near-Term Prospect

As indicated at the outset of this chapter, there is no basis for questioning the conventional military superiority of the republic in relation to any foreseeable combination of independent African states. Table 2 provides a crude quantitative sketch of the force relationship as of 1978.

TABLE 2

INDICATORS OF THE SOUTHERN AFRICAN MILITARY
BALANCE 1978

Country	Total Armed Forces	Combat Aircraft	Naval Combatants#	Tanks	Def. Bud. Mill. $
Angola	33,000	31	11	210	98
Botswana	1,000 (?)	NA	NA	NA	?
Lesotho	1,000	NA	NA	NA	?
Malawi	2,400	NA	NA	NA	9*
Mozambique	21,200	47	7	150	109
Swaziland	2,000	NA	NA	NA	2*
Tanzania	26,700	29	23	34	140
Zaire	68,400**	49	26	60	164
Zambia	14,300	30	NA	10	310
Subregional	170,000	186	67	464	832
Nigeria	221,000	24	13	140	2,670
Subregional + Nigeria	391,000	210	80	604	3,502
South Africa	65,500 (404,500 incl. reserves)	345***	26	260	2,620

Source: The Military Balance 1978-79 (London: IISS).

All armed naval units counted equally.

* Data for 1976 from World Military Expenditures and Arms Transfers, 1967-76 (ACDA).

** Includes paramilitary forces.

*** Does not include armed helicopters, transport and utility aircraft, or training aircraft convertible to combat role.

Table 2 only begins to suggest the extent of the disparity in armed strength. The South African and Nigerian navies are the only ones possessing units heavier than patrol craft, and the former far outranks the latter in fighting capability. The South African Air Force is the only one listed with the trained pilots, logistic support, and numerical depth to be considered an operational force. Comparative strength in tanks does not reflect South Africa's substantial inventory of armored cars and personnel carriers, nor does it convey the extraordinary complexity of maintaining armored vehicles in serviceable condition, particularly in combat situations.

Troop totals presented in aggregate form are virtually meaningless without an analysis of the parties' capacity to deploy, maneuver, and resupply actual combat units, to say nothing of such critical factors as leadership, training, and morale. None of the African states represented in Table 2 could deploy more than a token combat force to a potential combat zone on South Africa's periphery without substantial outside logistic support.[39]

To these disparities, one must add the enormous political and logistic advantages accruing to South Africa from a unitary command structure were it to face a wartime coalition of African states. As in the Rhodesia/Zimbabwe conflict, there is no basis for presupposing that the African "frontline" is capable of joint military action. Not only are the African states militarily weak, they are also autonomous political units that are unlikely to adopt a more common stance for long toward an issue affecting their tangible interests, as distinguished from their ideological positions. In addition, the fragility of political and economic institutions and the continuing internal security problems of many states listed rule out the possibility of a liberation offensive led by African conventional forces. As the remaining bastions of white power contemplate their immediate neighbors, they see an extensive vacuum of conventional military power for either offensive or defensive purposes. These are the factors that explain the almost total freedom of action for cross-border operations enjoyed by Rhodesian forces up through late 1978, despite their miniscule size and modest hardware.

So far, however, this discussion has omitted several key variables affecting the near-term military balance. A major constraint on the African conventional challenge to South Africa itself is the prevalence of other conflicts that must first be somehow resolved: continuing civil strife in Angola, the Namibia and Rhodesia/Zimbabwe struggles, and the uncertain state of Zairean internal stability and Zaire-Angola relations. Until at least some of these problems are settled, it will remain impossible for geographic and military reasons to mount a threat against the republic. Consequently, the projected military balance of the early 1980s depends entirely on one's estimate of the timing and outcome of other, more immediate conflicts. This judgment pertains equally to the prospect of conventional and guerrilla challenges to the republic. As Mozambique's actions demonstrate, South African–oriented nationalist guerrillas are unlikely to obtain the sanctuary and support required from neighboring states that are themselves preoccupied with other wars.

Such factors partially explain Pretoria's own involvement in the current phase of the Angolan conflict and its crucial financial and hardware support for the Rhodesian war effort. South African policy in Namibia may be similarly influenced by the calculation that continued resistance to militant nationalist demands will buy more time.[40] After several years of reacting to the shock of rapid regional change, South Africa's potential to influence its timing and direction appeared to be improving as of late 1978. This is not to say, however, that it is capable—acting on its own—of monopolizing the process of southern African change in order to establish a new, nonhostile order in place of the current unsettled one.

Another crucial variable is the level and nature of external involvement in southern Africa in the near-term future. Large-scale Soviet-Cuban combat involvement in the Namibia or Rhodesia/Zimbabwe conflicts would accelerate the political and military pressures on the republic. At the same time, such activity could trigger Western counteractions, and this prospect may deter the Communist powers, depending on the type of opportunity offered them by circumstances on the ground in those two territories. In addition, substantially increased Soviet-Cuban involvement could trigger a major South African military response, necessitating a level of military effort and risk beyond that deemed prudent in Moscow and Havana. Absent the achievement of internationally recognized settlements in the two conflicts, it appears most likely that Communist support for the Southwest African People's Organization (SWAPO) and the Patriotic Front guerrilla armies will continue to expand incrementally. However, such support is not likely to grow beyond the level actually desired by the guerrilla movements and by the African front-line states hosting them. To put it another way, such support may be restrained by the desire to avoid the charge that an African struggle has been transformed into a Soviet-Cuban liberation war. The experience of recent years does not suggest that Moscow and Havana are willing to extend their African activities beyond the point when they become controversial in the OAU and other African diplomatic fora.

An additional restraining factor is the capacity of the guerrilla movements to absorb, maintain, and use effectively substantial new infusions of military assistance. This suggests that the pace of military escalation in Namibia and Rhodesia/Zimbabwe will be governed above all by the rate at which the guerrilla movements themselves can develop the basis for successful "people's war."

Assuming, again, that negotiated settlements remain beyond reach, the time may come within the next two or three years when nationalist guerrillas succeed in breaking the will of the existing authorities in Salisbury and Windhoek (whether they be white or black). A sudden white exodus and a collapse of government authority could ensue, leading to a scramble for control and a belated South African effort to forestall the installation of a Marxist government with the direct help of Communist arms in the Angolan fashion. Alternatively, before that point is reached, military frustrations in Salisbury or Pretoria could prompt a sharp expansion of escalatory, cross-border strikes into neighboring African-ruled countries. A third possibility might be the emergence of a critical threat to a neighboring African government (Botswana, Swaziland, or even Zambia) from Communist-supported guerrillas, leading to overtly or tacitly invited South African intervention. In any such scenario, the Communist powers could perceive an inviting opportunity for a more frontal military challenge to the existing order. The issue in each case would be a Soviet-Cuban confrontation with South Africa (with or without Western diplomatic support or mediation) over who would control events in the disputed territory; these scenarios do not address white rule within South Africa proper.

There is no adequate precedent against which to judge Pretoria's military capacity to deal with a sophisticated conventional opponent. Nor is there any hard evidence of the likely black South African response within the republic should such circumstances develop, though the timing of the 1976 Soweto rioting in the wake of the 1975-1976 Angolan conflict may not have been wholly fortuitous. What the Angolan conflict demonstrated was the extent of Pretoria's diplomatic and political liabilities, not its military power. In fact, there is reason to suppose that the military lessons of Angola have given pause to

Havana as much as to Pretoria. South Africa experienced some difficulties in coordination and control over long lines of supply, and its forces would have had an easier time with more helicopters, heavier artillery, and better antitank weapons. But the 1,500 to 2,000-man South African expeditionary force acquitted itself well, taking only a small fraction of the casualties suffered by the Cubans, before the political decision to withdraw.[41] Thus, it would appear that neither Havana nor Pretoria would slide casually into a rematch. But neither is it likely that Pretoria is, in fact, deterred by the prospect of tangling with a strictly Cuban-African force—even one of some size (25,000 to 35,000 men)—provided the stakes are considered important and the technological balance has not changed substantially in the meantime.

On the other hand, there is no doubt that South Africa could be forced to back down in such a scenario by a sudden and large-scale application of Soviet (or East European) and Cuban military power. A naval screen could be thrown around the republic's coast to interdict or interfere with South African trade, while the Soviets and their allies brought sophisticated air and naval power to bear from Brazzaville, Luanda, or Maputo to take out its air and maritime defenses. On a less dramatic scale, Communist ground and air forces could seek to extend Pretoria's supply lines to the north and get it bogged down on several geographic fronts. Such an approach would offer opportunities to force South Africa to spend its scarcest military resources. Given its technological limitations, a modest stockpile of key consumables such as helicopters and fixed wing aircraft, and the high value placed on white lives, it is unlikely that South Africa would choose to participate in a prolonged war of attrition beyond the borders of the homeland itself.

By the same token, however, it may also be unlikely that the Western powers would let matters get so far out of hand without making a determined effort to limit the conflict. From the standpoint of the Soviets and their allies, one wonders whether they are prepared to commit major air and naval forces—or, alternatively, a sizable ground force (a minimum of 40,000 to 50,000 men) backed by squadrons of aircraft, tanks, and surface-to-air missile batteries—which the prudent military planner might request.

A final variable affecting the near-term military balance is the possibility of meaningful internal dissidence within the republic. Urban riots, demonstrations, and strikes occurred sporadically in the 1970s and will surely occur from time to time in the next few years. Terrorist incidents and small-scale infiltration attempts also seem destined to increase in frequency, as a function of the growing population of self-exiles from the republic. The South African system offers an abundance of sparks for potential unrest within an overall environment of sullen and apparently growing frustration at the failure of African aspirations to date. Three years before the riots of 1976, African workers had begun to demonstrate their potential bargaining power in a series of strikes, leading the *Rand Daily Mail* to plead, "South Africa dare not live with this kind of risk. We must provide proper trade union machinery for black workers. . . . This year they have sensed the nervousness of the whites and it will be surprising if they do not begin to take full advantage of it."[42]

Five years later, evidence of new potential vulnerabilities is not hard to find. Botswana, a geopolitically important element in South African stability, has begun to experience the impact of the spreading Rhodesian insurgency and the influence of political exiles passing through from the republic.[43] The Swaziland government has been obliged to crack down on internal elements pressing for an end to cordial relations with the republic, while several homeland governments have become caught up on domestic tensions and clashes with armed militants from urban areas.[44] One scholar of African nationalist politics considers that "the possibility of violent upheaval appears very strong" and questions how effective the state's repressive machinery would be "if blacks could unite in applying the leverage of their numbers, their economic strength, and their potentially superior morale." Pointing to a "revolution in popular attitudes" as a result of the Black Consciousness Movement, Soweto and its aftermath, she argues, "Today . . . it appears from the widespread outbreaks of urban violence and the ever-escalating level of coercion required by the regime, that the South African order is becoming increasingly unstable—and that one of the prime causes of this instability is the ideological reorientation taking place among the younger generation of urban blacks.'[45]

To this observer, however, violent upheaval does not appear to be imminent, in the absence of some external cataclysm capable of profoundly shaking the will and morale of white South Africa. The term "upheaval" implies a completely different order of events from anything yet seen, an uncontrollable wave of violence (whether spontaneous or organized) that cannot be contained short of a reordering of basic power relationships. The South African state, on the other hand, is structured politically and organized militarily to withstand significant levels of unrest by international (and especially Western) standards. There are many explanations for this state of affairs, but the internal military balance is prominent among them. In raw, physical terms, the white minority possesses overwhelming firepower to sustain an administrative apparatus designed, if necessary, to break black organization and seal off the black majority from the essentials of life. At the present juncture, it seems likely that this capacity could be used successfully before violence became uncontrolled or triggered direct international intervention.

This admittedly impressionistic view is buttressed by both history and revolutionary theory. Analysts differ over the respective roles played by attitudes, objective hardship, and political organization as triggers of revolutionary violence. However, few would dispute Lin Piao's dictum on the critical importance of organization and arms in a revolutionary struggle. In addition, the actions taken by the state also appear to influence the extent to which politics becomes transformed into violence, thus leaving open the question of when and if an upheaval will occur. Finally, the revolutionary process depends on the capacity of insurgent organizations to gain support by coercion and the offering of tangible rewards—a capacity that remains underdeveloped in black South Africa.[46]

Some scholars stress the importance of indigenous leadership and organization and safe sanctuaries in African anticolonial wars, downplaying the role of external aid, especially from the OAU. Describing the struggle in Portuguese Africa, one concludes:

The three simultaneous wars were sufficient to drain the human and material resources of Portugal, to impose an increasing financial burden on an authoritarian regime whose revenues declined for civilian programmes at home, and to sow dissatisfaction amid its own population and most crucially in the armed forces. Waiting for despondency and dissension to develop within the enemy's ranks proved all that was necessary.[47]

But white South Africa's circumstances differ drastically from those of Portugal, and it would be unwise to project a predictable or easy road ahead for would-be insurgents. The evidence from Rhodesia underscores the point that the nature of the incumbent regime is of decisive importance, while it also suggests that rebels require large amounts of both patience and unity. In the post-Soweto period, there is little evidence to suggest that nationalist guerrillas have succeeded in tackling the enormous logistics, training, and morale problems that confront them. Efforts to launch any form of sustained urban terrorism or rural-based guerrilla activity have failed to date. South African officials estimate that about 4,000 black guerrillas are in training in neighboring and more distant African states, three-quarters of them members of the African National Congress. Some nineteen noteworthy incidents were reported over the twenty-six months up to January 1979, concentrated primarily in the Transvaal.[48] These events must be interpreted as strictly preliminary rounds for a future contest that cannot get under way on a serious scale until the turmoil in neighboring Africa is somehow resolved.

Longer-Term Projections of the Balance

A host of imponderables confronts the analyst looking beyond the next two to three years in southern Africa. The preceding discussion suggests that among the states of the region South Africa may retain its military predominance during this period. Only some combination of South African and Soviet-Cuban miscalculation would appear able to upset this projection, unless the Western powers seek to bring Pretoria to its knees through overwhelming economic pressure—a contingency deemed possible but unlikely in this time period. Looking ahead to the mid-1980s, the same judgment about the balance of military strength could be projected, but only subject to a longer list of conditions. It could be argued, moreover, that purely military factors may be of declining importance over time in relation to such other factors as global and South African economic trends, white migration patterns, and domestic political reform or repression in the republic. However, military variables will remain important.

Whatever one concludes about the republic's internal future, the country is located in one of the world's least stable regions where a new pattern of external involvement has been inserted. The region's traditional Western relationships are marked principally by hesitation and ambivalence—in black Africa, white Africa, and the West. Starting from a low base relative to other regions, African (including South African) arms imports rose nearly tenfold in the decade up to 1976 in real terms. During the same period, the portion of total imports devoted to arms purchases rose from 1.4 percent to 5.7 percent, and there is every reason to expect that it continues to rise. Although Africa, including southern Africa, remains one of the least militarized regions, it is the world's most rapidly militarizing region.[49]

This trend reflects a dramatic rise in the role of Soviet arms supplies to Africa where Moscow provided 56 percent of total arms imports during the same period. Much of the influx is concentrated among twelve states where the USSR is the sole or predominant arms source, including Angola and Mozambique and the guerrilla movements aided at overthrowing minority rule.[50] Thus, in a very real sense, the pace at which southern African conflicts become militarized is a function of Soviet foreign policy, as well as the decisions of the local actors. Given the limits on the absorptive capacity of African arms recipients, any marked increase in their ability to challenge the military position of Pretoria will depend directly on the participation of the Soviets and their allies in training, logistics, intelligence, and combat roles.

Assuming that settlements of today's conflicts are achieved by the mid-1980s, two types of outcomes (or some combination of them) could face Pretoria. In the first scenario, the insurgent nationalist movements seeking power in Rhodesia and

Namibia are successful, with Communist support. One by-product of this process might be significant political change in one or more of the other major black-ruled states (Botswana, Zambia), leading to a proliferation of governments committed to a militant stance against Pretoria. Soviet influence over the economies and security forces of the region would expand, together with the development of a serious South African guerrilla effort armed by Moscow. In the second scenario, some of the same African pressures would be present but to a lesser degree owing to Soviet restraint, Western involvement on a substantial scale as an alternative partner of some African governments, or the continuing economic and military influence of the republic itself. For whatever reason, the Communist powers and the advocates of confrontation would face greater obstacles in mobilizing African support for military options. Hence, the African front line would come to resemble the Arab front line facing Israel for much of the past thirty years. The arms supplied to African states would be used to buttress regimes and control resident guerrilla movements, as much as to confront apartheid; South Africa might itself be an integral participant in the process, serving as an alternative source of arms for governments or groups the Western nations are unwilling to support.

Decision makers in Pretoria can hope and plan for the second scenario, but must be prepared for the first. If the West disengages from the region and it becomes impossible politically for black governments to do any form of business with the republic, the first scenario *will* emerge. A period of prolonged cross-border escalation could ensue, culminating at the point when Pretoria would be ready (perhaps too late) to engage in serious bargaining about a sharing of power. (This assumes that another form of internal bargaining is not already under way, as a result of white recognition that sheer military power has been overtaken by black economic and political power.) How long it might take to force Pretoria to bargain is a matter of guesswork, but the conflict would be shortened by South Africa's failure to remedy potential gaps and vulnerabilities in its stance. It cannot assume, for example, that the border areas most suitable for guerrilla operations—Rhodesia/Zimbabwe, Mozam-

bique, Swaziland[51]—will remain indefinitely neutralized or
friendly as at present. Nor would whites be safe in assuming an
indefinite continuation of the military backwardness so preva-
lent in Africa today. Even if African governments take a decade
or more to develop substantial combat capabilities, African
guerrillas will have a more compelling set of incentives to become effective. Besides, effectiveness need not hinge on seizing
territory; it may be measured also by the casualties inflicted on
government troops and the costs imposed on the modern
economy and white standard of living. Hence, the racial self-
assurance or arrogance so intimately connected with the survival
of white rule to date could, over time, become a source of miscalculation and surprises.

Surprises could also flow from unexpected shifts in the military technology arrayed against Pretoria. This will be all the
more likely if official planners are inwardly counting on a
return to the days of Western arms supplies and indefinitely
continued access to military-related technology. From the
South African standpoint, "worst case" planning must assume
that, at best, the Western powers will pursue their regional
interests through diplomatic means backed by naval presence in
surrounding waters and arms transfers to friendly African governments. Any direct form of Western military support for
Pretoria itself—perhaps in reaction to unrestrained Soviet behavior—must be considered an unlikely bonus.

The republic possesses or is developing the arms inventory
and arms production capacity to meet most threats projected in
the previous section of this chapter. Among the locally produced items in which there is a high degree of local content (as
distinguished from reliance on embargo loopholes or previously
stockpiled kits and subassemblies) are armored cars, mine-
clearing vehicles, and personnel carriers; patrol boats and other
light naval vessels; most ammunition types, bombs, fuses, and
propellants; communications equipment; light ground-attack
fighters (Impala I and II) and utility aircraft; guns, mortars, and
light to medium artillery; chemical weapons, napalm, tear gas;
some engine types and electronic equipment; air-to-air missiles;
and some aircraft alloys.[52] Bearing in mind the critical importance of a few unavailable components, it is by no means cer-

tain that these items are all producible if the embargo is strictly enforced, except after long lead times needed to duplicate (by hand) foreign technology. Even assuming they are, potentially important gaps may remain. Heavy artillery and tank guns, heavy armor, helicopters, various missile types and homing devices, avionics, fire control radar, and modern jet strike air- craft (beyond the Mirages already completed under license) are not known to be in production in the republic. Time and great expense would be required to develop significant production capability in many of these areas. Thus, Pretoria faces hard choices about how and when to use its existing equipment. Similarly, it faces choices about where to invest its funds in local production, what items to stockpile, and how great an effort to make to keep up with the ever-increasing sophistica- tion of military technology.

The analysis in this chapter contains the implication that the South Africans must make such investments on a major scale if they wish to maintain some degree of regional supremacy into the mid-1980s. So far, the evidence suggests that they are doing so. Though arms imports have necessarily declined since 1977, the level of production and employment at Armscor plants has been growing at a minimum of 25 to 30 percent annually. There is no reason to project that the build-up of domestic armaments industries will soon level off. However, technological variables that constitute so visible an element of its present superiority appear destined to decline in relative importance as neighboring Africa, with outside support, catches up. A context of steadily increasing escalation would only accentuate the fact that the republic's technological base, however impressive by regional standards, is finite. When and if this happens, the southern African balance would come to rest more clearly on the less tangible strengths and weaknesses of the white position.

Notes

1. As reported in SIPRI's *World Armaments and Disarmament: SIPRI 1978 Yearbook* (New York: Crane, Russak and Co. for the Stockholm International Peace Research Institute, 1978), pp. 232-33. Using different

data, sources, and methodology, Sean Gervasi concludes that as much as two-thirds of the South African defense budget is spent on imports, a conclusion that would mean that it imported arms in 1975 alone greater than the SIPRI total for the years 1970-1976 inclusive. See his "The Breakdown of the Arms Embargo against South Africa," testimony before the Subcommittee on Africa, U.S. House of Representatives Committee on International Relations, July 14, 1977, reprinted in *Issue* (Quarterly of the African Studies Association) 7, no. 4 (Winter 1977):29. Official U.S. government figures on arms imports for the years 1970-1976 total $756 million, compared with the SIPRI total of $779 million (both in constant 1975 dollars). See Arms Control and Disarmament Agency, *World Military Expenditures and Arms Transfers 1967-76* (Washington, D.C.: ACDA, July 1978), p. 148. Gervasi's account appears to be based upon a debatable interpretation of South Africa's *White Paper on Defence, 1977* (Cape Town: Department of Defence, March 1977), p. 12, which could be read to imply that 55 percent of the defense budget was spent externally. The more likely interpretation is that 55 percent of arms *procurement* was external.

2. ACDA, *World Military Expenditures*, pp. 29, 61.

3. SIPRI, *World Armaments and Disarmament*, Appendix 7B, pp. 203-22; see also Gregory R. Copley, Michael Moodie, and David Harvey, "Third World Arms Production: An End to Embargoes?" *Defense and Foreign Affairs Digest*, August 1978, pp. 10-13, 30-31; and *Strategic Survey 1976* (London: International Institute for Strategic Studies, 1977), p. 22.

4. *The Military Balance, 1978-79* (London: International Institute for Strategic Studies, 1978), country data.

5. Gervasi, "Breakdown of Arms Embargo," p. 32.

6. Pauline H. Baker, "South Africa's Strategic Vulnerabilities: The 'Citadel Assumption' Reconsidered," *African Studies Review* 20, no. 2 (1977):90.

7. The most prominent exponent of this school is Sean Gervasi. In addition to his testimony cited above, see his "The United States and the Arms Embargo against South Africa: Evidence, Denial, and Refutation," *Southern Africa Pamphlets*, no. 2 (Binghamton, N.Y.: Foundation of State University of New York at Binghamton, 1978), which contains his July 1977 testimony, a reply by a Department of State spokesman, and subsequent evidence presented by Gervasi to the United Nations Committee against Apartheid, May 20, 1978. Much of the recent data alleging post-1963 U.S. embargo violations is derived from a volume by his brother Tom Gervasi, *Arsenal of Democracy* (New York: Grove Press, 1978). For related work conforming to Gervasi's view, see the chapters by

Michael Klare and Eric Prokosch, Ronald Walters, and Robert Sylvester in Western Massachusetts Association of Concerned African Scholars, eds., *U.S. Military Involvement in Southern Africa* (Boston: South End Press, 1978). The major work suggesting a Western "conspiracy" on matters of nuclear cooperation is Barbara Rogers and Zdenek Cervenka, *The Nuclear Axis: The Secret Collaboration between West Germany and South Africa* (New York: Times Books, 1978). See also Ronald Walters's earlier "The Nuclear Arming of South Africa," *Black Scholar*, September 1976.

    8. Sean Gervasi, "United States and Arms Embargo," pp. 45, 47.

    9. Ibid., p. 35.

    10. SIPRI, *World Armaments and Disarmament*, p. 233.

    11. See Robert Sylvester, "U.S. Observation of the Arms Embargo," in Western Massachusetts Association, *U.S. Military Involvement*, pp. 221-43; and Michael T. Klare and Eric Prokosch, "Getting Arms to South Africa," *Nation*, July 8-15.

    12. An official overview of South African defense cooperation with the Western powers in World War II, the Berlin airlift, and the Korean War is found in "Partners in Combat," backgrounder issued by the information counsellor, South African Embassy, no. 7 (Washington, D.C., 1978). A British view of the pre-1960 period is offered by W.C.B. Tunstall, *The Commonwealth and Regional Defence* (London: Athlone Press for the University of London, 1959), pp. 47-51. On the provisions of the Simonstown Agreement and the role of the Simonstown facility see the analysis in "South Africa and the Defence of the West," *Round Table* (London), January 1971, reprinted in *Survival* 13, no. 3 (March 1971):79-83; and D.C. Watt, "The Continuing Strategic Importance of Simonstown," *U.S. Naval Institute Proceedings* 95, no. 10 (1969):51-54. A fuller treatment of Anglo–South African military cooperation is presented in Dennis Austin, *Britain and South Africa* (London: Oxford University Press, 1966), Chapter 5.

    13. See, for example, Geoffrey Ripon, "South Africa and Naval Strategy," *Round Table* (London), July 1970; various articles in *NATO's Fifteen Nations*, April-May 1972; and *International Defense Review* 3 (1969).

    14. A recent example of such argumentation, by the former NATO commander in chief of Allied Forces Northern Europe, is (Gen.) Sir Walter Walker, *The Bear at the Back Door: The Soviet Threat to the West's Life-line in Africa* (Surrey, U.K.: Foreign Affairs Publishing Co., 1978), pp. 9-15, 123-38. See also Robert L. Schuettinger, ed., *South Africa—The Vital Link* (Washington, D.C.: Council on American Affairs, 1976), chapters by James Dornan, (Lt. Gen.) Daniel O. Graham, and (Sen.) Carl T. Curtis; Patrick Wall, "The West and South Africa," in Patrick Wall, ed., *The Indian Ocean and the Threat to the West* (London: Stacey Interna-

tional, 1975), pp. 39-64.

15. Quoted in Daan Prinsloo, *United States Foreign Policy and the Republic of South Africa* (Pretoria: Foreign Affairs Association, 1978), p. 131.

16. Ibid., pp. 117-22.

17. Peter Lock and Herbert Wulf, *Register of Arms Production in Developing Countries* (Hamburg: Study Group on Armaments and Underdevelopment, March 1977), pp. xi-xii and Table 1 and country registers for Africa, pp. 55-73. The concept of military dependence is explored more fully in the author's "Military Dependence: The Colonial Legacy in Africa," *Journal of Modern African Studies* 12, no. 2 (1974).

18. Although not yet a significant exporter, except to Malawi and Rhodesia, the parallel with other third world arms producers and the limits of the domestic market strongly suggest a growth of South African interest in exports of both components and end items. See Anne Hessing Cahn, Joseph J. Kruzel, Peter M. Dawkins, aud Jacques Huntzinger, *Controlling Future Arms Trade* (New York: McGraw-Hill for the 1980s Project of the Council on Foreign Relations, 1977), pp. 87-88.

19. The primacy of security considerations in fostering indigenous arms production is by no means confined to South Africa. See Michael Moodie, "Defense Industries in the Third World," in Robert Harkavy and Stephanie Newman, eds., *Arms Transfers in the Modern World* (New York: Praeger, 1979), p. 5.

20. This writer has been unable to obtain such confirmation in extensive interviews with official and unofficial sources. See also the caveat on this alleged transaction in Michael T. Klare and Eric Prokosch, "Getting Arms to South Africa," *Nation*, July 8-15, 1978. The initial source of the F-104G claim is Sean Gervasi, *United States and Arms Embargo*, pp. 42-44, whose only identified source is the previously cited work by his brother Tom Gervasi, *Arsenal of Democracy*, p. 73.

21. *White Paper on Defence and Armament Production, April 1969* (Pretoria: Government Printer, 1969), p. 2. Some force data for the early 1960s is contained in Neville Brown and W. F. Gutteridge, "The African Military Balance," *Adelphi Papers*, no. 12 (London: Institute for Strategic Studies, August 1964), pp. 9-10.

22. Union of South Africa, *A Record of the Organization of the Director-General of War Supplies (1939-43) and Director General of Supplies (1943-45)*, cited in Deon Fourie, "The Military Environment in Southern Africa," unpublished paper in author's possession (1977), p. 9.

23. SIPRI, *World Armaments and Disarmament*, p. 158.

24. *White Paper on Defence and Armament Production*, pp. 2-3.

25. A full description of the stages toward self-sufficiency is contained

in Moodie, "Defense Industries," pp. 5-6.

26. Assessment by Geoffrey Kemp, "South Africa's Defence Programme," *Survival* (London: IISS, July-August 1972), pp. 160-61.

27. Richard Booth, "The Armed Forces of African States, 1970," *Adelphi Papers*, no. 67 (London: IISS, May 1970), p. 2.

28. Neville Brown and W. F. Gutteridge, "The African Military Balance," *Adelphi Papers*, no. 12 (London: IISS, August 1964), p. 3.

29. For an earlier and still useful attempt at scenario development, see Charles W. Petersen, "The Military Balance in Southern Africa," in Christian P. Potholm and Richard Dale, eds., *Southern Africa in Perspective* (New York: Free Press, 1972), pp. 300-01, 316-17.

30. *Paratus* (monthly journal of the SADF), February 1977, pp. 15, 17, and February 1977 Supplement to same issue, p. vi.

31. Estimate of Kenneth W. Grundy based on South African parliamentary sources in "The Use of Blacks in the South African Armed Forces" (Paper presented to the 21st Annual Meeting of the African Studies Association, Baltimore, November 1-4, 1978), pp. 17-18.

32. *White Paper on Defence, 1977*, p. 31.

33. Ibid., p. 18.

34. *Military Balance, 1978-79*, p. 49; and *The Military Balance, 1977-78* (London: IISS, 1977), p. 47.

35. On the lingering impact of the U.K. legacy, see Richard Dale, "The Legacy of the Imperial-Commonwealth Connection for South African Defense Policy: A Tentative Appraisal" (Paper prepared for the Biennial Conference of the Section on Military Studies, International Studies Association, Charleston, South Carolina, November 8-10, 1978).

36. *White Paper on Defence, 1977*, p. 23.

37. Ibid, p. 26.

38. *Military Balance, 1978-79*, pp. 88-91.

39. Logistics, including the ability to transport and resupply troops and to move and maintain equipment, is of decisive importance in considering actual combat operations, especially over long distances. The discussion by W. F. Gutteridge in David Wood's "The Armed Forces of African States," *Adelphi Papers*, no. 27 (London: IISS, April 1966), pp. 3-4, remains substantially valid twelve years later. On the centrality of political, rather than military, roles played by the African military, the fullest account is in J. M. Lee, *African Armies and Civil Order* (London: Cuatto and Windus, 1969), especially pp. 52-85.

40. See the discussion of Pretoria's Namibian options in Chester A. Crocker and Penelope Hartland-Thunberg, *Namibia and the Crossroads: Economic and Political Prospects* (Washington, D.C.: Center for Strategic and International Studies, Georgetown University, 1979), pp. 9-11, 27-29.

41. An official South African account of these operations is contained in "The Nature and Extent of the SADF's Involvement in the Angolan Conflict" (Pretoria: Defence Headquarters Press Release, February 3, 1977). A fuller and less partisan account is found in Robin Hallett, "South African Involvement in Angola" (Cape Town: University of Cape Town Africa Seminar, October 1977), pp. 6-11.

42. Cited in *Africa Research Bulletin*, Political, Social and Cultural Series (September 1973), pp. 2989-990.

43. Richard Dale, "The Challenges and Restraints of White Power for a Small African State: Botswana and Its Neighbors," *Africa Today* 25, no. 3 (1978):15-18.

44. On recent Swaziland and Bophuthatswana internal events, see the reports in *Africa Research Bulletin*, Political, Social and Cultural Series (August 1978), pp. 4962-963.

45. Gail M. Gerhart, *Black Power in South Africa: The Evolution of an Ideology* (Berkeley: University of California Press, 1978), pp. 17, 300.

46. See Bernard A. Nkemdirim's review article "Reflections on Political Conflict, Rebellion, and Revolution in Africa," *Journal of Modern African Studies* 15, no. 1 (1977):83-84, 87-90. Though dated, much useful analysis and background are contained in Sheridan Johns, "Obstacles to Guerilla Warfare—A South African Case Study," *Journal of Modern African Studies* 11, no. 2 (1973).

47. Thomas H. Henriksen, "People's War in Angola, Mozambique and Guinea-Bissau," *Journal of Modern African Studies* 14, no. 3 (1976): 398. A far less sanguine view of the potential for rural-based guerrilla warfare is in Claude E. Welch, Jr., "Obstacles to 'Peasant War' in Africa," *African Studies Review* 20, no. 3 (1977). Welch specifically limits his basic conclusions to situations in which "alien rule" is not a major factor; despite this, his observation that urban outbreaks are more likely than rural revolution may have pertinence to South African conditions.

48. *Rand Daily Mail*, June 2, 1978; *Argus* (Cape Town), January 29, 1979.

49. ACDA, *World Military Expenditures*, pp. 29-31, 116-18.

50. Joseph P. Smalldone, "Soviet and Chinese Military Aid and Arms Transfers to Africa: A Contextual Analysis," in a forthcoming volume on Soviet and Chinese policy in Africa by Warren Weinstein and Thomas H. Henricksen, eds. (New York: Praeger, 1979).

51. On terrain features affecting guerrilla operations, see Petersen, *Military Balance in Southern Africa*, pp. 300-01.

52. This list is confined to publicly reported items. See Lock and Wulf, *Register of Arms Production*, pp. 63-67; and SIPRI, *World Armaments and Disarmament*, pp. 210, 220-21.

5
The African States
as a Source of Change

I. William Zartman

Change in South Africa will be primarily an internal matter. It will, however, have many causes, interacting with each other in ways that are often difficult to separate. African states are a distinct, and interested, group of forces and therefore deserve a special focus of attention, even though such special attention should not be taken to imply that they will be a major or conclusive cause for change. African states—it will be suggested here —will provide the necessary background of pressure for change, but this pressure will not be sufficient or even immediately productive of the desired outcome. Yet their role of background pressure cannot be abandoned if change is to result.

To arrive at this conclusion, this chapter will examine the past, the present, and the future. It will begin with a rapid review of past African policies toward South Africa, although here too it is frequently difficult to separate the South African target from other steps in the decolonization of the continent. It will then look at the major ingredients of policy choice, in an effort not only to show what policy is made of but also to show that African states' responses to the situation are not likely to be united or homogeneous. Thus, African states will not only be reacting against South Africa but also interacting in a policy debate over appropriate strategies, as they have in the past but even more so. Finally, the chapter will examine the nature of five such prospective strategies to evaluate both their impact and their chances of being adopted in part or in whole.

In the basic document of the liberation struggle for southern Africa, the Lusaka Manifesto, issued on April 16, 1969, by the heads of state of central Africa and adopted by the 1969 heads of state meeting of the Organization of African Unity (OAU) at Addis Ababa, the independent African states declared the political equality of citizens in southern African states to be their goal and "peaceful methods of struggle even at the cost of some compromise in the timing of change" to be their preferred means. "But while peaceful progress is blocked by actions of those at present in power in the States of Southern Africa, we have no choice but to give the people of those territories all the support of which we are capable in their struggle against their oppressors."[1]

The organization of this support and the choice of strategies were begun on the continental level as early as 1963 with the founding of the OAU, although in fact liberation was a major theme of the first Conference of Independent African States in Accra in 1958 and of the subsequent meetings of "groups" of states that finally led to the founding of the OAU. The OAU Charter identifies the "eradication of all forms of colonialism" as one of its purposes,[2] and the founding summit at Addis Ababa established an African Liberation Committee (ALC) of eight states (Algeria, Zaire, Ethiopia, Nigeria, Uganda, Tanzania, Senegal, Guinea, and Egypt, with the subsequent addition of Zambia and Somalia in 1965).[3] The ALC immediately went to work to form a list of effective, cooperative, reliable liberation movements for recognition by the OAU.[4] In South Africa, two organizations qualified—the Pan-African Congress (PAC) and the African National Congress (ANC). The committee also established a budget of $4.2 million, which was never attained, and decided to turn over coordination of support to the host countries of the liberation movements, thus giving up most of its functions. In the following summit at Cairo in 1964, the OAU called for a communications boycott of South Africa, but subsequent summits included resolutions deploring the lack of compliance with such decisions to boycott South African trade and communications. The early years of OAU established a pattern that has continued throughout the shrinking of the southern redoubt—a wide gap between decisions and performance, and continuing problems with financial support, coordination of liberation activities, compliance with common policy,

and effectiveness with outside powers. The low mark in liberation activities of the OAU came in 1965, when the breakaway
Rhodesian government misappropriated the sacred name of
"independent" and the African foreign ministers, in a pique of
impotence, recommended the rupture of diplomatic relations
with Britain if it did not reestablish its colonial rule over the
territory. For the following decade, the OAU was paralyzed by
its awareness of impotence, reducing its effectiveness even in
those areas of inter-African relations in which it had been most
competent.[5]

This decade was interesting from one point of view in that it
was filled with explorations of very different kinds of policy
toward South Africa as African states searched for an appropriate answer to their impotence. In the late 1960s, the focus was
on Rhodesia until finally the OAU session at Algiers in 1968
declared that force was the only applicable means of liberation
in Rhodesia, a position maintained until the Council of Ministers at Dar as-Salaam of 1975, which declared armed struggle
and negotiation should go hand in hand toward the liberation of
Zimbabwe. In 1970, the ALC, the Council of Ministers, and
then the summit at Addis Ababa began a concerted campaign in
favor of an arms embargo on South Africa, finally adopted by
the United Nations as a recommended action in 1975 and as a
mandatory policy of the Security Council in 1977. Again, in the
same series of meetings in 1970, repeated by the ALC in 1973,
the OAU made an important decision to concentrate its efforts
on the Portuguese territories, the first such tactical plan recommended by the organization; although it would be hard to maintain that this action felled the Portuguese colonial regime, it was
in the direction of coming events. On the other side of the contest, in 1968 the OAU decided to withhold its support and
recognition of the PAC as pressure for resolution of a leadership
contest, and then to restore recognition when resolved.

Two other policies were explored during this period. In the
early 1970s, Ivory Coast, Chad, Liberia, Dahomey, Gabon,
Malawi, Rwanda, Burundi, Uganda, and Madagascar proposed a
change of attitude toward South Africa to explore the possibility of influence through direct contacts. South African officials,
including the prime minister, visited some of these states' capi-

tals as their leaders sought to show South Africans that majority government worked and to learn about ways in which they could foster integration by lessening hostility. But in 1971, the OAU summit at Addis Ababa cut short such explorations by condemning the policy of Dialogue,[6] and the military coup in Madagascar the following year, which had some of its roots in the popular feelings against the policy, brought home the lesson to African leaders.

The following year, following a plan reactivated by the Council of Ministers at Addis Ababa in 1970, the ministers meeting and summit at Rabat recommended the creation of a joint unified command and the preparation of all states' military units for support of another African state that would request assistance. Unlike the policy of Dialogue, the military plan was not specifically disavowed, but, like other international organizations' plans for a common defense force, it has never been implemented.

In 1975, Mozambique and Angola became independent, without much of a debt toward the OAU or at least to most of its members. With their own struggle ended, they sought to overcome the weakness of the OAU through coordinated action with the other Frontline States—Botswana, Tanzania, and Zambia—to set African policy toward southern Africa. The same year, the ALC urged an immediate concentration of attention on the three remaining territories of southern Africa and asked that all assistance be channeled through the committee. The African states then undertook a number of actions that had some influence on the southern liberation struggles. On Zimbabwe, in 1977, they recognized the Patriotic Front of the Zimbabwe African National Union (ZANU) and the Zimbabwe African People's Union (ZAPU) and the following year rejected the internal settlement of the United African National Council (UANC) (which it had previously recognized as a legitimate nationalist movement), thus applying an effective veto on the latter arrangement. On Namibia, the Security Council waited in 1978 until the OAU agreed to the Western Five's proposal for a process of arriving at independence, a plan that for the moment seemed to have good chance of implementation, although South Africa was later to renege on it. In regard to South Africa, the OAU and its members launched three campaigns to bring in outside support.

In the mid-1970s, they sought to establish in a number of resolutions a tie between the nature of the Israeli and South African regimes and to warn against mutual support between the two states (the second point was more solidly based in reality than the first). By this means, African states hoped to enlist Arab and OPEC support in their campaign against South Africa, as the Arab states had persuaded them to cut their ties with Israel and support the Arab League at the time of the October war. The OAU also condemned France in 1976, at the Mauritius summit, for supplying nuclear reactors to South Africa. It thus involved its own members in a campaign against the most active former metropole, a campaign that finally brought about the termination of French arms sales and other support of South Africa and also made it a more willing member of the Western Five in their efforts in Namibia. More than any other European state, France's South African policy in its changes is a result of pressure from French-speaking African states. Further, African states, notably through an OAU resolution of 1976, were effective in interrupting international sports exchanges, including Olympic participation, by South Africa, not only bringing along other states' support of their campaign of ostracism, but also making a small dent in South African practices on a subject of importance to them. Finally, Japan stands as a case where African pressure through implied withholding of raw materials was able to cause an important industrial state to reduce economic relations with South Africa.[7] Although a Japanese boycott has not been imposed, its 1974 decision to avoid investment and reduce trade marks a reversal of previous trends between the two countries.

Although these have been the major policies of the independent African states, others have been tried or discussed as well. African states were able to have South Africa expelled from membership in the Technical Cooperation Commission for Africa (CCTA) in 1963 and excluded from its successor, the Economic Commission for Africa (ECA); from the International Labor Organization (ILO) and the Food and Agriculture Organization (FAO); from the World Health Organization

(WHO), the International Civil Aviation Organization (ICAO), and UNESCO in 1965; and from the Commonwealth as well. They have tried to exclude South Africa from membership in the United Nations, but were prevented by a triple Western veto in 1974 in the Security Council. There is continuing discussion of using the Uniting for Peace Resolution in the General Assembly to accomplish the same goal.

African states have also made use of the International Court of Justice, in 1966 and 1971, against South Africa on the matter of Namibia, although it may be less useful on domestic affairs in South Africa. Finally, to complete the list, African states have given sanctuary and direct support to guerrilla movements in other territories struggling for independence, although the battle line had not yet moved far enough south before the end of the 1970s for this policy to be directly applicable to South Africa.

To this review of independent African states' policies should be added the fact that none has been without discussion and dissent among the African states themselves. Indeed, the whole history, as enumerated, can be seen as a search for an appropriate policy under changing conditions, with many being tried and some rejected. Probably more symbolic has been the criticism of the ALC itself. The committee began under fire in 1963, when its initial decisions won it attacks from both the moderates and the activists the following year. At the end of the decade, a special committee was charged with reviewing the entire operations of the ALC; but when it reported in 1970, the report was shelved without action. Even in the 1970s, when hopes might have been expected to rise as the target area was reduced, the African Liberation Fund continued to be seriously undersubscribed.

The Ingredients

There are at least six factors that are involved in assessing the prospects for different roles for independent African states in bringing about change in South Africa in the coming decade. In evaluating these factors, two assumptions will be made. One is that all Africa north of the Orange and the Limpopo rivers will be independent, whatever that means—that is, the independence of Zimbabwe and of Namibia may be under either an "internal" or an "external" settlement. Whether these states under an internal settlement will be admitted as members of the OAU or not is another matter, and one that is likely to enter into the tactical debate among African states. But this chapter will focus on the Republic of South Africa as the target of liberation efforts. The other assumption is a "no surprise" type of projection in regard to the East-West struggle, in which détente is the "name" of the game but a wide range of variants are admissible under it.[8] It is therefore assumed that whatever the momentary client relations, neither side will have satellites or allies on the continent that would engage automatic defense reactions in case of attack. It is always delicate to distinguish between temporary tactical support and firm advance commitment, to be sure, but the assumption is that the level of commitment operative at the end of the 1970s will not have changed.

Liberation begins at home, and the first factor influencing policy is the domestic political stability and economic well-being of already-independent African states. These are the elements that go into the choice among various policy alternatives and the support accorded to the policy chosen. The second aspect is more directly foreseeable: States need to have the ability to make sustained and coherent policy choices. One of the basic tenets of international relations points out the necessary balance between ends and means. A policy unsupported by implementing strategies and appropriate means will not go far. Although these considerations are particularly important in deciding a military policy against South Africa and only slightly less important in supporting indigenous liberation movements with external African resources, they are also relevant to the much cheaper diplomatic track, since the effectiveness of a strategy of borrowed power from non-African states depends on the sanctions that can be imposed if those states do not lend their support readily. Moral appeals have varying effects according to the times and are not to be discounted, as the human rights campaign and Carter's election and subsequent African policy have shown; but their holding power is transient, as limitations on the same phenomena have also shown.

It is more difficult to relate domestic fortunes and policy choices unambiguously. It has often been held that popular foreign campaigns can be used for the purpose of domestic consolidation, and that distractions abroad can shift domestic concern from economic insufficiencies. But to conclude that the worse independent African political and economic fortunes become, the stronger the campaign against South Africa will be, or that the campaign will be stronger in those states that have greater domestic troubles, is to ignore opposite conclusions of equal logic. A stable regime with a mission can also lead to a tough policy; a high degree of domestic well-being can give rise to the guilt feelings over brothers' conditions and an equally hard-line position.

In the presence of such ambiguity and in the absence of a reliable theory of motivation, it seems most promising to return to the element of morality and conviction to find the link between domestic fortunes and policy choice. Policies decided by a weak domestic system are unlikely to go far;[9] the effectiveness of an African strategy against South Africa will depend on the engagement of the richer, stronger, developing states of the continent behind it. But that, in turn, will depend on their degree of commitment, built up over a period of years. The emergence of support for a Nigerian role of weight in African affairs ever since the All-Nigerian People's Conference of 1961, the long-standing commitment of a stable Tanzanian regime behind liberation movements, and the fifteen-year struggle of the Mozambican nationalist movements that formed the Mozambique Liberation Front (FRELIMO) are evidences of a commitment that is as much a necessary condition for a firm contribution to a liberation policy as are domestic stability and domestic well-being. This combination of factors already begins to create a distinction among African states.

A second factor that is a foreseeable characteristic of coming inter-African politics, as it has been in the past, is the impending leadership struggle, which is related to the previous domestic considerations.[10] Some African states are doing significantly better than the rest in the process of development—in their ability to generate, accede to, and utilize their own resources. Algeria, Nigeria, and possibly Zaire and Morocco have a good base for continuing development that sets them apart from others, with a sizable GNP and population that provide the means and aspirations for leadership roles in Africa. Another group of states also has a high economic growth rate and is active in African politics, but without the weight and hence the drive of the first group. These states include Libya, Ivory Coast, Tunisia, Cameroon, Kenya, Malawi, Liberia, Botswana, and perhaps Zimbabwe, Angola, and Mozambique. But a much larger group of states has had a per capita growth rate of 1 percent or less over the 1960s and 1970s, with a low base to begin with, and its prospects for changing these characteristics are dim. Thus, already African states are spreading out more and more on the economic development spectrum. As they continue to do so, they will constitute stronger and weaker states. The first will not only have capabilities and resources at their disposal but also a sense of leadership for having found answers to the problems of growth and development on the continent; and the second will be potential followers.

As small elite factions in the poorer states fall out over the distribution of the unexpanding resources of the country, and as opposition movements make redistributive appeals, the chances for external interference in domestic affairs are increased. Furthermore, the distributional crisis in Africa provides an issue on which aspiring continental leaders can try to lead other African—and like-minded third world—states against the developed countries of the North, much as Algeria has already been doing in the 1970s. In this situation, the liberation of South Africa has an appeal that is difficult to deny and is a further issue of the leadership struggle. In the earlier period of leadership struggles at the continental level, in 1960-1963, when the leadership aspirants did not yet have the resources to lead or the power differentials to play on, the degree of commitment to the liberation of the remaining colonies was an issue of contention between the two—Casablanca and Brazzaville—groups. This phenomenon can be expected to return.

The interaction between the leadership on continental issues and other issues is also an important consideration in assessing the effect of the coming leadership struggle. Some issues are likely to line up parties on one side or another of a "radical"-

"moderate" split, reinforcing the leadership issues, even though they are not inherently germane to the content of the leadership struggle. Such a case is the Saharan issue as of 1978, which has exacerbated the formation of moderate and radical camps behind Morocco and Algeria, respectively, even though there is nothing inherently radical or moderate about the sides taken on the issue. Such issues reinforce the struggle, and, by the appeal of the liberation issue, tend to strengthen the radical pressure for stronger measures against South Africa. Other issues, however, can cut up camps, sap energies, and destroy momentum. They may not be easily predictable, but once observed they help explain a sudden collapse in joint efforts. An example, also from 1978, was the ill-timed Ugandan attack on Tanzania over the Kagera region in November, which completely undercut Tanzanian efforts at a crucial point in the Zimbabwe and Namibian negotiations. Coalescent and disruptive issues may be hard to sort out beforehand, and hence hard to evaluate in their overall effect on change in South Africa, but they can certainly be expected to fuel and fog the leadership struggle on the continent.

A third factor concerns regional divisions. The first two factors have pointed to divisions among African states on the basis of their internal strengths, compounded on the continental level by a leadership struggle. The third factor indicates that subregional considerations—between the state and the continental (regional) level—and geographic location will also contribute to policy differences.[11] If African states have been getting better acquainted on the continental level—especially across colonial linguistic barriers—a less-noticed phenomenon has been the increase of contacts and ties on the subregional level. If subregional organizations have generally broken down or remained weak, subregional interaction—most of it cooperative, even if ad hoc—has increased.

Subregionalism means working together with neighbors on common development efforts and common problems, but it also means, by that very fact, pulling away from the efforts and problems of other subregions, and hence of the continent as a whole. Although liberation may be a condition for development, the two have generally proven to be antithetical issues. Thus, liberation is likely to have less appeal for subregions further from the battleline, particularly those middle-sized states mentioned above that are not contenders for leadership but that are beginning to get their development problems under control. Already the Zimbabwe struggle has become essentially a subregional issue, where the Frontline States—Angola, Botswana, Zambia, Tanzania, and Mozambique—generally act and decide for the OAU, with only an information liaison back to the continental organization. (The only other states regularly involved in front-line activities are Nigeria and the current presiding state of the OAU, showing that geography must be combined with the previous two factors.)

In dealing with South Africa in the 1980s, however, the front-line (southern) subregion may become more complicated. A South West African People's Organization (SWAPO) Namibia and a Patriotic Front Zimbabwe could join the present Frontline States and reinforce their general outlook and firm approach. On one hand, both are militant nationalist movements, even more so than at least Botswana and Zambia, and perhaps more so than some of the others if the younger military leadership of ZAPU and ZANU were to replace the current political leadership as the war goes on. On the other hand, like Mozambique, Botswana, Zambia, Malawi, and others in the 1970s, the two new states will continue to feel the military and economic weight of South Africa and will be less radical than their leadership might wish.

But if the new states are independent through an internal settlement, the second consideration will be present but not the first, and the two states will be as welcome in the front-line subregion as Malawi. They will form a physical and ideological buffer zone between the current front line and the enemy. The more they are pressed by the African neighbors, the more support they will need from South Africa; the reverse is not as likely to be true. At some point, the question of their membership in the OAU will arise, complicating the policy debate, as some members will want to reinforce their African nature and enlist them in the struggle against South Africa, whereas others will find them not African enough to qualify for membership. In the OAU, they will complicate the tactical debate as well, by joining the moderate side. Put outside the OAU, they will still break up the solidarity of the southern subregion and, if ostracized in strong enough terms, will divert the thrust of the campaign against South Africa.

It is, of course, impossible to foresee which type of settlement will bring independence to Zimbabwe and Namibia, although the consequences of each are rather clear, as indicated. Yet in terms of relations between the southern subregion and the continent, the effects are similar. Governments from an external settlement will fit in well with the other members of the subregion but will pull away from other subregions into their own interests and policies. Governments emanating from an internal settlement will also have different interests and will be involved in some major policy differences with other members of the African region.

The previous factors have indicated the bases for different policy positions among African states; the fourth factor is the tactical debate itself. Even if there were no differences in motivation, resources, interests, and groups, there would still be a legitimate disagreement over the means to accomplish the end. Since the other differences exist too, these policy differences become associated with external factors that make a free debate more difficult.

Yet the policy debate is wide open. It cuts across many dimensions—proper targets, proper roles, appropriate means, appropriate allies, necessary sacrifices. One question asks whether African states can best effectuate change in South Africa by focusing directly on the republic or by working for maximum change within its neighbors, notably Namibia, Zimbabwe, and possibly Botswana as well. The question is most relevant in the case of internal settlements in the two newly independent states. Should the new governments be bypassed, or even accepted, and the campaign be aimed directly on South Africa, or should South Africa be put on the defensive for its role in the two neighboring situations rather than for its internal policies? Can the Bantustans such as Transkei and Bophuthatswana with their fictitious "independence" be turned into allies, or must they be locked into the arms of South Africa?

A second question asks whether African states should be the prime movers of change in South Africa, as the mobilizers of pressure, or whether they should simply be the agents and allies of internal forces of change. The wave of nationalism has been a succession of internal movements with international ties, but as it rolls its way unevenly down the continent, there is increasing pressure of conviction, frustration, and opposition for African states to bring liberation to South Africa.

A third question concerns the much broader matter of means: Is southern African liberation the last occasion for a clear-cut decisive conflict between the forces of the past and the forces of the future, is it a situation of natural evolution where time with a little prodding will bring about the maximum possible in due course, or is there some middle ground of means, with a less coherent image to justify its choice? This matter will be the subject of the final section of this essay and so is only posed here.

A fourth question refers to the choice of allies. As a rule in international relations, any state, or any group of states tied together by a common sense of identity, would prefer to attain its goals singly. Allies are needed, however, when the means are inadequate, but allies tend to bring their own needs, interests, and goals. In any case, as the struggle moves into the core area of the South, where both the stakes and the power of resistance are highest, the need for tangible support grows. African states in general would doubtless prefer to borrow power from the West, since they know Western states best and still feel culturally close to them. But Western states are not eager for the honor and are not sure enough of their own goals in the situation to be wholehearted partners. The remaining candidates are the Communist states, and their presence raises questions and reluctance among many though by no means all African states, as the debates at the 1978 OAU summit showed. Egypt's experience with Russian aid also shows that the Russians are unsure allies, inconstant in support of supposedly common goals, balky and cumbersome in their administration, awkward and offensive in their relations, and troublesome in the encouragement of domestic opposition. This is not to say that African states would be well advised to steer away from Communist countries, or that they will inevitably learn this lesson if they were to enlist Communist support; it is only to suggest that there are enough grounds to sustain a real difference of opinion among such states over the costs and benefits of borrowing power from the East.

A final question about policy concerns the sacrifices policy choices require. If, as seen, African states tend to greater commitment in the liberation struggle, the closer they are to South Africa, they also increase their dependency in the same direction. Furthermore, if that dependency tends to decrease as the years of independence increase, the stakes in a peaceful developing society and economy also increase in the same direction. Finally, beyond these typical relations concerning costs and sacrifices in the support of the campaign against South Africa are the continuing unavowed ties of trade, communications, and other relations that link South Africa to other African states beyond its regional sphere of influence. Costs in terms of South African dependency, of domestic development, and of incidental ties are ingredients states will have to weigh in evaluating their commitment to liberation.

The fact that such questions of means must be faced in a choice of policies should not be taken to imply any division on the ultimate ends, a majoritarian or egalitarian outcome in South Africa. But neither should the agreed goal be interpreted to imply an absence of division on means. Such divisions are natural, inevitable, and, in the end, healthy in fostering the selection of the best policy in terms of costs and benefits.

The fifth factor affecting the African states' role in producing change in South Africa concerns their ability to generate power. For all the economic development, international connections, military self-sufficiency, domestic repressive capacity, and dominant regional position of South Africa, the other African states are not powerless. Their power is directed toward two arenas: toward South Africa directly, and toward third states in order to generate power over South Africa indirectly. Some types of power within these arenas are likely to remain excluded: African states' direct military power is insufficient to sustain a war against South Africa, and African states are unlikely to offer their own economies for investment by South Africa in exchange for South African cooperation in policies of change. The same range of inhibitions is unlikely to limit African power toward third states.

African power toward South Africa is neither unknown nor untried. It involves both threats and promises. African states can threaten South Africa with guerrilla sanctuary, a threat that has a military answer whose consequences might be politically counterproductive. They can also threaten with an international diplomatic campaign, but a threat is not very useful for bargaining if its termination is not credible. Ironically, African states may exert more power through a cooperative vein with South Africa than through threats, although effectiveness is not assured and the power of contingent gratifications implies some compromise on goals whereas the power of deprivation can be pursued—even if ineffectively—without yielding on goals. Even after the end of Dialogue, in 1972, a number of African states have maintained contact with South Africa, but it would take a real reversal of South African policy on apartheid to remove its international pariah status in the eyes of the Africans; Dialogue was abandoned, in part, because it was producing no results. Trade and advice are the two main commodities that African states can offer to South Africa, not a rich fare of inducements to change, to be sure.

As a result, Africa's power is likely to turn toward third parties capable of lending power to the African campaign. Again, threats and promises are available. The greatest threat is the old nonaligned ploy of playing off sides, and it is an ideal threat since it becomes more credible the more it is pursued. A threat to turn to the other side can be an effective inducement to any of the three protagonists in the cold war, and it becomes even more effective if an initial presence or cooperation is already inaugurated.

The cooperative basis of power is found in the growth of African economies.[12] At the end of the 1970s, the Nigerian GNP is about the same size as the South African. There is already twice as much American trade with Nigeria as there is with South Africa. If South Africa holds the largest percentage of American investment on the continent, the rest of the continent taken together holds half again as much. Since South Africa has a large trade deficit with the United States, efforts to improve the American trade balance will concentrate on independent African states that have a large trade surplus. If South

Africa is in a strong position as American supplier of chrome, platinum, antimony, and vanadium, other African states are main American suppliers of columbium, manganese, cobalt, and petroleum. Many other figures could be produced to show that, for all South Africa's economic weight, independent African states have as much or more, and it is growing.

The final factor is the degree of restiveness in the South African black population itself. The revolution can be considered to have begun on June 16, 1976, when it was clearly shown that there were large numbers of urban youth who finally felt they had nothing to lose by picking up the weapons of violence, and therefore to whom state violence was no longer a threat. They also showed that organization was available, even though the South African State Security Bureau did its best to remove the organization of the moment. The following year, the South African goverment showed that it accepted the challenge in these terms by banning the important remaining moderates. As a result, polarization continues and the difficulty of finding *interlocuteurs valables* (effective mediators) increases. Thus, even if South Africa moves toward internal African opinion in a reformist turn of policy, there will be no one in the middle with whom to talk, and the old problem of negotiating in changing social situations will again appear—when yesterday's solutions become today's proposals, the other side has already gone on to look for tomorrow's solutions.

If the revolution contines to grow, it will give the lead that external African states have been awaiting, and the pattern of external support for internal nationalist revolt that the rest of the continent has seen (albeit not usually in revolutionary terms) will be resumed. Much of the business of external accreditation of a national liberation movement consists of a series of steps by which the movement is promoted to government status and statehood, corresponding to various levels of success on the domestic terrain. Recognition by the OAU, support by the African Liberation Committee, observer status at the United Nations, recognition by the United Nations, recognition as government-in-exile, and recognition of government status in liberated territory are all examples of these steps, each with its political campaigns and diplomatic maneuvering, and each requiring its accompanying evidence of domestic support in order to prevent the external signs from outrunning the internal substance.

There are two major internal problems in this process—beyond the problem of overcoming South African opposition! One is the problem of unity, or of overcoming internal opposition. A conclusive study still remains to be done about the conditions of splintering, but it appears that the greater the stalemate and frustration, the greater the chances of tactical debates and counterleadership revolts and hence of splintering.[13] Since such events do not take place from a tabula rasa, even when momentum picks up the movement has to contend with the splinters of past doldrums. The national movement of Zimbabwe is a painfully apt example of these problems, and the ANC-PAC split, followed by SASO and other organizations, is only less complex to date. Truistically, such splits weaken support, reflect external tactical debates, and sap strength with cross-fighting where there should be united assistance.

The other problem concerns the urban-rural nature of the nationalist movement. Typically in the past, tolerated nationalist movements in a reformist context have tended to be urban; guerrilla movements have tended to be rural.[14] The type of assistance African states can offer differs in each case. The classical elements of sanctuary and supply are not as applicable to an urban revolt, and a prolonged urban resistance is likely to be unlike any other in contemporary—or indeed, in all—history. As a result, the urban-rural problem is likely to throw a greater burden of leading, rather than following, the revolution from outside on the independent African states, a situation whose difficulties and divisions have already been noted.

Of course, under the threat of administering its own country as a wartime occupied land, South Africa may embark on a reform policy, less than desired by almost any African group inside or outside the country but still with enough change and momentum—and a successful enough repression of opposition—to make a difference. Although such a policy may be considered unlikely, it is worth examining. Such a policy would include piecemeal incorporation of the African population into the political process in the urban areas, as well as continuation of the homelands policy as a no-longer-exclusive framework for African participation. It would pose two challenges to African states: the challenge of taking their lead from participant African leaders, essentially regarded as Uncle Toms, and the challenge of coming to terms with the Bantustans. The latter is a long-term problem that would involve major changes of attitudes on both sides; the former will doubtless not take place for a long time either, leaving African states as critics whose active role will be to keep the co-opted African leaders on their toes, although it may discredit them entirely. Nonetheless, these two challenges will also add to the policy debate among African states if South Africa should ever choose the way of reform.

The preceding six factors will be the basic ingredients determining the role of African states in promoting change within South Africa. The main point in enumerating them has been to show the many bases of difference and debate where a solid front might have been anticipated. Such differences help explain—and also reflect—a certain ineffectiveness, but they also indicate the components of final policy choices. The last section of this chapter will indicate the elements of five different policy choices and evaluate their prospects. As to their implementation, it is likely that all five will find their protagonists, and, to some extent, that all five will be adopted by different groups, as the preceding discussion suggests. Which will finally dominate is a question this essay will not reveal, lest all further room for choice, chance, and betting be eliminated in the process. In the present state of African power, the effectiveness of any strategy depends on its ability to involve other states. This involvement, of course, takes different forms along the spectrum of policies.[15]

Prospects for African Involvement

Prospects for Borrowing Power—The Russian Connection

As in the Middle East, the one thing that local states can expect from the Communist countries is military support. Most likely it will continue to take the form of arms aid to national liberation movements and neighboring states' armies, but its extreme form could be actual military participation. Implications for South Africa are examined in the following chapter; implications for African states are briefly touched on here. There is no doubt that a military policy on the part of independent African states, unlike the Middle East, will depend on significant outside involvement for its success for years—or decades— to come. As much or more than military organization, logistic support is required, and that means Soviet involvement. Furthermore, there is little doubt that African states are aware that the current marching wing of the Soviet Union—the Cuban overseas brigades—is not simply a force to be lent lightly to any cause, but rather one that operates within defined territorial limits, under specific sovereign units with a recognized ideological commitment, and in a carefully delimited military role. This means that direct involvement in an operational military role would come only after a long period of advising and training or as part of an advanced state offensive into South African territory.

Prospects for Guerrilla Support and Sanctuary—The Cuban Connection

Among the hard-line policies, the guerrilla support option is patently the most attractive to African states, although it will only appeal to a minority of them. Guerrilla support allows African states to pick their internal South African allies and reinforce them directly, even with outside support. It allows them to create the conditions of escalation that have put South Africa into an increasingly difficult position diplomatically and that have an innate momentum of their own. It also provides a tangible object of support that does not directly expose most African states, thus removing the emptiness of pious declarations without bringing in the dangers of direct military action. Despite all these apparent advantages, such support will also make gradual change impossible. That will not be the fault of the African states, to be sure, but it may not be in their interest either.

There are only four states that can provide sanctuary, because of their location on South Africa's northern border. Of these Namibia and Botswana provide only inhospitable terrain, Zimbabwe is bordered by an easily defensible river, and only

Mozambique (including Swaziland) offers a penetrable guerrilla border and hospitable sanctuary. By the same token, the chances of effective South African reprisals and hot pursuit into Mozambique are great. Furthermore, the distances are great enough that there is little possibility of sanctuary being located in a state once removed from the border and merely using border states as transit buffers. The laager is in place.

Nonetheless, the channels for African states' support through the African Liberation Committee to guerrilla groups, or direct support bypassing the ALC, are in existence. The place for third power support, such as that offered by the Cubans, in training and arming the guerrillas is also found in this strategy. There are no accurate parallels in current African history to date, but the best approximation is SWAPO with its role more symbolic than military that nonetheless qualifies it for designation as the authentic spokesman for its country, as well as for foreign and OAU support.

The example of SWAPO is useful in pointing out that, even in its current position of limited military capability, it has been the justification for South African raids across the border. The more effective an African-supported guerrilla movement, the more likely that South Africa would riposte militarily, and the threshold is low. Such raids would strengthen the arguments of hardliners on both sides of the border. They have frequently been the occasion for some mild diplomatic knuckle rapping through the United Nations when practiced by South Africa, Portugal, and France in past conflicts, but at some point they can have immense repercussions on the domestic body politic, as the French military revolt of 1958 and the Portuguese military coup of 1974 have shown. Thus, the greatest hope of the guerrilla strategy may not lie in the effectiveness of guerrillas either as a military force of liberation or even as a hard-line alternative to evolution, but as a catalyst for some kind of change within South Africa itself.

Finally, guerrilla support conceived as pressure for change does have its own limitations. Not only is it likely to produce harder reactions within the laager, but it removes the possibility that African states will recognize and support evolutionary alternatives that conceivably might arise under the guerrilla pressure. Once a militant force has been accredited, a black spokesman who emerges from a reformed electoral system is out of the running for international African support.

Prospects for Boycott—The Western Connection

The policy of sanctions seeks to combine two unusual bed-fellows—morality and economics. The chances of sanctions being voted in the Security Council are slim and will be so until South Africa commits such a loathsomely offensive act that governments cannot resist public pressure. Even then, the chances of their being fully applied by private companies remain small. In this light, sanctions frequently appear to be moral statements rather than practical measures. At the end of the 1970s, however, there was discussion beginning about lesser sanctions and the like—such as air travel bans, or slowdowns in stock market reports—that are less inconceivable.

Unfortunately, the tactics of such a policy require putting pressure on the pressurers as much as on the pressured, and therefore pushing the West into the category of object when it is wanted as ally. In this tactic, the East is not of much use, and neither is the South. The campaigns for disinvestment, mobilizing part of the West against itself, have been gaining momentum and will continue to do so, but the road is long. Although African states' economies are growing, as noted, they are unlikely to want to put development on the line as a threat to bring about sanctions. Those with the least to lose can create an atmosphere of pressure for their neighbors, but in the process the pressure chain becomes longer and weaker.

Yet in the middle run, there is a prospect of effectiveness in this policy. From scattered investment moratoria to the mandatory arms boycott, there are more sanctions in place at the end of the 1970s than at the beginning, and this gradual pressure can be expected to continue, even if it never reaches an economic or oil boycott. It may well serve to push people into the laager, to unite the white factions, as is often claimed, but it may well turn out that the South African reflex is to go into the laager but not to feel comfortable there in the long run. Such possibilities are more properly the domain of the first chapter in this work, but are raised here to point out that the boycott policy through pressure on the West is at best a context for African states, but not a policy for change in the early 1980s.

Prospects for Dialogue—The South African Connection

Much of the preceding seems to indicate that dialogue is necessary if African states are to be able to recognize African spokesmen that might emerge from South African reforms under external pressure. This conclusion is only warranted if a new meaning of dialogue is introduced. It is improbable that any policy of discussion, normalized relations, and friendly advice from independent African states to South Africa can produce anything but a conning of the former into inaction and a reinforcement of the latter's sense of self-righteousness. Some states may be able to "dialogue" with Pretoria, and indeed Western states should make sure that some communications channels are open, but that is not Africa's role. It is hard to see what African states can get in exchange for diplomatic relations, just as it is hard to imagine what changes in South Africa should be paid for by African ambassadors. If representations need to be made, they can be done so just as effectively on an ad hoc basis.

African states do need a policy of dialogue with the African leaders of South Africa, beyond the contact provided through recognized liberation movements. Somehow, if progress is to be made, it must be remembered that the South African situation is not one of political change where a simple transfer of power is to be negotiated, whereupon the colonizer will go home; it is rather a situation of social change in which power is to shift within an expanded political system. It therefore becomes much more difficult to identify a sole authentic representative of the African population. It is the Buthelezis and the Mantanzimas as well as the ANC and PAC leaders (not instead of them, to be sure), the SASO and black power figures and any possible leaders of intermediate stripe, who need to be contacted by African states, not as national spokesmen but as African leaders among many, in order to keep the chances of change alive. Not all African states will make such contacts, any more than all

African states will support guerrilla groups, but both options are possible and useful.

Prospects for Disengagement—The Disconnection

The possibility that some African states will simply grow tired of the liberation activities going on at the far end of the continent and fix their entire attention on domestic development and other issues closer to home should not be dismissed. Such a policy could be the result of an explicit decision, or it could be the implicit outcome of a situation where the means of a more active policy are simply not available, beyond an occasional UN or OAU vote. This is not to imply that any state will come out and approve of the South African political system; they may simply find other issues to be of overriding importance. Individual defection may not be significant, but it is also likely that groups of states north of the equator will find themselves too far from the conflict to make it meaningful for them. Their disinterest in the liberation campaign may weaken it more than the debates and infighting over competing strategies.

This section has sought to portray and evaluate the spectrum of strategies that the previously analyzed ingredients can produce. The main conclusion points to an intensification of the policy debate, and at the same time the adoption of each strategy by some group of African states. A second conclusion indicates that the road to liberation is still long, for even those strategies that are available require an alliance with third powers in the absence of sufficient African capabilities. Third, the frustrations of slow effectiveness and of reliance on outside support are likely to contribute to continued policy shifts and renewed debates, in a circular search for an effective stance. Fourth, change in South Africa in response to these policies and their outside concomitants is likely to be highly uneven, combining times of shift and periods of holding out. Since African states can neither effectively reward the shifts nor combat the resistance, their role is essentially given and constant. The onus of change is on black and white South Africans, and the onus of pressure is on the West.

Notes

1. The Lusaka Manifesto is included in Martin Minogue and Judith Molloy, eds., *African Aims and Attitudes* (New York: Cambridge University Press, 1974), pp. 268, 270. For other attempts, similar to the first part of this chapter, to portray African policies toward South Africa, see Mohammed El-Khawas, "Southern Africa: A Challenge to the OAU," *Africa Today* 24, no. 3:25-41; Christian Potholm, "The Effects on South Africa of Change in Contiguous Territories," in Leonard Thompson and Jeffrey Butler, eds., *Change in Contemporary South Africa* (Berkeley: University of California Press, 1975); Leonard Kapungu, "The OAU's Support for the Liberation of Southern Africa," in Yassin al-Ayouty, *The Organization of African Unity after Ten Years* (New York: Praeger, 1975); Yashpal Tandon, "The Organization of African Unity and the Liberation of Southern Africa," in Christian Potholm and Richard Dale, eds., *Southern Africa in Perspective* (New York: Free Press, 1972); and Kenneth Grundy, *Confrontation and Accommodation in Southern Africa* (Berkeley: University of California Press, 1973).

2. Also reprinted in Minogue and Molloy, *African Aims and Attitudes*, pp. 195-99, quotation from p. 196.

3. Committee membership was again altered in the 1970s.

4. See Kenneth Grundy, *Guerrilla Struggle in Africa* (New York: Grossman, 1971), p. 138; I. William Zartman, *International Relations in the New Africa* (Englewood Cliffs, N.J.: Prentic-Hall, 1966), p. 36; and Zdenek Cervenka, *The Unfinished Quest for Unity: Africa and the O.A.U.* (Boulder: Westview, 1979).

5. For a discussion of this evolution, see I. William Zartman, "Africa," in James Rosenau et al., eds., *World Politics* (New York: Free Press, 1976), pp. 369-96. For a convenient but selective chronological review of OAU activities, see Michel Crouzet, "Le Journal de l'OUA," *Jeune Afrique* 914 (12 July 1978):67-75.

6. The OAU declaration on dialogue is reprinted in Minogue and Molloy, *African Arms and Attitudes*, pp. 278-280.

7. See *African Research Bulletin* 6, no. 9 (1972):2497.

8. On this assumption and its larger implications, see W. Howard Wriggins and Gunnar Adler-Karlsson, *Reducing Global Inequalities* (New York: McGraw-Hill, 1978).

9. This point is the basis of W. Scott Thompson, *Ghana's Foreign Policy* (Princeton, N.J.: Princeton University Press, 1969).

10. For further development of this point, see I. William Zartman, "Social and Political Trends in Africa in the 1980s," in Zartman et al., *Continent in Crisis* (New York: McGraw-Hill, 1979), pp. 73-85.

11. For further development of this point, see ibid., pp. 91-100.

12. For a careful evaluation, see Gordon Bertolin, "US Economic Interests in Africa," in Jennifer Seymour Whitaker, ed., *Africa and the United States: Vital Interests* (New York: New York University Press, 1978).

13. For a good study of this problem, see Richard Gibson, *African Liberation Movements* (New York: Oxford University Press, 1972).

14. See treatments of the Algerian and Guinea-Bissau wars of national liberation; a good list of references to the latter are found in Joseph Smaldone, *African Liberation Movements: An Interim Bibliography* (Waltham, Mass.: African Studies Association, 1974).

15. For other attempts to look ahead, see Grundy, *Guerrilla Struggle*, Chapters 6-7; Grundy, *Confrontation and Accommodation*; Leonard Thompson, "White over Black," in Thompson and Butler, *Change in Contemporary South Africa*; Andrew Nagorski, "U.S. Options vis-à-vis South Africa," in Whitaker, *Africa and United States*; Christian Potholm, "Toward the Millenium," in Potholm and Dale, *Southern Africa*; and Herbert Vilakazi, "The Last Years of Apartheid," *Issue* 7, no. 4 (1978):60-64, special issue on Africa 2000.

6
South Africa in Soviet Strategy

W. Scott Thompson
Brett Silvers

Our cardinal assumption about developing Soviet strategy toward South Africa is that it is characteristic of, and parallel to, Soviet foreign policy as a whole as we interpret that. Though long-term, strategic aims are shaped by and informed with doctrinal and ideological considerations, foreign policy on a month-to-month or even year-to-year basis unfolds in response to opportunities that become available. These opportunities, however, must be seen relative both to regional contexts and to the world "correlation of forces," in addition (obviously) to the situation existing in the particular country object of Soviet policy. This means first of all that Moscow will continue to be cautious in its development of a strategy for destabilizing, or otherwise affecting, South Africa, until the region is, from a *strategic* point of view, under its control. By this we do not imply a Soviet "occupation," but rather a position in which Moscow *can* control the sea-lanes around South Africa (principally by deterring American naval opposition), has the capability to project sufficient forces into the region to tie down (or deter) substantial South African forces, and has firm alliances with South Africa's neighbors, from which sabotage and guerrilla operations may be launched with impunity, so long as the abhorrent practice of apartheid continues.

The Soviets, secondly, will remain cautious until the world correlation of forces has moved sufficiently far in its favor to permit it to take large risks in distant theaters—for example applying a naval blockade on South Africa. Thus while Soviet aims remain that of "helping history along" in its progress

toward Communism, and in the short and medium term of assisting "national liberation movements" where these enhance Soviet
prospects, Moscow will for the moment be respectful of such a
relatively powerful state like South Africa while continuing to
use it as a Western whipping boy in its propaganda and escalating its involvement in military (guerrilla) conflicts on the immediate periphery of South Africa as opportunities north of the
Limpopo arise.

In this essay we will first of all analyze the factors in the
international and regional contexts that bear on Soviet policy
and longer-term intentions toward South Africa. We will then
consider the political-economic stakes. We will thereafter
examine the existing balance of forces in the region before
attempting, finally and cautiously, to foresee the possible
patterns of development of Soviet policy toward South Africa
in the 1980s.

I

The correlation of forces worldwide has shifted meaningfully,
if not yet decisively, in recent years. From a position of gross
inferiority at the strategic level, the Soviet Union advanced to a
position of parity: having achieved such rough balance in the
early 1970s, it continued its qualitative and quantitative buildup to the point where it either moved beyond the United
States or put itself into a position where such could not be prevented by the early 1980s, given the slowing down or cancellation of many American advanced weapons programs. Whether
that event occurred by 1979 is less important than that the
trend is agreed upon by virtually all analysts. It is, after all,
trends against which policies of reaction by smaller states are
set.[1]

How does this affect Soviet South Africa policy? It does so in
two ways, strategic and what we will call power projectional,
the former affecting how the Soviets can constrain American
reactions, the latter how they can affect events in distant lands
themselves. At the strategic level, it is worth noting that every
superpower crisis of the nuclear age—those of 1961 in Berlin,
1962 in Cuba, 1970 and 1973 in the Middle East—were ulti-

mately determined by the strategic balance.[2] Thus in the unlikely event that the United States wished (for example) to
counter a Soviet blockade of South Africa, using its still
superior ability to project power afield, it could be dissuaded
from doing so by a Soviet "upping of the ante" in the crisis
to a higher strategic level where Moscow's superiority was
unquestioned.[3]

The Soviets are quick to see the relationship. As two of their
analysts put it in 1972, "At present, the main factor which
restrains the imperialist aggressors in all regions of the world is
the ability of the USSR to reach any point on the world's
surface with nuclear missile weaponry."[4] In other words, the
strategic balance is intimately related to a superpower's conventional capability.

At the power-projectional level, changes in Soviet capabilities
have been as dramatic as at the strategic level. As recently as
1960, Moscow failed to sustain some otherwise potent forces in
the Congo (as it then was) owing to its lack of large transport
aircraft. But following the Cuban missile crisis it undertook a
massive buildup—of its airborne divisions, its large aircraft, its
amphibious craft, and numerous other exotic weaponry.
"Unlike the United States," the same two analysts wrote,

> the USSR has its own particular historical, economic and geographic
> features which neither gave it the possibility nor occasioned the need
> for it to secure a military presence in areas of the world distant from
> the USSR. In the situation, the Soviet Union finds that *the need has
> arisen, as has also a certain possibility,* for the solution of this
> problem. The need, one may observe, is in response to the global
> aggressive policy of imperialism; the possibility is determined above
> all by the state reached by the USSR's own economy, by the devel-
> opment of its armed forces, by its international political links, etc.[5]

Thus in 1975 Moscow was able to take advantage of the pa-
ralysis of American will and move swiftly to buttress its ally in
Angola, the minority-Marxist party (the Popular Movement for
the Liberation of Angola—MPLA), despite the apparently
greater projectional capabilities America had for that theater.
By quickly establishing a sizable presence, the Soviets raised the
cost of any counterintervention. A convoy of five ships, in addi-

tion to their intelligence and supply functions, advertised the
Soviet commitment to Africa. The use of an air corridor and
fuel stations involving Algeria, Mali, Guinea, and Congo Brazzaville tested and exercised Soviet logistic capabilities.[6]

In 1978 the Soviets made their next great test relevant to the
South African theater, this time in the African Horn. A Soviet
strategic presence in the Horn is a prerequisite to an effective
interventionary capability in southern Africa (in addition to the
other utilities of such a presence). Having been expelled from
Somalia in 1977 as they saw, and acted on, the larger opportunities in Ethiopia, the Soviets began building up their logistics
base in Addis Ababa, began bombarding Red Sea ports where
this was necessary to get their matériel unloaded, and of course
brought in the requisite Cuban allies. It was the largest airlift
in African history, one that made possible the largest military
operation in Africa since the World War II battles decades
earlier. Between one and two billion dollars' worth of arms were
brought into Ethiopia during 1978.

Having helped defeat the Somalis and having been instru-
mental in breaking the back of the army they had themselves
virtually created, the Soviets then turned on their erstwhile
allies in Eritrea, the two socialist guerrilla groups that controlled
the region's population. By the end of 1978, they had completed the job, helping the Ethiopians to mop up the last
organized military resistance. No doubt those impressive groups
in Eritrea, the ELF and EPLF, would struggle on. But from a
strategic point of view, the Soviets had for the time being accomplished their theater objectives. "There is no disguising the
magnitude of the recent Eritrean defeat," John Darnton wrote
in the *New York Times* on December 7.[7]

It was thus only at the beginning of 1979 that the Soviets
could truly contemplate intervention in white-controlled
southern Africa, now that they had a secure air corridor to
South Africa in prospect, intermediate fueling stations and
dependable allies along the way, and a strategic superiority over
the United States that was bound to widen. The change in the
environment was felt, if not analytically perceived, in most
quarters. By late 1978, for example, it was already apparent
that the initiative on Zimbabwe was no longer in Washington or

London, but in Moscow and Havana, to which guerrilla leaders repaired in order to obtain the largesse that would determine the outcome of that long struggle.[8]

Moscow's position toward South Africa has always been one of implacable opposition, dictated not just by the South African involvement in the international free-market system, but also by the principled opposition in Marxist doctrine to racism. Such would be insufficient, however, to explain the large role South Africa appears to play as an object of Soviet strategy—judging from the large amount of press coverage, serious discussion in Soviet periodicals, and political-military movement in that direction.

Our argument is that Soviet strategy toward the West has evolved, in recent years, toward the ultimate goal of *resource denial* to the West, something that explains the Soviet preoccupation with the Middle East and southern Africa—and in this strategy South Africa's place is nearly central.

II

Russia's strident Africa policy in the last decade is probably just a hint of things to come in the struggle for southern Africa, and, as we argue in this section, the stakes are large. Although the Soviet leadership and its Cuban ally confront a much more powerful local adversary in Pretoria than any yet encountered on the continent, the potential gains also far outweigh those of previous engagements; at the very least, they include near monopoly power over the production and distribution of strategically vital minerals, an opportunity to undermine the financial health of some of capitalism's largest multinational enterprises, added problems for the United States and Great Britain's ailing balance of payments, control of the West's main access route to oil-producing countries and the Far East, and use of the southern hemisphere's most sophisticated shipping and defense infrastructure.

South Africa's enormous reserves of metal and nonferrous minerals have prompted one analyst to call it "the Saudi Arabia of the 1980s."[9] Over 80 percent of the world's platinum and chrome deposits are located in the republic, along with the largest known reserves of vanadium, gold, manganese, fluorspar; significant quantities of nickel, zinc, copper, lead, coal, and iron ore are also present. More is continually being discovered; in August 1975, the minister of mines stated that no other place on earth can match the Aggenys-Gamsberg (northwest Cape Province) find of these minerals in quantity or value, although its full dimensions are not yet public knowledge.[10] In addition, as Peter Jancke has pointed out, in ten years South Africa may replace Canada as the non-Communist world's second largest producer of uranium, next to the United States.[11]

Unlike many southern hemisphere countries in the aftermath of OPEC's oil embargo, South Africa does not pursue economic policies that are antagonistic to free trade and foreign investment; it has, sensibly, chosen to eliminate any irritants to the industrial West beyond apartheid itself. Thus, as a mineral supplier, the republic's importance to the West is enhanced by the fact that its leaders refuse to cut back production in order to raise prices, or to reduce shipments abroad for political reasons. This is despite continuing Western pressure over apartheid: for example, America's observance of the UN arms embargo, its refusal to use the country's port and to extend Ex-Im Bank credits to companies doing business there. The United States currently relies on Pretoria for at least six out of the twenty minerals of which she imports more than 30 percent, including antimony, chrome, manganese, platinum, vanadium and vermiculite; figures for uranium are not available, but are presumed to be high. If South Africa's mineral exports were ever curtailed by domestic strife or Soviet influence, other countries would no doubt find it much easier to organize (with Russian encouragement) producer cartels and price-stabilization schemes damaging to the West.

Strategic control of South Africa's production by the Russians would enable them, in effect, to control 90 percent of the platinum, 75 percent of the manganese, 80 percent of the gold, 60 to 80 percent of the diamonds, 50 percent of the chrome, and 50 percent of the copper produced in the world.[12] Moreover, a sizable cadre of geologists and engineers would have access to sophisticated techniques developed in South Africa for the conversion of coal to oil at relatively low prices. South

African scientists have already outlined the country's most promising areas for future mineral exploration, another potential boon to the Soviet economy.[13]

Communist domination of South Africa, or of large parts of it in the event of a breakup of the republic along racial lines, would also entail substantial losses of physical capital and profits for hundreds of private multinational corporations headquartered in North America and Western Europe. Although Angola's Soviet-backed Marxist government has allowed Western companies such as Gulf to explore for oil, radical third world nations as a rule impose harsh terms on foreign investors, including minority ownership, heavy taxation, restricted transfer of profits, and sudden, uncompensated nationalization of property. Once Angola has the technical expertise to manage its oil interests, one should hardly expect it to permit Gulf to remain on the relatively advantageous terms it now enjoys.

As of 1978 American investment in South Africa exceeded U.S. $1.8 billion, or 37 percent of total American investment in all of Africa. The lion's share is in long-term projects, with thirteen firms accounting for more than 75 percent of American-owned assets. Among these subsidiaries of General Motors, Ford, Mobil, Chrysler, General Electric, ITT, and Texaco own assets worth over U.S. $30 million each. The operations in South Africa constitute an important profit center for the two largest automobile manufacturers, with 14.1 percent of the total American investment there being GM's and 11.0 percent being Ford's.[14] British capital is even more entrenched in South Africa, comprising an estimated U.S. $6 billion, split evenly between short-term bank loans and longer-term direct investments; other Western countries are similarly involved, with German and Japanese banking houses providing a significant amount of short-term investment. The International Monetary Fund, directed by the United States and other big industrial powers, supplied 60 percent of South Africa's short-term financing in 1972.

Foreign capitalist involvement in the republic is, as we have noted, a pervasive theme in the Soviet press. In January 1978, TASS rather blandly reported, for example, that at the present time over three hundred American monopolies are doing business in the Republic of South Africa. They exercise control over 43 percent of its oil market, 70 percent of the production of electronic computers, 23 percent of car sales, etc. The total sum of American investment in South Africa has reached almost 2,000 million dollars.[15]

The plant and personnel of Western companies in South Africa thus could be priority targets of Soviet-assisted terrorism in the 1980s.

South Africa's imports and exports represent a significant (and strategically vital) part of the Western powers' trade with the Southern Hemisphere. In 1978 the United States purchased nearly U.S. $2.3 billion in raw materials, manufactured goods, and technology from South Africa in return for U.S. $1.08 billion worth of capital equipment, technology, and services.

In addition to minerals, South Africa has provided this country with innovative technologies for mining, uranium enrichment, and coal gasification, as well as a water purification system that, apparently, virtually saved the tanning industries of Pennsylvania and Georgia from extinction. A source, admittedly not the least biased, contends that 66,000 jobs in the United States depend directly on trade with South Africa, and many more than that if one takes into account the multiplier effect;[16] whatever the number is, analysts will agree that it is substantial. Certainly Jimmy Carter's refusal to make Ex-Im Bank financing available for American investors in South Africa has prevented some profitable trade and exacerbated the United States' balance of payments crisis (thereby indirectly serving Soviet interests at both ends). According to John Chettle, South Africa's acceptance of French bids for the construction of a nuclear reactor followed troubles with the United States over regulation and cost Americans several hundred million dollars and 4,000 jobs in California.[17]

South Africa's largest trade partner is still the United Kingdom (U.S. $2.4 billion in 1977), followed by the United States, West Germany, Japan, and France. Overall, the West's trade with the republic (including NATO, Japan, Australia, and New Zealand) exceeded U.S. $10 billion in that year, or 49.2 percent of Pretoria's exports and 82.4 percent of her imports.

South Africa's primary geographical resource, proximity to the Cape sea route, enables it to monitor "the most crowded shipping lane in the world."[18] Eighty percent of Western Europe's oil supplies, and a growing proportion of America's, pass through the Indian Ocean and along this route. Political control of Pretoria would thus enable the Soviet Union to disrupt Western access to energy in a crisis situation. Even an open Suez Canal does not reduce the NATO countries' dependence on Cape transport, given its physical inability to accommodate modern supertankers and its location in a politically volatile region. For the 20,000 non-Communist ships passing the Cape of Good Hope every year (10,000 to 13,000 of which call on South African ports), a pro-Western, militarily competent government on shore, willing to defend their right of passage, is essential.

One should not assume that the Soviet Union's virtual self-sufficiency in raw materials diminishes the importance of South Africa for its global strategy. In the first place, Russian leaders are attempting to conserve these resources against the contingency of international crises, and against the day when its own resources have dwindled. There is some evidence that Russia has already surreptitiously purchased large amounts of chrome ore from Rhodesia, at the same time Moscow loudly condemned the United States for doing so on the open market.[19] The more salient point, however, is that Russia's Africa policy is not driven by its own resource needs, but rather those of NATO, which as we have seen is heavily dependent on South African supplies and would be weakened by Soviet control of this source.

In fact resource denial has been at the cornerstone of Soviet strategy vis-à-vis the West in third world theaters since 1957, when Major General A. N. Lagorsky formulated his "weak link" principle—namely that the Kremlin could extract political and economic concession from America because of its dependence on external sources of chrome and other high-technology minerals.[20] The major producers of strategic minerals were then, and still are, Rhodesia, South Africa, and the Soviet Union itself.

Communist ideology as the Kremlin practices it dictates

patience in the face of Western strength, combined with physical and psychological pressure against the Western defense perimeter's "unlocked doors." Not only is Western strength visibly paling beside Moscow's growing capability, but nearly every industrial democracy is becoming ever more dependent on distant, easily subverted third world countries for their energy and mineral imports. With the removal of Zimbabwe and Namibia as buffers to direct intervention, South Africa would become a logical target for Moscow's subsequent blow against Western power on its quest for world hegemony.

South Africa's defense infrastructure, particularly the Simonstown, Westlake, and Durban naval-communications facilities, would give those powers enjoying access to it significant advantages in any conventional war east of Suez. At present NATO (by its own choice) does not include areas south of the Tropic of Cancer in its sphere of activity. The West's use of South African dockyards ceased with the abrogation of the Simonstown Agreement of 1955, although Pretoria is willing to make formal defense arrangements with NATO members.[21] By ignoring South Africa's entreaties, the West is greatly constraining its potential position of influence in the Indian Ocean (where, since January 1972, the Soviet Union has continually deployed at least thirty warships) and Southeast Asia.[22] As Chettle points out,

> During the Vietnam War, destroyers based on the east coast of the United States made heavy use of Luanda, Angola and Maputo, Mozambique on their way to Vietnam, due to U.S. refusal to use harbors in South Africa. The time required enroute for refueling added two weeks to the voyage, and the 2,800 mile gap between Luanda and Maputo left the destroyers dangerously low on fuel. . . .
> It is unlikely that the United States could depend on the hostile Marxist governments of Angola and Mozambique in another crisis. The United States is, in fact, losing access to bases along the Cape route.[23]

Avoidance of South African bases further complicates Western security because unfriendly or unstable governments (such as Libya, Ethiopia, Sudan, Iran, and Turkey) control air routes to the Indian Ocean region and could close them to NATO in a crisis situation. Harbors, repair areas, radar stations, and naval industries are among South Africa's vital resources, and cannot be divorced from our analysis of Soviet strategy and motives.

III

The Soviet Union's stake in South Africa is thus nothing less than an opportunity to control some of the world's most important strategic resources. We will now examine the operational military threat that the Soviets could pose to South Africa. Western leaders should expect Russia to pursue its goals in a fashion typifying ambitious states throughout modern history, namely with various forms of political and economic pressure and, failing these, by ultimately resorting to, or sponsoring the use of, military force against the republic.

In the last decade, nonmilitary sanctions aimed at toppling the anti-Communist regime in Pretoria have not only foundered, but have had the opposite effect of strengthening successive governments' commitment to internal security and national defense; until recently, they have also increased white support of the policy of apartheid. Since the UN Security Council called, with Soviet inspiration, for an embargo on arms shipments to South Africa beginning in 1963, Pretoria has increased defense spending more than 1,000 percent, to the point where it now represents one-fifth of total government expenditures.[24]

Moreover, the embargo provoked massive official investments in an indigenous arms industry. Considerable progress has been made in making the country self-sufficient in the production of small arms, ammunition, and other instruments of counter-insurgency, although Pretoria still relies on external suppliers for such sophisticated weapons systems as supersonic aircraft.[25] Until recently the embargo also failed to prevent weapons sales from several NATO members, particularly France, Britain, and Italy. As late as 1975, South Africa had a U.S. $350 million contract with France to manufacture components for the Mirage III fighter on its own territory.[26]

The ineffectual results of passive (nonmilitary) sanctions against South Africa increase the possibility that the Soviet Union (and Cuba) will ultimately resort to military threats and the application of force to secure their regional objectives. Certainly most of the environmental contraints on overt military action that were present even five years ago no longer exist. Soviet warships dominate the Indian Ocean as the British once did and venture far from their home shores to complicate Western security in the North Sea, Mediterranean, and North Pacific.[27] Owing to NATO's apathy, the Russian navy has set an important precedent for coercive maneuvers off the north, east, and west African coast in recent years.[28] In addition, as we have seen, Soviet flyers gained considerable experience shuttling weapons and advisers to clients waging "revolutionary" war in Angola, Mozambique, and the Horn. Cuban troops armed by the Kremlin now roam the continent wherever an opportunistic faction has invited them, in the process becoming a disciplined and battle-ready force at the disposal of Soviet planners. All this has taken place at a time when most countries in the West (with the exception of France) eschew active military roles in Africa, even though the potential losses in terms of access to minerals and sea routes are huge. Until recently the possibility of military confrontation between South Africa and Communist powers would have been ruled out as fantasy. This is no longer true. Indeed Soviet-Cuban intervention must now be considered as a real possibility in the early 1980s, for reasons that will become clear.

Where, and in what form, such intervention will occur depends on four factors: (1) the Soviet Union's ability to project naval power into waters adjacent to South Africa and utilize bases situated on the African continent (the Kremlin's desire to continue adding to its capability can be taken for granted); (2) the Cuban expeditionary army's capabilities with respect to land operations—a major offensive, commando missions, or support of local guerrillas—against South Africa across its northern border; (3) the Western powers' willingness to intervene in hostilities between Communist intervenors and the republic (ironically, the salient factor here is just the reverse of the Soviet case: NATO's capabilities can be taken for granted, only its commitment is tenuous); and (4) the size and quality of South Africa's military and internal security forces. The frontline black states in southern Africa are too small and poorly equipped to sustain independent missions against South Africa, and so do not figure significantly in regional force calculations, except insofar as they provide logistical bases and sanctuary. By examining the current regional balance of forces and assessing the "political will" of the parties involved, we may construct alternative scenarios of military confrontation in the 1980s.

The worst possible case from South Africa's perspective is a large-scale invasion and seizure of important mineral-producing areas by Russian naval, air, and infantry units. There is little doubt that Soviet leaders have the hardware and transport capabilities at their disposal to conduct a sizable overseas operation, although probably not for an extended period of time given the logistical problems.[29] As of 1978, Soviet fleets included five naval infantry regiments, each with three infantry battalions and one tank battalion. This gives them an option of quick intervention, in the third world, similar to America's with its marines,[30] since no third world state can match that Soviet projectional power, however much smaller it may still be than America's. Brezhnev's readiness to send combat troops of the airborne divisions to the Middle East in October 1973 indicates great confidence in the ability of Soviet forces to undertake missions abroad.

Several factors make a Soviet invasion of South Africa, in the form of southern and western beachheads and/or a land offensive from the north, a remote contingency. With respect to the first two operations, Russian commanders have no historical or practical experience with Normandy-type applications of naval, air, and infantry power; it is unlikely that their initial attempt will be against a rugged coastline in bad weather and choppy seas. Although South Africa's seaward defenses are weak relative to the northern perimeter, we can discount a massive Russian assault from offshore positions. An invasion from the north, using Soviet troops based in adjacent territories (Mozambique, Angola, independent Namibia, and black-ruled Zimbabwe), is also improbable. The republic's standing military force of 65,500 men can be mobilized in a short time to over 400,000, including a land force of forty infantry battalions equipped with tanks, rocket launchers, and antitank weapons.[31] Supplemental units designated as "Joint Combat Forces" can deliver 500 men to any spot in the country within ninety minutes.[32] The air force is equipped with first-rate tactical weapons including thirty-six French Mirage III and forty-eight F-1 fighter planes, providing close support for troops on the ground.[33]

Viewed objectively, South Africa's military is strong enough to put up a good fight against an all-out Russian attack from any direction. Official statements reflect the Soviet leadership's appreciation of Pretoria's strategic depth. For example, TASS noted in February 1978, that

> with the help of NATO member-countries, the apartheid regime is steadily building up its military potential. South Africa's military industry can now produce many types of small arms and heavy armament. Military-transport planes "C-130 Hercules" were purchased in the United States. France and Israel supply the regime with submarines. South Africa's army is fitted out with British Centurion tanks, French, West German and Israeli missiles.[34]

The Russians' scrabble in late 1977 to publicize what appeared to be an imminent South African nuclear weapons test suggests (among other things) that they are also deterred by the republic's nuclear potential (and ability to raise the costs of intervention). According to TASS,

> The press in the independent African countries expresses concern over the fact that in the face of the expanding national liberation struggle in the south of the continent the racists are capable of resorting to any reckless ventures, even including the use of nuclear weapons. The Pretoria regime . . . is hell-bent on getting hold of the nuclear bomb at all costs.[35]

Another obstacle to a Russian invasion is the strength of Afrikaner nationalism, which, it is often forgotten, is the oldest nationalist movement on the African continent. Territorial defense of the republic would involve most whites directly or indirectly; it is not unthinkable that it would elicit enough sentimentality (and pragmatic thinking) in the West to trigger a military response from at least some NATO members.

The most compelling reason for Soviet "prudence" in the

1980s, however, will be their ability to secure objectives in South Africa *without* launching a risky invasion. Thus, Russia's military profile in southern Africa is more likely to hinge upon the magnitude of terrorist activity inside South Africa and incursions from neighboring countries. If, in this 1980s scenario, guerrillas managed to sabotage the republic's industrial infrastructure, pin down its armed forces, and spark nationalist fervor in black townships, the Soviet Union could support their efforts with air strikes and naval bombardment. Precedents exist for both tactics. In May 1978 Soviet warships shelled Eritrean coastal positions while the Ethiopian government opened a major drive against the secessionists.[36] Russian pilots flew missions for the Egyptians and Syrians in the Middle East (1970-1971), aided the MPLA in its conquest of Angola,[37] and took part in the coup d'etat in South Yemen in 1978. The Russians already have a sophisticated air base in Conakry, Guinea, and are developing long-range offensive capabilities from Luanda; Soviet *Bear* aircraft staged their first oceanic flights from an Angolan airfield in 1977. By the decade's end, Namibia and Zimbabwe will presumably be hostile staging grounds as well.

Another high-probability scenario, one that could be linked to the previous one as well, is a blockade of South Africa by the Russian fleet, ostensibly in fulfillment of UN aid and trade embargoes against the republic. NATO countries are on a cleft stick here; the momentum that has built up in most industrialized countries in the campaign against South Africa will make it increasingly difficult for them to oppose such a blockade.

The blockade itself would be accomplished from convenient naval bases in Mozambique, Angola, and Namibia, if Walvis Bay, a South African enclave, is taken over by Windhoek. The Russians would not impede oil shipments around the Cape in the initial phases, in order to avoid provoking a Western military reaction; but their advantage in an East-West crisis situation would, from that moment on, be a foregone conclusion.

South Africa does, of course, have forces to oppose a blockade. Three French-built *Daphne* submarines, ten coastal minesweepers, and four helicopter-carrying ASW ships provide the country with formidable coastal sea-denial capabilities (these are aimed at infiltration as well as international intervention or blockade).[38] Beyond coastal waters, defenses are limited to seven old *Shackleton* reconnaissance aircraft, one bomber squadron of *Buccaneer* S-50s, and three missile-armed Israeli *Reshef* patrol boats (with three more on order)—hardly sufficient to defend the long Cape route. According to former Defense Minister P. W. Botha,

> South Africa is a medium-size power. . . . Our objectives are therefore limited, and we have clearly defined them as follows: 1) We must defend our land frontiers and our coasts, and we think we can do so; 2) Within limits we can contribute to defense of the sea routes which run close to our shores. But in view of our resources—the South African Navy long ago defined its tasks as antisubmarine warfare and minesweeping—we cannot defy a great power. Nor is that our policy.[39]

Even more likely is that Soviet forces will supply, train, and airlift Cuban and irregular black nationalist troops to positions along the South African frontier as they did in the Horn, Angola, and Mozambique. As Soviet proxies escalate the level of tension within South Africa, fleet maneuvers off the coast could offer moral and symbolic support to the insurgents. Detachments of Soviet capital ships for the purpose of coercive display are also a familiar tactic.[40]

The fall of the shah will also, of course, have a dramatically deleterious effect on South Africa. No successor government is likely to continue supplying Pretoria with oil, and Moscow will be able to supply Iran with increasing credits, weapons, and the like in return for an Iranian South Africa policy complementary to its own. South Africa is a frequent victim of Arab-instigated oil boycotts, and it has weathered the storm of international unpopularity largely because of Iran's supposedly apolitical stance in selling petroleum—a stance that derived from the shah's affinity for South Africa (where his father was exiled) and his geopolitical interest in Israeli strength. *To the Point International*, a South African publication, estimates that 90 percent of the republic's oil imports came from Iran.[41] South Africa's mineral resources will be as important to the Soviet economy in the near future as Iran's oil fields, so a trade-off between points of political-military pressure is not inconceivable. Control of the Cape would give the Soviet Union leverage over Iran's production of crude, since shipments to the West must pass along this route. Thus, if it plays the diplomatic game wisely, the Kremlin could realize two major foreign policy goals at the same time.

Latent Soviet threats to Pretoria are compounded by the presence of 40,000 Cuban soldiers on African soil, who figure in at least two scenarios for which South Africa military strategists must prepare. The first involves a large Cuban offensive across the northern border, out of bases in hostile adjacent countries and with cover from Soviet air and naval forces. The Cuban army waged a determined campaign against the Somalis in Ethiopia's Ogaden region from January to March 1978. With critical Soviet help, the Cubans demonstrated remarkable airlift and mobilization capabilities in assembling its expeditionary force of nearly 20,000. This force was supplemented by hundreds of Russians and other Warsaw Pact nationals (especially East Germans and Bulgarians), but the hard chores were carried out by Cubans.[42]

Most U.S. government analysts discount almost totally the possibility of a Soviet-Cuban demarche against South Africa of any sort. Indeed, there is a remarkable unanimity in views of the most senior U.S. intelligence and diplomatic officials charged with responsibility in these matters—namely that the logistical and other related problems make a Soviet-Cuban intervention in South Africa, Angolan-style, most unlikely. The reasons cited are real enough. South African defenses would make intervention on the scale required much more complicated than it was in Angola, as we have already seen.

It is also true that Cuba has "enough" problems on its hands in Angola, as administration experts note. They are bogged down in some regions with insufficient matériel and foodstuffs, resentment of them abounds in others, and many are getting killed by the continuing efforts of the União Nacional para a Independencia Total de Angola (UNITA). The intervention established a new level of anxiety in centrist regimes in Africa over Soviet-Cuban goals, which the Soviet-Cuban duo presumably would not wish to exacerbate further.

Is the conclusion that there will be no additional intervention in South Africa wishful thinking or sound analysis? A Defense Intelligence Agency (DIA) intelligence appraisal notes that "increased efforts (by the Cubans) have apparently been required to ensure continued MPLA rule. As recent press reporting indicates, the Cubans are willing to insert additional troops and equipment to provide this necessary support. However, Cuba's capabilities have been severely strained by the effort, and Havana, in concert with Moscow, may eventually decide that the costs outweigh the benefits of continued support to the MPLA."[43]

The fallacy in this appraisal is the same as that in many analyses of the potential for intervention: it is a projection by Americans, onto the Soviet-Cuban duo, of American problems in Vietnam and elsewhere. The biggest American constraints in Vietnam were political sentiment at home and the not unrelated problem of military morale in the field. (Western intelligence appraisals of the Cubans in the field would indicate similar problems.) But the Cubans can ignore sentiment at home, and they need not indulge their troops with R and R, one-year tours, and extravagant accommodations. The Soviets have shown again and again that, where they have an important objective, they will keep to it, however frequent and numerous the setbacks. (They have been ejected from Guinea twice and most recently had their base rights for surveillance flights over the South Atlantic severely restricted.)[44]

Moreover the Cubans, unlike the Americans in Vietnam, are not free agents. They are not wholly Soviet puppets, not wholly mercenaries at the Soviets' beck and call—but they are to a considerable extent. So sending another expedition to Africa, when another—greater—nation is paying the bills and coordinating (if not always calling) the shots, is something less than an adequate analogy to American freedom of maneuver at the time of the Vietnamese imbroglio. Fidel Castro is certainly not constrained by domestic opinion from sending more of his country's 160,000 soldiers to fight against the racists. On the contrary, given Cuba's internal economic problems and inability to subvert other Latin American regimes, escalation might be a useful diversion.

Arrayed against Cuba's army on the South African side would be the same well-equipped, mobile force that deters a large Soviet attack. There is little doubt that South Africa, with 170 tanks, over 1,500 armored personnel carriers and batteries of Cactus surface-to-air missiles, would make short work of its Cuban opponents. A more likely scenario, therefore, is one similar to Cuban activities in Angola and the Eritrean campaign. For years Cuba has organized and trained guerrilla groups on Angolan soil, including the MPLA, SWAPO, and Katangan cadres that periodically invade Zaire. Havana has also deployed in Angola some 700 "teachers" whose primary task is political indoctrination of the population about the virtues of revolutionary Communism.[45] Prior to 1978 Cubans taught Ethiopian pilots to fly relatively advanced MiG-21s, and there is evidence that they actually participated in bombing missions against the Eritrean separatists.[46] With bases in Namibia and Zimbabwe in the 1980s, Cubans would surely be organizing black nationalists for incursions into South Africa, supported in their efforts by a lavish supply of Soviet tanks, artillery, and airplanes. As with the Russians, the temptation for Cuba to engage its own combat forces against South Africa will increase as the situation within the republic deteriorates. It is unlikely that these would fight central South African defense forces in classic conventional battle, but rather that the Cubans would contend with badly divided and well-dispersed troops, in a situation where the republic had already partly disintegrated. For this is a process already ensuing.

Despite reassurances by police officials to the contrary, inhabitants of the sparsely populated northern Transvaal report that guerrillas regularly ford the Limpopo River into the republic; a rash of incidents through the summer of 1978, including burglaries and murders, seems to substantiate their claims.[47] In response to the situation, Agriculture Minister Henrik Schoeman recently announced that farms in border areas could be subdivided down to one hectare units, provided there is a house and permanent occupant on each parcel.[48] This reverses a decade-old policy of consolidating small farms for economic reasons, since an estimated one-third of all cultivated holdings are too small to be economically viable. The government is even considering a plan to expropriate lands used as vacation retreats and sell them to young, permanent farmers for a fraction of their real value. According to army chief General Constand Viljoen, without such measures the drift of whites away from rural areas would eventually lead to terrorist control of the countryside.[49] Partial solutions include a radio alert network that will soon link remote farms to each other and security command posts. In the long run, however, economic freedoms regarding the ownership of land along the frontier may give way to the country's security requirements.

IV

Prophecy, which usually involves tea leaves, unscholarly risk, and ignorance of the very multiplicity of variables that can play in any complex setting, is nonetheless rather easy, in the broad, with respect to South Africa. Labor unrest, communal violence, and the rising threat on South Africa's borders hardly make the republic an investment haven for the eighties. And given the apparent unwillingness of the republic's elite to take the requisite risks in the area of interracial relations that would make support possible from potential friends in the political center in the West, Pretoria is likely to remain a pariah. But these are variables that have in fact been rising in strength over a longer period of time than is generally realized.

Yet analysis of South Africa's future is curiously beclouded on both the Left and Right by strangely similar mind blocks. On the Left the horror of apartheid is such that it is assumed on faith alone that the miserable situation will disappear of its own volition—a logic not generally applied to Communist regimes whose violation of human rights is orders of magnitudes greater. On the Right is a smug confidence in the republic's sheer competence, especially its military capability. South Africa has been able to build up "an impressive military capability . . . far bigger than any of the publicly available estimates made by military watchdogs such as the International Institute for Strategic Studies. I am convinced that the South African armed forces possess both the means and the will to defend their country's territorial integrity," wrote a British general.[50]

This sort of logic blinds these advocates to scenarios that borrow from the fall of South Vietnam, or from the confusion of Angola in 1975-1976. In this logic it is forgotten how political miscalculation led to military disaster for the republic in late 1975 (or the blame for the disaster is laid elsewhere, usually Washington), and how internal political-military consequences might flow from a deterioration of public order on the level that has occurred in the 1975-1976 period.

More specifically, can we argue that Soviet-Cuban intervention in South Africa is a serious prospect? We feel from the foregoing—the change in the correlation of forces worldwide, the disintegration of order in the region, the growing Soviet willingness to take military risks in view of the large stakes— that such a prospect should not be ruled out, if and when Nkomo's ZAPU forces are installed in power in Zimbabwe and Sam Nujoma's Marxist SWAPO forces are in Windhoek.

Of course the obstacles to an intervention would be considerable, but there are always economic or logistical reasons for thinking that an adversary will not do what he desires politically. The main variable has always been political will. The arguments used in Washington today against the possibility of further Soviet intervention in Africa are quite similar to those argued against the likelihood of the original Soviet-Cuban Angolan intervention; by others against the 1964-1965 U.S. involvement in Vietnam, indeed against virtually every military demarche any power has ever attempted, none of which has ever been deemed cost-effective by those who hoped it would not happen or who had an interest in a different outcome.

Ultimately, the Soviets and Cubans are likely to intervene precisely because of their long-vaunted commitment to "liberation." The capital amassed from past posturing and support on southern African questions could be dissipated in strategic parts of Africa were the duo not to put their troops where their rhetoric has been. Moreover, Moscow moves on *momentum*, working greatly in their favor owing to U.S. policy and the movement of events in the southern African theater. Failure to intervene, at the time of a UN blockade and large-scale uprisings in the republic, for instance, both of which are highly possible, would be the classic failure of will at the moment of "truth"—

as Africans would see it. The Soviets are now seen as having "history" on their side. They dare not lose it. Furthermore, the Soviet willingness to arm guerrillas, combined with the guerrillas' own perception of growing Soviet strategic and conventional superiority, has resulted in the *fact* of superior arms being turned into a whole doctrine of superior arms.

The only pertinent variable that we have not examined and that bears heavily on the outcome of the southern African crisis, is the "American card," as it impinges on Soviet strategy. The administration of Jimmy Carter, Walter Mondale, and Andrew Young—to list the key formulators of its African policy—is deeply committed to bringing about an end to apartheid in South Africa. This is not to say that such a commitment has been thought out with respect either to implementation or implication; indeed Vice-President Mondale is said to have shocked the German chancellor with his boasts in 1977 of "leaning on Vorster until apartheid collapses." "What will you put in its place when this happens?" Helmut Schmidt is reported to have asked. "We will worry about that when the evil is gone," Mondale is said to have replied.

Numerous constituencies have refused to believe that Jimmy Carter would in fact do what he promised to do in his presidential campaign—whether it was related to military weaponry, China, or troops in Korea. These constituencies have one by one revised their skepticism. Moreover, radical policies develop their own constituency and momentum, leading to further such decisions. Thus on Zimbabwe the Carter administration has already made clear that the "internal solution" will never garner American support, and the brunt of American diplomacy has been to achieve the same outcome as that supported by Moscow. Whether in fact Washington will be seen as having played into Moscow's hands depends, of course, on how the next phase of southern African developments turns out; in 1979 it was nonetheless tempting to see the Carter administration as having unwillingly advanced the interests of the chief American adversary, as far as southern Africa was concerned.

The extent to which the context and assumptions of American diplomacy have changed, insofar as these relate to Soviet strategy, can be seen in the Namibian case. American diplomats involved were proud of their success in applying compelling pressure (in conjunction with four Western partners) on South Africa in 1977 by implying the threat of sanctions against it. The specifics of UN Resolution 385 were bought in toto by the Western coalition: free elections under UN control, a release of all political prisoners, a repeal of all discriminatory laws, permission for all exiles to return, and a total withdrawal by South African troops. The quid pro quo, of course, was that SWAPO must not impede a political settlement; but, despite the absence of convincing proof that it would not do so, the Americans pursued their South African quarry anyway. Indeed, the Americans found Nujoma ubiquitous and impossible to find, as if this was a treatment meted out equally to all comers—rather than a shrewd stratagem of a trained Marxist-Leninist who knew which side had the ultimate cards. Nujoma's benefits from and loyalty to Moscow are exceeded by few third world Soviet clients.

In effect and in sum, the American administration remains committed to changing the status quo in South Africa, irrespective of its repercussions. Like-minded journalists praise the change of policy and help blind the administration to the irrelevance of its efforts in Rhodesia and the willfulness of its policy toward South Africa. When the possibility of Soviet intervention is mentioned, it is both denied as a possibility and rationalized in advance. William Beecher reports that a "Western diplomat says that when he talks to Soviet officials on the subject [of a Soviet intervention], they generally say, 'Just as the United States got over Angola and Ethiopia, so will they get over what we do in Rhodesia.'"[51]

What would induce Moscow and Havana to get off their present course? Only one thing: an abrupt change in American policy. America's policy of nonintervention will change, simply because it is unresponsive to reality and to American interests. But to what end? When government policies are out of joint, there is necessarily a lag before the shift in course. Carter is too far out on a limb to come back in time to turn American policy around. After the fall of the shah, the Marxist coup in Afghanistan, the Soviet-supplied Vietnamese victory in Cambodia, and the strident posturings of Soviet leaders in the presence of American senators and other visitors, the Carter administration was beginning to consider that a danger did exist. By 1979 it became possible to believe that following a massive duo intervention in Zimbabwe, the administration would not "get used to" the presence of Soviet and Cuban troops on the Limpopo. But as in Angola, the first party on the scene would have an enormous advantage; it would take ten times as much force to blow an interventionary force out as to keep it out in the first place. And because the object was a racist regime in southern Africa, it would require a vastly heightened sense of threat before Washington would attempt to come to the rescue. In any event, Moscow would have long since consolidated its ties in Mozambique and Angola, and, through the strategic superiority it would have advertised through the unequal SALT II accord, Moscow would be able to tell Washington and the world that it was simply too late for its gains to be contested.

Notes

1. As an example of the trends, see for example Santa Fe Corporation, "Measures and Trends: U.S. and U.S.S.R. Strategic Force Effectiveness," Washington, D.C., Defense Nuclear Agency, February 1978. Of the forty-three indices, the United States was ahead on all in 1962. By 1978, the Soviet Union was ahead on all but eleven.

2. See Paul H. Nitze, "A SALT I Negotiator Challenges SALT II," *Christian Science Monitor*, March 27, 1978.

3. A point owed to Admiral Elmo Zumwalt.

4. Candidate of Military Sciences A. M. Dudin and Candidate of Historical Sciences Yu. N. Listvinov, in V. M. Kulish, ed., *Voyennaya sila i mezhdunarodnyye otnosheniya*, 1972, p. 136, cited in "Soviet Aims and Activities in the Persian Gulf and Adjacent Areas, by Alan Berson, Klaus Luders, and David Morison, for Abbott Associates, Inc., November 1976.

5. Ibid., p. 137.

6. See W. Scott Thompson, "The Projection of Soviet Power," Rand Paper Series (Santa Monica, Calif., August 1977).

7. John Darnton, "Ethiopia's Victory Also Proves to be Russia's Gain," *New York Times*, December 17, 1978.

8. Joshua Nkomo, for example, the leader of ZAPU, visited both Communist capitals in November 1978 for the purpose of soliciting weapons and public support for his guerrilla organization's efforts against the Smith regime.

9. U.S., Congress, Senate, Subcommittee on African Affairs of the Committee on Foreign Relations, *Hearings*; "South Africa: U.S. Policy and the Role of U.S. Corporations," prepared statement of John M. Chettle, director of the South Africa Foundation, 94th Cong., 2nd sess., September 1976, p. 42.

10. Ibid.

11. Ibid., p. 43.

12. Ibid., p. 42.

13. W.C.J. van Rensburg, "Africa and Western Lifelines," *Strategic Review* 4, no. 3 (Washington, D.C.: United States Strategic Institute, Spring 1978), p. 49.

14. Ann and Neva Seidman, *South Africa and U.S. Multinational Corporations* (Westport, Conn.: Lawrence Hill and Co., 1977), p. 79. 1978 figures from "Corporate Activity in South Africa" (Washington, D.C.: Investor Responsibility Research Center, 1979), p. G4.

15. TASS report on January 13, 1978 (the eve of Henry Ford II's eight-day visit to South Africa to talk with officials about expanding the Ford Motor Company's operations in the republic), in *F.B.I.S.* 3, no. 10 (January 16, 1978).

16. Senate Hearings, op. cit., p. 24.

17. Ibid.

18. Patrick Wall, "The Vulnerability of the West in the Southern Hemisphere," *Strategic Review* 4, no. 1 (Washington, D.C.: United States Strategic Institute, Winter 1976), p. 45.

19. van Rensburg, op. cit., p. 46.

20. Senate Hearings, op. cit., p. 43.

21. Paul Giniewski, "South Africa and the Defence of the Cape Route," *NATO's Fifteen Nations* (Amstelveen, the Netherlands) 17, no. 2 (April-May 1972):25.

22. Steward Menaul, "The Security of the Southern Oceans: Southern Africa the Key," *NATO's Fifteen Nations* (Amstelveen, the Netherlands) 17, no. 2 (April-May 1972):44.

23. Senate Hearings, "South Africa," p. 44.

24. Michael T. Schieber, "Apartheid under Pressure: South Africa's Military Strength in a Changing Political Context," *Africa Today* 23, no. 1 (January-March 1976):34; and *The Military Balance, 1978-1979* (London: International Institute for Strategic Studies, 1978), p. 49.

25. Schieber, "Apartheid," p. 37.

26. Sammy Kum Buo, "Fortress South Africa," *Africa Report*, January-February 1975, pp. 11-17.

27. See Worth H. Bagley, "Sea Power and Western Security: The Next Decade," *Adelphi Papers*, no. 139 (London: International Institute for

Strategic Studies, 1977), pp. 12-34.

28. See, for example, David K. Hall's unpublished manuscript "Soviet Military Power in West Africa" (Ph.D. diss., Political Science Department, Brown University, July 1978), pp. 1-103.

29. Bagley, "Sea Power," pp. 12-34.

30. See W. Scott Thompson, *Power Projection, a Net Assessment of U.S. and Soviet Capabilities* (New York: National Strategy Information Center, 1978), p. 17.

31. *Military Balance*, p. 49.

32. Schieber, "Apartheid," p. 38.

33. *Military Balance,* pp. 49-50.

34. Report by TASS correspondent Alexsandr Osipov on February 7, 1978; in *F.B.I.S.* 3, no. 27 (February 8, 1978).

35. TASS report of December 30, 1977; in *F.B.I.S.* 3, no. 1 (January 3, 1978).

36. See W. Scott Thompson, "The African-American Nexus," *Horn of Africa* (1978), pp. 5-21.

37. See ibid.

38. *Military Balance*, p. 49.

39. Giniewski, "South Africa," p. 25.

40. Hall, "Soviet Military Power," p. 16.

41. "South Africa's Oil Lifeline Threatened If Shah Overthrown," *To the Point International* (Sandton, South Africa), November 10, 1978, p. 12.

42. Roger W. Fontaine, "Cuban Strategy in Africa: The Long Road of Ambition," *Strategic Review* 6, no. 3 (Washington, D.C.: United States Strategic Institute, Summer 1978), p. 23.

43. W. Scott Thompson, "Cuba and the Soviet Union in Southern Africa" (Unpublished paper), pp. 16-17.

44. Thompson, "Cuba and the Soviet Union," p. 17.

45. Fontaine, "Cuban Strategy," p. 20.

46. Fontaine, "Cuban Strategy," p. 24.

47. "Terrorist Threat Grows along the Limpopo," *To the Point International* (Sandton, South Africa), November 10, 1978, p. 60.

48. "Unoccupied Border Areas Vulnerable," *To the Point International* (Sandton, South Africa), November 10, 1978, p. 57.

49. Ibid.

50. General Sir Walter Walker, *The Bear at the Back Door* (Surrey: Institute for Conflict Studies, 1978), pp. 131-35.

51. *Boston Globe*, October 29, 1978.

7
Evolving American Views
of South Africa

Bruce J. Oudes

The pattern of migration and commerce that has produced societies so similar—and yet so different—as South Africa and the United States surely must be one of the more acute and complex ironies in the human experience in the past four centuries.

The American traveling to South Africa and the South African visiting North America share an experience that those who do not make the diagonal journey across the Atlantic can never wholly comprehend. The travelers pass through a kind of looking glass and to one extent or another invariably find themselves drawn to Carrollian imagery in their attempts to understand and relate what they have experienced.

In such an extraordinarily kaleidoscopic situation so heavily laced with passion, the task of arranging these attitudes into a relatively coherent American foreign policy is rendered even more difficult by the fact that comparatively few Americans have firsthand knowledge of South Africa. There are, of course, those who believe that such is an advantage rather than a disadvantage in the foreign policy development process. Some of these people are on the Right and essentially would like to develop policy in a clublike atmosphere. Others sharing this view constitute a frustrated club more to the Left who in the 1970s tended to conclude that, as one lyricist has put it, you don't have to see Johannesburg after you've seen Detroit.[1]

Such attitudes, however, may be changing. The South African government's visa policy, highly capricious in recent decades, may be taking a more open turn in the late 1970s.

There is in all probability a positive correlation between open-
ness on the part of the South African and American governments and the rate of the evolution of private attitudes and ultimately formal government policies on the bilateral relationship. The question, of course, is in which direction(s)? Powerful
forces and emotions within both countries and around the
world seek to influence the answers. Probably the only thing
that these constellations of attitudes and policies share is that
they are all too often simply reflexive and, alas, only too rarely
reflective.

One who would be so presumptuous as to attempt to analyze
even one side of that question—American attitudes—is best
advised to proceed with great caution. Although there is broad
enough agreement on the notion that American attitudes
toward South Africa have evolved over the past century and
even since World War II, the dispute begins when one attempts
to describe how they have evolved, the extent to which they
have evolved, and why that evolution has taken place.

Whether one is observing all this from a conservative, liberal,
or radical perspective, the question has to be posed primarily in
terms of its racial dimension for the fundamental reason that is
the way the vast majority of people in the United States and
abroad see it. The problem is the evolving relationship of racial
attitudes, political power, and government in both countries.
The world has come some distance since both Wilsonian self-
determination and the Russian Revolution were born in the
ashes of World War I. The philosophical, administrative, and
economic systems of the United States and the Soviet Union are
astride the world, but their exalted status has not shielded
either of them from serious failures in foreign policy. Some of
these have not been entirely unrelated to problems of racial
attitudes and perceptions.

If Wilson's idea can be seen as the foreign policy corollary of
Lincoln's domestic proclamation, then we should quickly also
recall that it was Lincoln who finally recognized the independence of Haiti, the second independent nation in the Western
Hemisphere. Although the independence of much of Africa,

some of Latin America, and many parts of Asia was spawned by the evolutionary and revolutionary themes of this century, Haiti owes its independence to the French Revolution. Lincoln also recognized Liberia, a permanent reminder of America's melancholy history, but it is from Haitian independence that one might date the long history of the influence of American racial attitudes on American foreign policy. Had the Haitian population been largely white, such a revolutionary government seeking recognition from the United States probably would not have had to wait for sixty years and a Lincoln for a favorable American nod.[2] Lincoln, nevertheless, also was a staunch advocate of black American expatriation. As president he made an arrangement with Haiti to accept a black American colony. More than a century later South Africans would call this the "homelands" concept.

Essentially American policy toward the Haitian Revolution was ambivalent, what diplomatic analyses often characterize rather inelegantly as a "straddle," in which regional considerations were secondary to the global politics of the era, namely pressures from Britain and Napoleonic France. Two centuries later, of course, we continue to weigh moral and philosophical considerations together with regional and global considerations in developing our particular "straddle" toward South Africa.

The evocation of Haiti is also important in another respect. The failure of Haiti to have achieved democracy and/or prosperity as it approaches its own bicentennial is grouped together with the failures of Africa, real and imagined, in the past two decades as a reason why reasonable people might view the "liberation" of South Africa with concern. Such a view can be described as tending to racially stereotype Africans and their descendants, but the Haitian example influences too many people to be swept quietly under the rug.

Although, of course, the tendency of many Americans and South Africans to share a frontier spirit and settler mentality can be dated from the Dutch settlements at New Amsterdam and Cape Town, the development of the essential duality in the American attitude toward South Africa can best be dated from the nineteenth century when black and white Americans began to be lured to South Africa by opportunities there as each saw them. Some Americans were drawn to South Africa by its gold, diamonds, and other minerals, while others went to pursue religious proselytization. That missionary/mercenary strain in contemporary American attitudes toward South Africa is well grounded in the sweat of history. American policy at the turn of the century straddled the war between the Afrikaners and the British, but a large segment of American public opinion was emotionally attached to the underdogs and against the British.[3] However, in that age in which American foreign policy was also emulating Britain to a degree by experimenting with imperialism, American opinion was also ambivalent about the underdogs among its own citizenry. In 1896 the United States Supreme Court upheld the "separate but equal" doctrine in *Plessy* v. *Ferguson.*

In this century American–South African fraternity reached a memorable pinnacle called the "Spirit of Monte Cassino" during the Allied invasion of Italy when South Africans played an important role. Then the divergent themes reasserted themselves. Even while participating in the San Francisco conference, General Smuts was only too well aware of the implications that the founding of a new United Nations would have eventually for his own country. As President Truman campaigned for human rights at home and abroad, the National party came to power in South Africa. Although the Supreme Court in 1954 led the government into saying emphatically that racial separation is inherently unequal, the South African government's disagreement with that approach—in the midst of the cold war and at the same time that much of Africa was being granted its political independence—led to a clash with American policy that essentially is the departure point for analyses of the evolution of contemporary American attitudes toward South Africa.

In March 1957, Vice-President Nixon led the American delegation to ceremonies marking the independence of Ghana, the first black African state to achieve sovereign status in the twentieth century. There was none of the hesitation and ambivalence that earlier had marked the American response to

Haiti, Liberia, and Ethiopia. In Accra Mr. Nixon, at his own personal request, briefly met for the first time a black American preacher who was winning a widening reputation. The young minister was Martin Luther King, Jr. That little noted meeting remains a symbolically important sign of the unity and evangelical nature of the American foreign policy of the times. It is little wonder that by the early 1960s there was serious concern within the South African government that the United States might actually invade southern Africa militarily, if only in the context of a UN action and then only in South-West Africa (Namibia).

As we begin to gain some perspective on that period in American history, we can in fact understand how our internal anxieties and conflicts interacted with our anxieties about Soviet intentions in the third world. Certainly the state of domestic racial détente and the foreign policy version of détente are the two most important variables at any given moment influencing American attitudes toward South Africa. The relative détente in both Soviet-American relations and domestic American race relations as the 1970s draw to a close explains why there is a considerable degree of psychological breathing room enabling a more measured view of American attitudes toward South Africa and how they might evolve in the years ahead. The third important variable at any given moment is the status of tension in the Middle East, and the fourth is the now historic fact that the buffer insulating South Africa from the rest of the continent, the Portuguese colonial empire, has disintegrated, thus focusing many minds in a way previously impossible. To comprehend the extent of the evolution that has taken place, we only need recall the spectrum of attitudes possible toward South Africa in the late 1960s and early 1970s when both domestic and cold- and hot-war tensions raged while Israel and South Africa were perceived by many to have had much more pronounced regional superiorities.

In articulating the nature and extent of this attitudinal change, the comparison of public opinion polls does not begin to convey its scope. Presidential documents are helpful, but even when fully declassified they in and of themselves will not tell the whole story. Instead the most relevant device of all may be simply to use the sequence of public statements of policy by American officials on policy toward South Africa that, in diplomatic jargon, "cut new ice," and then ask ourselves again why could we not bring ourselves to say these things earlier. Certainly what we tell ourselves and the world reveals a good deal about our attitudes past and present.

Getting Down to Brass Tacks

The United States defined a considerable amount of policy toward South Africa in the 1976-1978 period. In the previous two decades policy articulation had consisted of variations on the standard theme of American abhorrence of South Africa's racial policies, a low-key interest in South African nuclear restraint, and during the early 1970s an initial yet demonstrable interest among the professional ranks of the State Department in the question of the employment practices of American firms in South Africa. Throughout these years there was sporadic concern with the appropriate level of contact with the South African government and whether the fact of these contacts should be openly disclosed or closely held.

Secretary of State Kissinger launched the era of policy development on March 22, 1976, by expressing American concern for minority rights in South Africa.[4] Minority rights—human rights—are, of course, a recurrent theme in American foreign policy, one with broad support within the American public. Because of the state of domestic race relations, East-West relations, and the apparent stability of the South African buffer in the 1960s, it was not until 1976 that the United States could bring itself to articulate with respect to South Africa this standard principle of American foreign policy. Dr. Kissinger's statement was revealing in that it shed light on the state of American opinion in 1960 in the wake of the Sharpeville riots as well as in 1976, the year of the Soweto riots. The secretary of state's two trips to South Africa in 1976 also established new precedents. Publicly disclosed high-level meetings with South Africa would take place as often as the United States thought useful regardless of criticism that might emanate from third countries over that contact.

The Carter administration not only endorsed those principles of American policy, it went further. Surely someday historians would find of considerable interest the fact that more than two decades after the Nixon-King meeting in Africa, two men who had first come to national attention as their respective aides— Henry Kissinger and Andrew Young—would have such a major influence on the national dialogue determining the contours of the straddle in American policy toward South Africa. The general outline of that straddle has in fact been readily discernible for decades, but the process of articulation—filling in the blanks—has been slow and politically sensitive. The straddle, quite obviously, involves on the one hand keeping faith with the frustrated majority of South Africans who historically have been denied the right to vote on a common roll and on the other hand keeping the faith with and nurturing the growth of a responsible democratic process.[5]

The first major milestone of official American rhetoric on South Africa during the Carter years came, significantly, not from an official with a partisan domestic political constituency to please, but rather a career diplomat. For that reason, however, the statement at the time did not receive the public attention it deserved. It was delivered by William Schaufele, the assistant secretary of state for African affairs, to a Philadelphia audience on April 16, 1977. Ambassador Schaufele, who later became President Carter's envoy to Poland, said,

> Of all people, we Americans should probably be chary about providing excessive and unsolicited advice to others about how they should solve their racial problems. True, we have made impressive progress within our own country in removing the stain of injustice and discrimination based solely on race. But we must also admit that we have a considerable way to go before our achievements approach the ideals set forth in our Declaration of Independence and our Constitution. But perhaps more important, our recent history provides testimony to the fact that change in the racial sphere came about gradually, unevenly, perhaps even grudgingly, not because outsiders or foreigners told us what was right, but because the realization finally dawned on our people that the status quo was wrong and had to be changed for our own good. This self-realization must be given an opportunity to do its creative work in South Africa also, although

I will readily agree that the time for results is limited. It is in no one's interest if the South Africans move into an isolationist shell, closed against outside influences, there to defend themselves from all enemies, foreign and domestic. Such a development would have an effect opposite from the one we wish to achieve. Our diplomacy toward South Africa must, therefore, be carried out with a good deal of finesse and skill. We shall have to weigh carefully the relative merits of speaking out and restraint. . . . The United States is necessarily pursuing a nuanced policy vis-à-vis South Africa without compromising our principle.[6]

If the statement might strike some as indecisive, unremarkable, or bland, the fact remains that this was the first time the United States ever had articulated the theme of humility as a cornerstone of its policy toward South Africa. In and of itself the statement was an important barometer of the evolution of American attitudes toward South Africa. It was candid and confident, a signal that the United States would not be panicked by any rush of events in southern Africa and would be sensitive to both the people of South Africa and the obligation to stay in the straddle. If not used excessively, it also might be considered the perfect preface for whatever policies the United States might feel obliged to develop toward South Africa in the 1980s and beyond. It also, however, was another measure of the degree to which the cold war, domestic racial conflict, the Vietnam war, and the Congo (Zaire) crises had shaped American statements on South Africa in earlier years.

Building upon extemporaneous remarks made earlier in Johannesburg, Ambassador Andrew Young in a speech delivered August 25, 1977, discussed the American attitude toward guerrilla violence in southern Africa.

I don't believe in violence. I fought violence in my own country. I am determined that the United Nations continue as one institution that is devoted to peaceful change. And yet, I have never condemned another man's right to take up arms in pursuit of his freedom. Too often, however, the armed struggle is advocated most vigorously by those who are thousands of miles away and whose only contribution to the struggle is the rhetoric of bitterness and frustration.[7]

While Ambassador Young thus put considerable distance between himself and some opinion on the Left in the United States and Africa, he also went further toward expressing American empathy with the anguish of those in southern Africa who opt for violence than any previous American spokesman. He thereby filled in another dimension of the overall American straddle toward South Africa.

In the ballet of bilateral diplomacy the expression of the nuance of the straddle is formally couched in yet a third manner. Are relations "friendly" or "unfriendly" or somewhere in between? It is, after all, the most basic question of diplomacy. And yet because it is so elementary it has remained essentially overlooked and unexamined in the context of the American-South African relationship and, moreover, in analyses of American public opinion about South Africa as well. Most Americans who have any opinion at all on the subject feel *strongly* that South Africa is—or should be—either a friend or else an enemy of the United States. And yet, of course, there are all kinds of friends and enemies. There are, for instance, hostile friends, sick friends, friends in need, and staunch friends and allies, among others; and there are philosophical enemies, bitter enemies, mortal enemies, and just plain enemies. At the same time there are, as George Washington sought to remind us in his farewell, important shadings in between. All manner of nuance can be conveyed over time through this diplomatic vocabulary. Whether the United States in fact will do so in its policy toward South Africa in the 1980s will in turn depend in substantial measure on the continuing evolution of American public attitudes toward South Africa. How sophisticated will the public debate on South Africa become? How willing are Americans to discipline their profoundly differing emotions on South Africa for the sake of achieving a policy consensus? Those are some of the questions for which observers will be seeking answers in the 1980s.

In the 1960s it was essentially inconceivable that an American spokesman could suggest that the American motive toward South Africa was a friendly one. The formulation, however qualified, was considered an impossible one for American foreign policy in Africa as well as for American society, which was itself still in the process of coming to grips with the problem of insuring that every adult was guaranteed the right to vote. Although a substantial array of Americans ranging from cynics on the Left to those on the earnest Right, believed that American policy toward South Africa was essentially friendly, it was taboo in official prose. In 1968, for instance, when the first senior American official in years to visit South Africa completed his talks in Pretoria, a South African newspaper apparently erroneously quoted a U.S. spokesman as saying the talks had been "frank and friendly." The United States quickly took pains to issue a correction that described the talks only as "frank," according to an American official present at the time. Subsequent Republican administrations grappled with the semantic problem inconclusively for a variety of reasons in the years that followed. In sum, for many years those of earnest sincerity on the Left and cynicism on the Right shared the dominant view that there was little choice but to deal with racism in a foreign power with many cultural and economic ties to the United States in the same way that one dealt with Communism—relentless rhetorical hostility. Persuasion in that equation was necessarily of low priority.

But in October 1977, Vice-President Walter Mondale crossed a significant psychological Rubicon. Well into an interview with a South African journalist the vice-president said the United States was expressing its concern with South Africa as a "good friend" and "as one friendly country to another." The United States, he added, would like "to continue to maintain good relations with South Africa that had been enjoyed in the past and which we would very much like to continue. We want a good relationship with South Africa."[8] Although it seems probable that senior U.S. officials had said much the same thing in private to South African officials several years earlier, this in fact was the first time since Sharpeville that an American spokesman had said so publicly. Certainly, many Americans and South Africans, conservatives and liberals, may have thought Mr. Mondale's statement had a tongue-in-cheek flavor, but the words, in fact, are on the record. A matter of days after the Mondale trial balloon, the Carter administration felt obliged to react strongly to the announcement by South Africa of a campaign of domestic repression; the stick replaced the carrot. However, in 1978 President Carter once again expressed his strong personal preference for the carrot and cut more new ice by inviting the South African prime minister to visit Washington if the Namibia problem were resolved satisfactorily.

Mr. Mondale had first become identified with American policy toward South Africa in the spring of 1977 when he committed what critics at the time described as a terrible blunder. After meeting South African Prime Minister John Vorster in Vienna, Mr. Mondale was asked by a journalist whether he saw any difference between "full participation" and "one man-one vote." "No," the vice-president replied. "It's the same thing. Every citizen should have the right to vote and every vote should be equally weighted."[9]

The uproar in the South African press quickly spilled over into the U.S. press. And yet in all the commentary that followed,[10] there was no mention of the uncanny parallel to be drawn between that incident and the cause célèbre sixteen years earlier at another press conference when G. Mennen Williams, President Kennedy's spokesman on African affairs, was quoted as having endorsed the idea of "Africa for the Africans." The Williams flap came not long after Sharpeville; the Mondale flap not long after Soweto.

In psychological terms the two incidents could be described as a testing by South Africa of the depth of popular support for the position taken by two American spokesmen. In the 1960s the evolution of American attitudes toward South Africa ground to a halt not long after the Williams episode, but in the late 1970s the Carter administration seemed determined to keep the ball rolling.

Certainly the Mondale "faux pas" illustrated some important aspects of American attitudes. Since it has been a couple of centuries or so since Americans wrote a constitution, South African ideologies such as the one surrounding the phrase "full participation" seem to most Americans to be a form of Scholasticism—counting the angels on the head of a pin. While for many in southern Africa the writing, and rewriting, of constitutions is such a recent and regular part of life that it may be the region's second most popular indoor sport, Americans limit their constitutional horizons to the crossing and dotting of the *t* and *i*. Can, therefore, an American urging that "every vote should be equally weighted" be talking about anything but an essentially evolutionary process of change rather than a revolutionary one? It was not too long after the Williams flap that white South Africans began to make the transition to calling themselves African rather than European. If that sequence is any guide, then it may not be all that long before the tempestuous Mondale "watershed" is seen to have been no larger than a teapot.

The Search for Handles

The tendency of some South Africans to project their problems into the United States worries some South Africans and Americans, but that essentially is a prerogative of free debate. Perceived American policy was the major issue in the 1977 South African elections, another prerogative of those eligible to vote in South Africa. Yet it is the reverse of those equations that has received all too little attention in the United States. Not long ago a senior American diplomat with long experience in American–South African relations observed that it would be worthwhile to explore the question of just why and how we Americans "project our problems" into South Africa. Since he was addressing a generally liberal group, he cited as examples of this "our guilt feelings and our bitterness." Had he been addressing a more conservative group, he might also have cited our concern for order, stability, and property rights. He was in essence proposing the essentially sound idea that carefully formulated sociological research and analyses of American attitudes toward South Africa could be of considerable assistance to the process of the development of official policy toward South Africa. It is, one would suspect, yet another way of raising the question of the degree of seriousness of American public support for America's venerable official policy of "peaceful change" in South Africa.

American attitudes toward South Africa frequently focus on two essentially ancillary aspects of mainstream policy development, embargoes and the practices of American firms in South Africa, to such an extent that an analysis of the evolution of these attitudes in the past may furnish some clues to the future. The limited American economic embargo on trade with South Africa launched in 1962 and revised several times since then is a fascinating contemporary counterpart of a theme in British and American diplomacy rooted in the nineteenth-century idea that the denial of trade privileges can be a valid and meaningful adjunct in the struggle of Africans and those of African descent for human rights. While Victorian Britain won considerable applause in progressive circles for using its navy in the attempt to halt the Atlantic slave trade, some American entrepreneurs went to great lengths to continue their commerce in human cargo. Consciously or unconsciously the thinking of many interest groups and policymakers in the United States, Britain, and Africa continues to be deeply influenced by this history. The League of Nations imposed sanctions on Italy for attempting to destroy the sovereignty of Ethiopia, an African nation. While not a league member, the United States nevertheless paid lip service to the embargo. However, the entire exercise essentially was a charade; American oil continued to flow to Italy. Britain ultimately liberated Ethiopia militarily.

When President Kennedy imposed an embargo on American arms sales to South Africa in 1962, he told leaders of some other countries at the time that he did not think this was a very important decision since U.S. arms sales to South Africa in fact were modest and their termination could not be expected to produce a change in South Africa's racial policies.[11] Four years later Britain and America slapped a somewhat more comprehensive set of embargoes on rebellious white Rhodesia in order to avoid the difficult choice of either doing nothing at all or else putting down colonial insurrection by military means. The sanctions, however, had no decisive political impact. Britain and the United States wrote the sanctions, which they then ran through a rather skeptical UN Security Council in such a way that British and American firms operating abroad were not obliged to halt exports to Rhodesia if the country in which they were operating, South Africa, for example, chose not to enforce the sanctions. Since some of these firms in South Africa were oil companies, commerce in what could be called a twentieth-century version of black gold was not halted. Meanwhile, a lone

British navy vessel, periodically rotated, patrolled uselessly for years off the African coast, its only cargo being the ghosts of past British decisiveness.

In 1977 Anglo-American policy plowed additional symbolic ground by making the UN embargo on arms sales to South Africa as "mandatory" under Chapter 7 of the charter as the embargoes on Rhodesia. South Africa, unlike Rhodesia a sovereign state and UN member recognized by both Britain and America, called the action an act of war but continued to acquire arms one way or another.[12] South Africa's considerable arms buildup in the 1962-1977 period had, of course, been spurred in part by the original embargoes of the early 1960s.

While it appears certain that the embargo ballet between South Africa, the international community, and world opinion would continue into the 1980s and beyond, it seemed clear also that Britain, the United States, and other governments found themselves locked into a cyclical pattern of behavior that they were reluctant to review in any candid but thorough manner. The votes for embargoes were somewhat useful as a means of persuading third countries and certain groups within the United States of the earnestness of the American resolve to "do something" about South Africa and to convince public opinion of American "clean hands" in its policy toward South Africa. Egged on by conservative expressions of alarm about the possibility of Communist inroads in southern Africa, many liberal activists have been only too willing to argue that some form or other of additional sanctions would somehow or other prevent those Communist inroads.

Certainly it was understandable that the United States in the global climate of the early 1960s might have gotten itself rather quickly and casually into the southern African sanctions muddle. There was a widespread belief in the United States, Africa, and even in some parts of South Africa that the South African government would collapse precipitately either of its own inequities or else as a result of some presumably imminent military invasion. However, as time passed and nothing happened, attention turned elsewhere. A wide array of liberal and conservative political leaders in the United States, Britain, and other countries for years turned cartwheels to avoid the central issue of the damage done by their southern Africa charade to the integrity of the UN mechanism.

As the widespread sentiment that the apocalypse in South Africa was imminent faded in the mid-1960s, public interest in the more decisive types of action in the embargo field tended to be replaced by a surge of interest in corporate responsibility in southern Africa. This movement in fact could not have developed momentum as rapidly as it did without that growing sense in public attitudes that South Africa in fact was a long-term question. The corporate responsibility idea also was indirectly spurred by the civil rights atmosphere of the 1960s, which tended to promote black participation in the American economic system. Although it was developed as an issue by congressional Democrats, there are indications that President Nixon was intrigued by the subject as well.[13]

By 1978 the idea had enough support on Capitol Hill that Congress instructed the Export-Import Bank to link its willingness to finance exports to South Africa to the willingness of private firms to proceed toward the implementation of fair employment practices there. Its future in the mainstream of American policy toward South Africa seemed assured.

One way to measure the evolution of this American economic, social, and political thought with respect to South Africa is to compare these recent events to a Marxist platform, published in 1931 in English, that was explicitly pitched toward black workers. This was in the first issue of the *International Negro Workers' Review*, which, interestingly enough, was published in Hamburg just two years before Hitler took power.[14] A large percentage of what amounts to a manifesto is devoted to South Africa, but it is also targeted explicitly toward black workers in the United States, the Carribean, and other parts of Africa including the Gold Coast. For the most part the publication has a historical flavor befitting its age. After all, 1982 marks the twenty-fifth anniversary of those ceremonies attended by Dr. King and Mr. Nixon at which the Gold Coast became Ghana. White American opinion seemed to have surmounted many of its fears about the attraction of Communism for black Americans. And yet the "demands and conditions" that the *International Negro Workers' Review* says should be achieved in

South Africa retains a distinctly contemporary flavor. The first of its eleven demands is for the complete freedom of trade unions in South Africa; the second demands "equal pay for equal work (Natives with Europeans) for men, women and youth." If this can be taken as a measure of just how limited South Africa's progress toward equal justice in industrial relations has been in the past half century, the fact that a broad coalition of the American political leadership can be brought together in support of that goal indicates that syntheses emerging from previous dialectical arguments do not have to be Marxist.

The 1931 Hamburg Marxist platform, it should be noted, did not include the concept of more recent origin that foreign—particularly American—firms should withdraw from South Africa. A philosophy that seeks to abolish private enterprise of course has to be wary of using it as an instrument of political change. The withdrawal notion essentially originated in the post-Sharpeville era when liberals came to the conclusion that the structure of South African society was not going to unravel precipitately of its own accord and when a revolving credit established by American banks was seen as having propped up the South African government at a critical moment. The fact that the origin of the withdrawal idea was in church groups seeking to call public attention to American involvement in South Africa illustrates its philosophical roots in the antislavery and nonviolent movements. It is essentially a part of the broader embargo idea and rationalized as a policy of "clean hands," putting moral distance between the United States and South Africa's racial policies. The withdrawal idea, in fact, was an essential component of the corporate responsibility movement, making it look comparatively tame, pragmatic, and responsible. In 1972 the withdrawal concept was embodied in the Democratic party's platform, which called for a withdrawal of U.S. tax credits to American firms in South Africa.[15] Some proponents of withdrawal in fact contend that it is essentially a centrist idea. For the United States to adopt the idea, they maintain, would not represent a tilt toward the black majority, but rather a continuation of the basic straddle of not choosing sides between black and white.

In the years since withdrawal first was proposed seriously, U.S. investment in South Africa has grown steadily despite the events of 1976 and 1977 in South Africa and anti-investment pressures in the United States.[16] Meanwhile, the 1978-1979 events in Iran suggest in part that the presence of U.S. business as a modernizing force in a given country can, at least under some circumstances, contribute to the development of a revolutionary atmosphere.

The 1980s: Variations on a Theme

How much more difficult is it to imagine a revolution that is to come—to space it properly through a long period of time, to conceive what it will be like to the people who live through it. Almost all social prediction is catastrophic and absurdly simplified. Even those who talk of the slow "evolution" of society are likely to think of it as a series of definite changes easily marked and well known to everybody. It is what Bernard Shaw calls the reformer's habit of mistaking his private emotion for a public movement.

Walter Lippmann
A Preface to Politics
1914

How then might all these strands of recent American attitudes toward South Africa arrange themselves in the 1980s? Some sense of conceptual order might be useful. Probably the best place to start is with the concern of the American diplomat about how we "project our problems" into South Africa. Over the years America's career diplomats have had ample opportunity to observe the projection phenomenon. In its most intense form—regardless of whether it comes from the Right or Left—it is not sustainable over time and therefore threatens the integrity of overall American policy. While the diplomat as a bureaucratic animal instinctively looks for the center, he is at the same time also warning lest the country take on an involvement, a commitment, it might later regret. These concepts, of course, are by no means novel, but they have not been adequately analyzed with reference to the South African context. This projection—or transference—challenges the efforts of the professional to keep a given nasty situation at arm's length. This is sometimes called distancing. In 1970 policymakers called it "tar baby."[17] These projections in fact can come from the Left as well as the Right. Regardless of provenance they threaten achievement of the diplomatic ideal, a visionary posture above the fray to which the local actors, as they are called, respond as anticipated through persuasive rather than coercive techniques.

Having dissected, then, the elements of American attitudes toward South Africa and the framework through which they are expressed, one can see that the chances a constituency of either the Right or Left might lurch policy precipitately and extensively in one direction or the other in the years just ahead appear rather slight. Essentially there seems to be a check and balance system at work, one that will permit and encourage the systematic evolution of progressive American policy, but nothing more radical than that. In addition there might also be a substantial realignment of traditional conservative and liberal American dogma about South Africa as a result of this process.

For instance, it is not impossible to envisage the emergence of an odd-couple coalition of activists on the Right and Left who will be ready to vote substantial appropriations for southern Africa to influence the situation. However, another odd-couple coalition could emerge on the other side of the fence consisting of Vietnam doves on the Left and Vietnam hawks on the Right who will scrutinize each appropriation request carefully, asking hard questions about the extent to which such expenditures might commit the United States to further action down the road.

The supporters of withdrawal can expect to be challenged more seriously than in the past to spell out the implications of their proposal to a wide range of skeptical American opinion, liberal as well as conservative, which will have to be persuaded that such increased government activism would not in fact contribute to an ill-defined but clearly bleak scenario for South Africa. On the other hand, those on the right who view South Africa uncritically as a bastion of Western security can also expect to have their views challenged by an equally wide range of skeptical opinion.

The tendency of a good deal of opinion on the Right and Left in South Africa and in the United States to assume that a future Republican administration will somehow revert to a kind of status quo ante bellum also may be unrealistic. Clearly a Republican party attempting to attract black voters would be hard put to explain a reluctance to move forward in the evolution of a responsible Africa policy. It does not matter whether there are in fact many blacks who vote Republican or whether the blacks who are Republican place a particular personal emphasis on Africa policy. Any president saying the United States must support a reactionary South African government for global economic or strategic reasons faces a major test of his or her persuasive powers.

However, the situation in Africa itself also leads to the conclusion that a Republican administration would pay closer, more visible attention to the continent than any of its GOP predecessors. Since Republican presidents have had more credibility with white South African governments than Democrats, it would seem reasonable to expect that white South Africa would listen especially closely to the counsel offered by a Republican administration. If it is true, because of domestic political configurations, that Democratic administrations have particular leverage with respect to the Middle East when they finally bite the political bullet, then it may be that somewhat analogous configurations would suggest a major, decisive role for Republican administrations in southern Africa.

Regardless of which party is in power in the United States at any given moment in the decade ahead, the history of evolving attitudes toward South Africa points toward a particular focus in the 1980s on the development of black trade unionism. American labor has a long-standing interest and self-interest in the development of free trade unionism in South Africa. With the increasing recognition by both foreign investors in South Africa and South African businessmen of the importance of such an evolution, the question of the rights of black workers thus moves to center stage, a test of the good faith of those in the system about the expansion of that system. In the formal sense, of course, black trade unionism and job reservation are internal South African questions, and the corporate responsibility issue is in fact an ancillary aspect of bilateral

American–South African relations. But the intellectual currents of the century cannot be blocked by national frontiers.

Nevertheless, one can expect the South African government in the decade ahead to continue making the argument in one way or another that South Africa is being unfairly singled out for attention. Workers are underpaid in countries other than South Africa, they note. Unemployment levels among black youth in America are astronomically high, white South Africans say after riots in Soweto. Despite all the decades of civil rights activity in the United States, South Africans note, there are still communities in and around many American cities that are racially segregated. Since it is also highly unlikely that Americans will stop dishing out their opinions of South Africa, the feedback from white South Africa could have some interesting implications domestically. Will fair-minded Americans gracefully accept such South African criticism of the United States and do something to correct those faults? In the 1970s Americans tended not to take such South African criticism to heart. That conceivably could change in the 1980s if America and South Africa really are the "good friends" that Vice-President Mondale suggests they are. In the 1980s the South African government will conduct two or three elections providing excellent opportunities for the world's democracies to observe and analyze South Africa's ostrich-politik in a fishbowl of international attention. In the same period the United States will conduct three elections, which in turn will convey to South Africans a great deal about the degree of American nervousness about foreign affairs, quite possibly including its policy toward South Africa. If the South African and U.S. governments cannot agree to refrain from financing each other's domestic elections, then perhaps the two could negotiate a Reciprocal Campaign Financing Agreement.

In 1985 South Africa presumably will mark its seventy-fifth anniversary as an independent state, having had a decade to adjust to the implications of the Portuguese coup. In 1978 the position of the Carter administration was that the United States had "no timetable" for change in South Africa. Given the existence of the projection phenomenon it might be reasonable to suspect the existence of certain domestic pressures suggesting that language be replaced by, in the artfully ambiguous language of the U.S. Supreme Court, the phrase "all deliberate speed."

It is also not unreasonable to expect that centrist American opinion might find particularly intriguing the question of whether and when South Africa will extend the full franchise on a common roll to its Coloured population. Certainly in the late 1970s there was a growing concern among some conservative Americans with firsthand knowledge of South Africa about the failure of that government to have taken that step. That reluctance tended to undermine the basic position of conservative Americans that the existing South African system could progress in an orderly manner.

If by the end of the 1980s South Africa has not been able to fully integrate politically a population group so closely identified with Afrikaner language and history, then centrist American opinion might have little choice but to reach the considered conclusion that the South African system is inherently incapable of significant and orderly improvement. A consequence of that in turn could be a fundamental reorientation of the visionary posture of American diplomacy toward South Africa launched in the late 1970s. Even the most ardent skeptic then could no longer doubt that South African "democracy" was hopelessly pigmentocratic. Although the limitations—even dangers—of analogy are readily evident, it would be useful in this context not to completely ignore the fact that the American Civil War broke out eighty-five years after independence from Britain and that the eighty-fifth anniversary of South Africa's independence from Britain will be in 1995.

Should South Africa have a military coup, American attitudes and presumably policy would be relieved of certain self-imposed constraints. Although obviously there would be considerable interest in the orientation of such a new regime, it would in fact be a military junta controlled by a minority ethnic group. Comparison would be invited with other African countries.

Obviously the advent of some variety of civil war in South Africa would titillate a wide range of American attitudes producing pressures on U.S. policy to tilt or at least lean one way or another. The U.S. government in such an eventuality would have to deal rapidly with a wide array of consular problems, humanitarian concerns, cease-fire initiatives, and pressures for UN Security Council intervention. Certainly a war with so many ideological and racial overtones would be of intense interest in the United States, providing unlimited opportunities for heroic journalism. It inevitably would be compared to, among others, the Spanish civil war. Might there be a new Abraham Lincoln brigade? Some American journalism of the late 1970s seemed to be lusting for just such a conflagration like an adrenaline junkie unable to get off its earlier wartime high.

In the 1980s many Americans will continue to think of civil war in South Africa as inevitable. How will activist lust for war account for the fact that in Spain the right wing won? Not until decades later did democracy finally replace fascism. In South Africa at the beginning of the century independence was gained only after war was lost. If civil war is adjudged by black South Africans to be their only alternative, they will have to undertake it in full understanding that while ultimately they will prevail politically—it might, in fact, be at the price of losing the war itself. Those advocating the war scenario will find themselves obliged to deal with the risk of a Black Holocaust as well as a separate-but-equal White Holocaust. In his 1960s ditty on nuclear proliferation, "Who's Next?" the sardonic Tom Lehrer suggested "South Africa wants two: one for the black and one for the white." Therefore, in the 1980s those Americans convinced of the inevitability and presumably the utility of civil war in South Africa as the way to win Johannesburg, the African Jerusalem, may find themselves asked to articulate their specific scenarios for American policy in more detail.

Although there are too many potential variables for any analysis of the possible evolution of black American attitudes on South Africa and American policy there to be meaningful and valid, it is reasonably certain that the black-Jewish relationship, a vital component of domestic tranquility in the United States, has now been sensitized with respect to American foreign policy in the Middle East and Africa. That black-Jewish relationship was strained by the urban violence in the United States in the late 1960s and then by the tendency of both Israel and the United States in the early 1970s to take black Africa for granted. This was gradually corrected in the wake of the 1973 Middle East war and the 1974 Portuguese coup, and a significant number of members of Congress with black and Jewish constituents began visiting Africa. The sometimes stormy relationship can by no means be described as a cabal; however, as applied to the Middle East and Africa it produces the implication that fairness in U.S. policy toward one of those regions should be reciprocated by fairness toward the other. This, in turn, is supportive of traditional American policy goals in those regions. In several respects of course, the extent to which the dynamics of domestic American ethnic politics have become a microcosm of the Middle East–African political dynamic is remarkable.

However, many black American and other experts on African affairs remain bitter about the failure of the society as a whole to heed their warning in the early 1970s about the deterioration of the integrity of American policy toward Portuguese colonialism. This, it is held, was an example of black cultural invisibility comparable to the lack of general attention accorded demonstrations in Harlem in the late 1930s against Italian Fascism. In each instance the integrity of overall American foreign policy would have more readily been maintained had this responsible and mainstream advice been heeded at the time it was given. This cultural invisibility in the 1970-1975 period contributed to the tendency of black American opinion toward stonewalling when confronted by the development of especially grotesque versions of the Haitian example in Burundi, Uganda, and Equatorial Guinea during the 1970s. The argument, quite explicitly stated on numerous occasions, was that if American foreign policy was going to stress sovereignty to the exclusion of all other considerations in its policy toward Portuguese imperialism, white Rhodesia, and South Africa, then why should it be critical of internal developments in independent black Africa?

If the essential thrust of the late 1970s in American policy in Africa is maintained in the 1980s, suspicions within the black community that official American interest in human rights travesties in black Africa is racially oriented may gradually diminish. Moreover, if this general evolution continues, one might also see an increased willingness to examine the use of sanctions by the UN Security Council more objectively. There can be no mistaking the usefulness of studying the applicability of the sanctions mechanism to problems involving human rights violations. The issues could be of considerable interest to liberals as well as conservatives in the years ahead, particularly since it is no longer thought feasible to send the U.S. Marines into the Haitis of the world. The 1978 action of the United States in establishing a legislated embargo on American trade with Uganda undoubtedly will be cited in the future as an important precedent justifying proposals for the establishment of similar sanctions toward other countries that violate basic human rights.

In the 1980s there also may be some evolution of American and African thinking on a question of more than passing philosophical and tactical interest precipitated perhaps by the flow of events within South Africa. What, if anything, should be done about those instances in which blacks in fact desire to live separately from whites? One dimension of the question is posed by the nominal independence of the Transkei and Bophuthatswana. However, the question also is raised by other black South Africans, perceived as more militant, who say that the future they envisage for South Africa does not involve living next door to whites. Moreover, the white South African political debate over federalism and confederalism also raises the issue in another form. How, if at all, should American opinion and policy respond to these sentiments? Although black American cultural nationalism in the late 1970s was not as prominent a part of the general public discourse as it had been a decade earlier, there is little doubt but that it remains a strong current of black American opinon. A given U.S. administration in the 1980s undoubtedly would be well advised to follow the evolution of African and American opinion on this volatile issue rather than to attempt to lead it, but it would seem likely that the question will be debated in many forms privately and publicly in the decade ahead.

In the 1980s both the South African government and those black South Africans who go beyond nonviolence probably will find American public opinion a far more elusive prize than either had thought possible at one time or another since 1960. At the same time, however, numerous previously unexplored avenues of communication will be available for those in South Africa willing to give self-realization an opportunity to do its creative work.

South Africans of non-English origin, for instance, share a powerful bond with influential non-Africans such as black Americans, Jewish Americans, Israelis, and South Asians. Blacks, Jews, and Afrikaners historically have known the sharp sting of discrimination, of gentlemen's agreements, and even physical subjugation at the hands of perfidious Albion, British imperialism, English colonialist exploitation, call it what one will. Israelis born in South Africa, such as the former foreign minister, Abba Eban, presumably will help their government evolve new policies toward Africa including South Africa. If a Gandhi inspired a generation of Americans, it is questionable whether in the 1980s his legacy will be entirely dismissed by a new generation of South Africans. They, of course, will not lose sight of the fact that Gandhi's thinking in turn was shaped by the experiences of his years in South Africa and studying the long history of African nationalist nonviolence there. There are many more strands waiting creative self-realization, but at the very least there should be mutual amusement that despite the vissicitudes of history the common denominator for the struggle remains the language of the impossible English.

It is not, in sum, surprising that in the 1980s South Africa should be at the cutting edge of America's intellectual interest in the evolving relationship between race and democracy and that this should be projected in a balanced fashion with such grace and dignity as the United States can muster through its looking glass relationship with South Africa. A country that presumably has profited a great deal from its past struggles, both foreign and domestic, has little need to be nervous about its future role with respect to South Africa.

If, however, Americans—black or white, conservative or liberal—display nervousness in private and public debate about policy toward South Africa, then invariably that nervousness will be communicated in many ways to South Africa, effectively reducing still further whatever chance it has for a relatively peaceful evolution to a just and stable government. And that nervousness also will be in itself a measure of how little Americans as a nation have learned from their own past.

Notes

1. In his song "Johannesburg" (New York: Arista Records, 1975), composer Gil Scott-Heron concludes "freedom ain't nothin' but a word: Detroit like Johannesburg." Although the thrust of what Mr. Scott-Heron says does not explicitly oppose American travel to South Africa, it does express deep cynicism that also is reflected in his comments about the coverage of South Africa in the American press. "They tell me that our brothers over there are defyin' The Man; I don't know for sure because the news we get is unreliable, man," he says. "What's the word? Tell me, Brother, have you heard from Johannesburg? " Mr. Scott-Heron's message, it should be noted, is neither a call for violence in South Africa nor an expression of vicarious pleasure in violence. He is "glad to see resistance growin'," but, he adds, "I hate it when the blood starts flowin'." Scott-Heron expresses identification with black South Africa in universal language: "I know that they ain't gonna free me; but we've all got to be strugglin' if we wanna be free."

2. The evolution of white American attitudes toward blacks in the first years of the Republic is brilliantly depicted by Winthrop D. Jordan in *White Over Black: American Attitudes toward the Negro 1550-1812*, New York: Pelican Books, 1969). Relations between Haiti and the United States are described in *The Diplomatic Relations of the United States with Haiti, 1776-1891* by Rayford W. Logan (Chapel Hill: University of North Carolina Press, 1941), *Haiti and the United States, 1714-1938* by Ludwell L. Montague (Durham, North Carolina: Duke University, 1940), and by other writers in more recent times.

3. Former President Richard Nixon linked South Africa to Vietnam in remarks to the Oxford Union on November 30, 1978. A great nation can always fight a large war, Mr. Nixon said, "but it is terribly difficult for a great nation to fight a small war. The British found that out in the Boer War. We found that out in Vietnam."

4. "Foreign Policy and National Security," an address by Secretary of State Henry A. Kissinger, in *Department of State Bulletin* 74:463. "The United States has made clear its strong support for majority rule and minority rights in southern Africa," Dr. Kissinger said.

5. In a broader, continent-wide or regional context, the American straddle in southern Africa, especially prior to the Portuguese coup, fre-

quently was described as being between two entities, one being "black Africa" and the other being "white Africa." See, for instance, National Security Study Memorandum 39 of 1969. However, the dissolution of the colonial buffer north of South Africa in the late 1970s made the phrase "white Africa" with its connotation of multilateral redoubt obsolete.

6. "United States Relations in Southern Africa," and address by William E. Schaufele, Jr., assistant secretary of state for African affairs, delivered April 16, 1977, at the American Academy of Political and Social Science, Philadelphia, in *Department of State Bulletin* 76:468.

7. Address by Ambassador Andrew Young to the World Conference on Action against Apartheid called by the United Nations at Lagos, Nigeria, August 25, 1977. Press release U.S.U.N. 59-1977.

8. Interview of Vice-President Walter Mondale in Washington, D.C., by Benjamin Pogrund, deputy editor, *Rand Daily Mail*, October 11, 1977.

9. News conference of Vice-President Walter Mondale at Vienna, Austria, May 20, 1977, in *Department of State Bulletin* 76:661-66.

10. See for example "Asking for Trouble in South Africa" by George Ball, former under secretary of state, in the *Atlantic*, August 1977.

11. According to the memorandum of a conversation between Mr. Kennedy and Julius Nyerere, president of Tanzania, in July 1963, "The president [Kennedy] commented that it might be possible to do something on the arms embargo question but sanctions seemed an unproductive line. He had been examining the statistics of U.S. arms shipments to South Africa. These totaled about $2 million in 1961 and perhaps a bit more in 1962. These quantities were not significant enough to produce a change in South Africa's racial policies. The president said he wished to consider the matter further."

12. John F. Burns, "South Africa Says It Is Getting Arms," *New York Times*, November 20, 1978. Some of the complexities of American embargoes toward South Africa are explored in *A Symposium on South Africa: Issues and Policy Implications for the United States* (Mount Kisco, New York: Seven Springs Center, May 1977).

13. The question of U.S. economic policy toward South Africa was the primary stimulus for Mr. Nixon's 1969 decision to review American policy in southern Africa, according to members of the National Security Council staff. Among the materials furnished Mr. Nixon to read at San Clemente in August 1969, was the special section on South Africa, "The Green Bay Tree" by Norman MacRae, published in the *Economist*, June 29, 1968, according to Roger P. Morris, Mr. Nixon's staff aide for African affairs in 1969. A major theme of "The Green Bay Tree" is that increased black participation in South African society would flow from increased black eco-

nomic prosperity. In September 1969, Sir Francis de Guingand, the South African industrialist, called on Mr. Nixon at the White House. In August 1970, Mr. Nixon modified the terms of the existing American embargoes toward South Africa in National Security Decision Memorandum 81. In late 1972 Mr. Nixon told the *Washington Star* that he was planning to review U.S. policy in Africa. Some American and South African officials have said privately that they believe Mr. Nixon had hoped to visit Africa including South Africa in 1973.

14. *International Negro Workers' Review* 1, no. 1 (January 1931), published by the International Trade Union Committee of Negro Workers, 8 Rothesoodstrasse, Hamburg, Germany.

15. The genesis of that Democratic party plank is discussed in "The United States' Year in Africa," *Africa Contemporary Record* Vol. 5 (New York: Africana, 1973):A73-A74.

16. During the first eight years of the 1970s American direct private investment in South Africa rose more than one billion dollars—almost twice the $556 million increase in American investment in all the rest of Africa combined. At the beginning of 1970 American investment in South Africa was $755 million, and that in Africa north of the Limpopo was $2,227 million. However, by the beginning of 1978 that gap had shrunk by almost one-third: American investment in South Africa was $1,791 million while U.S. investment in the rest of the continent had grown only to $2,783 million. If the trend continues, American investment in South Africa by the end of the 1980s conceivably could equal that in all the rest of the continent.

17. Anthony Lake, director of policy planning at the State Department in the late 1970s, used the phrase in the title of his book, *The Tar Baby Option: American Policy Toward Southern Rhodesia* (New York: Columbia University Press, 1976). In mid-1979, however, it remained to be seen whether the phrase ultimately might not also describe aptly the Carter administration's policy toward Rhodesia.

8

The European Connection: How Durable?

Lawrence G. Franko

The South Africa policy of the Carter administration has the Afrikaners worried. Unfortunately, they are not alone. Europeans, especially the British, Germans, and French wonder what effect U.S. South African policy may sooner or later have on them. For there is a European connection to the country of apartheid that the United States has passed over.

Many Europeans view present and possible unilateral U.S. moves with respect to South Africa as creating benefits for the United States but question marks for the South Africans—black and white—and risks to economic security for themselves. Their sense of foreboding and vulnerability, and for that matter that of the Japanese, is heightened not only by the lateral consultation on South Africa, but also by the fact that if the precise content of U.S. policy toward South Africa is somewhat obscure, the direction in which it is moving appears all too evident.

U.S. Policy

The United States is against apartheid, but it is less certain what it is for. What the current administration wants from South Africa has sometimes seemed dramatically clear, as when Vice-President Mondale stated that "one man–one vote" was the U.S. desire, or when Ambassador Young stated on British television that he personally was in favor of sanctions. Yet on other occasions the administration has backed away from the practical implications of such statements, to the point where South Africans complain that they are confused as to what the

This chapter appeared in a different form in *The Washington Review*, January 1979.

United States is really after, and members of the U.S. foreign policy community argue that the United States ought to consider doing forty-one more things in order to put pressure on South African whites.[1]

The lack of clarity in U.S. policy, and its open-ended character, has been defended by members of the administration on the grounds that it gives the United States "flexibility." To be sure, it can always be asserted, if not proved, that an unclear, one-step-forward, two-steps-backward, three-steps-sideways U.S. policy might promote peaceful social change in South Africa at least as effectively as, or maybe more so than, a U.S. policy of "the forty-one sticks," advocated in a recent *Foreign Affairs* article with the revolutionary title "South Africa: What Is to Be Done?" Yet if U.S. policy choices become polarized between vagueness and vengeance, the primary result may be less social change in South Africa (peaceful or otherwise) than a disruptive row with American's European, and perhaps Japanese, allies. The main strands of the U.S. debate over "what to do about South Africa" hardly recognize the existence of our allies' substantial interests in that country, and they largely ignore the possibility of engaging our allies in a multilateral approach to the problem.

Allies' Stakes

Doing away with the evil of apartheid in South Africa (assuming we knew exactly how) might, of course, be worth the costs of having yet another source of tension with our allies. The first year of the Carter administration produced so many tensions between the United States and Europe and Japan in nuclear, monetary, trade, arms control, and arms export policy that another disagreement would seem hardly to matter. Even so, a glance at South Africa's European connection might be worth the trouble before the United States plunges further ahead on its own. Perhaps what is to be done should not be done alone—or could be done more effectively in cooperation rather than in conflict with our NATO and Japanese allies.

What are the European and Japanese stakes in South Africa? A "worst case" comparison of the effects of such action by the United States draws the contrast most clearly. To be sure, few observers expect moves against South Africa to really result in truly effective international sanctions (that might require a prohibitively expensive naval blockade). Nonetheless, it is not unthinkable that the West has already begun to descend what some Europeans refer to as "the slippery slope" to disruption of trade. What would we lose; what would they lose in such an eventuality?

Trade and Investment

Comparative stakes in trade in goods are relatively easy to divine. U.S. import and export trade with South Africa are of roughly the same order as that of the United Kingdom and Germany: around $1 billion of exports, and similar amounts of imports in all three cases in 1976 (see Table 1). But a different perspective emerges when it is noted that the trade of the European Economic Community (EEC) as a whole, a region with a somewhat lower gross national product than that of the United States ($1 trillion in comparison to our $1.5 trillion in 1975), is some three times higher than that of the United States. Even these figures almost certainly understate European and especially British trade with South Africa: they include only trade in goods. British exports of services (insurance, freight, tourism) are not included; with little doubt they are quite substantial.

Something is also known about foreign investment in the South African economy, and what is known shows a U.S. stake of only some 16 percent of both direct and portfolio investment (or a total of some $3 billion), with Britain alone accounting for some 30 percent of the remainder (or perhaps $6 billion), and Germany, France, Japan, Switzerland, and the Netherlands accounting for virtually all of the rest (although even vehemently antiapartheid Sweden has a more than trivial stake in some twenty companies).[2] (See Table 2.) It is particularly remarkable that at least 10 percent of *all* British direct foreign investment—an amount not much different than British direct foreign investment in the United States—is located in South Africa.[3] Only 1 percent of total U.S. direct foreign investment is located in South Africa.[4]

These investment data are of interest in themselves, as

TABLE 1

UNITED STATES, EUROPEAN, AND JAPANESE EXPORTS TO AND IMPORTS FROM SOUTH AFRICA

(IN BILLIONS OF U.S. DOLLARS)

AREA	EXPORTS TO				IMPORTS FROM			
	1974	1975	1976	1977	1974	1975	1976	1977
U.S.	1.2	1.3	1.3	1.1	.7	.9	1.0	1.3
U.K.	1.2	1.5	1.2	1.0	1.3	1.4	1.1	1.5
Germany	1.4	1.4	1.2	1.1	.8	.9	.9	1.1
France	.4	.4	.5	.5	.3	.3	.3	.5
European Community	3.8	4.1	3.5	3.2	2.9	3.4	3.4	4.4
Japan	.9	.9	.7	.8	.8	.9	.8	.9

SOURCE: IMF, Direction of Trade, Annual 1971-1977.

TABLE 2

AMERICAN AND EUROPEAN INVESTMENTS IN SOUTH AFRICA: 1975

Total $bn (=100%)	U.S.	France	Germany	U.K.	Total EEC
Direct Investment 8.5	19%	1.97%	3-6%	20-35%	64%
Portfolio Investment 10.4	14%*	6.99%	n.a.	n.a.	56%
Total Investment 18.9	16%*	4.72%	11%*	26-34%	60%

NOTE: Where a range of figures is shown, the low figure is official, the higher figure is our estimate.

Estimates are marked (*):

U.S.: Assumes U.S. investment accounts for three-fourths of reported North and South American investment.
Germany: Assumes Germany accounts for $2.0 billion of the total
$11.3 billion EEC investment.

SOURCES:

U.S.: Dept. of Commerce Survey of Current Business, August
1976, p. 45.
France: Statement of South African Ambassador to France,
Louis Pienaar, to the Société d'Economie Politique, February 3,
1977, reported in "L'Afrique du Sud fait Appel aux Investissements
Francais," Le Monde, February 8, 1977, p. 42.
Germany: Federal Ministry of Economics.
U.K.: Ministry of Trade, Trade and Industry, February 25,
1977, pp. 532-533. Total figure cited in "British in a Quandary
over South Africa," R.W. Apple, Jr., New York Times, October 26,
1977, p. A6.
EEC: South African Reserve Bank Quarterly Bulletin, December,
1976, pp. S-64-65.

indicators of the degree to which South Africa can retaliate
against the West for pressures meted out to it. But a better measure of what the United States and its allies have at commercial
and economic risk would be some estimate of what trade and
investment with South Africa contribute to U.S., European, and
Japanese gross national products.

Estimates of the direct and indirect contribution to the GNPs
of the Western industrial countries are presented in Table 3:
they show that trade and investment with South Africa account
for a trivial proportion of U.S. GNP—less than three-tenths of
1 percent, that the European percentages are uniformly higher
(although in the case of France, not by much), and that the
German and British proportions take on important, and by the

TABLE 3

CALCULATION OF THE PROPORTION OF U.S., EUROPEAN, AND JAPANESE NATIONAL

INCOME DERIVING FROM ECONOMIC RELATIONS WITH SOUTH AFRICA

($ MILLIONS)

Item	U.S.	France	Germany	U.K.	EEC	Japan
Exports to South Africa,* 1975	1302	424	1382	1520	4080	873
Estimated returns on South African investment**	450	138	300	975	1702	
Subtotal	1752	562	1682	2495	5782	873
GNP, 1975	1,508,680	304,600	408,750	214,940	1,216,090	496,000
Resulting Direct Contribution	0.12%	0.18%	0.41%	1.16%	0.48%	0.18%
Direct and Indirect Contribution (assuming multiplier effects on income of two)	0.24%	0.36%	0.82%	2.32%	0.96%	0.36%

*IMF Direction of Trade, August 1977.

**Return on investment is assumed to equal 15% of back value -- the percentage actually reported by U.S. manufacturing firms from 1960-1975. The base figures used where of-ficial figures are not available are our own estimates as follows (See Table 2 for sources):

U.S.:	3000	U.K.:	6500
France:	920	EEC:	11329
Germany:	2000	Japan:	0

lights of most public policymakers, quite politically significant proportions of those countries' national incomes. Nearly 1 percent of German GNP and more than 2 percent of British GNP stem from economic intercourse with South Africa.[5]

With stakes such as these, it is only too evident why many British and German officials, industrialists, and labor leaders in export-oriented industries are likely to be ill at ease with any but the most careful, planned, multilaterally coordinated U.S. approach to changing South African society. But even the overall contribution of export and investment income to European GNPs is only part of the story.

Economic aggregates do not tell of the relatively greater diffusion of European economic, and therefore political interests in South African stability and prosperity. Many more European firms, and thus many more European people, have something to lose from disruption or sanctions. It has been estimated that there are some 400 German-owned companies alone active in South Africa, compared to only 300 American subsidiaries— despite the smaller dollar-investment stake of the Germans.[6] Moreover, the U.S. stake is particularly concentrated: 13 companies have some three-quarters of U.S. investment in South Africa.[7] Furthermore, European investment in South Africa is much more highly skewed to "smaller company" and labor, especially expatriate labor-intensive activities such as finance, insurance, real estate, and business services (nearly one-third of the total EEC direct investment of $5.3 billion in 1973) than is investment of American companies (13 percent of $1 billion).[8]

The Structure of Trade

More particularly, aggregates do not reveal much about the structure of trade, especially the extraordinary extent to which exports of modern manufactures by Great Britain depend on access to the South African market. South Africa is one of the world's leading exporters of agricultural products and minerals, consequently it purchases few such things from the outside world. Oil is the only noteworthy exception. (Even then, partly as an insurance policy against the threat of a political interruption in its oil supply, South Africa has perhaps the lowest percentage utilization of oil as a source of energy of any country in the world.) What South Africa buys are manufactures: they account for over 80 percent of South Africa's import bill in 1975.

In few product areas does South Africa take more than 1 percent of total U.S. exports, and in those few it does, basic, simple manufactures such as paper, textiles, and iron and steel predominate. (See Table 4 for a breakdown of the composition of U.S. and U.K. manufactured goods exports to South Africa.) The stake of British manufacturing industry is quite otherwise. In nine sectors, including electrical machinery and plastics and synthetics, the South African market takes between 6 and 9 percent of all British exports.

The British industries that are major exporters to South Africa are especially noteworthy in that—autos aside—they are among the handful of British industries that have been conspicuous by their absence from the long and well-publicized lists of U.K. industrial maladies. These are among the (all too few, as seen in Britain) industries that do not seem marked for extinction, either by Japanese and LDC price competition, or by U.S. or German high technology. The South African connection unfortunately may thus have had much to do with the ability of that segment of British industry to survive in the face of the alarming decline of British productivity and international competitiveness, which took Britain's share of world exports of manufactures from 15.3 percent in 1960 to 8.9 percent in 1975. These industries are among those with the largest economies of scale; in such industries, profits increase much more than proportionately with sales volume—at least up until some capacity limit. Thus, 6 to 9 percent of exports (in some cases, 3 to 5 percent of these industries *total* output) may account for vastly greater proportions of profit.

Raw Materials

As economic aggregates mask the structure of European and especially British exports to South Africa, they also obscure South Africa's role as a source of primary products to EEC

TABLE 4

U.S. AND BRITISH EXPORTS TO SOUTH AFRICA OF SELECTED MANUFACTURED

<u>GOODS AS A PERCENTAGE OF TOTAL U.S. AND BRITISH EXPORTS OF THOSE GOODS</u>[*]

Item (SITC Code)	U.S. Exports		British Exports	
	Percentage	Rank**	Percentage	Rank**
Chemicals (5)				
Organic chemicals (512)	2	14	2	12
Other inorganic chemicals (514)	3	10	8	1
Plastic, etc., materials (581)	2	9	8	3
Chemicals, n.e.s.***(599)	3	9	3	7
Basic manufactures (6)				
Paper and paperboard (641)	4	8	7	3
Woven textiles non-cotton (653)	6	3	3	13
Iron, steel, univ. plate, sheet (674)	4	4	1	17
Tools (695)	3	8	6	4
Machines, transport equipment (7)				
Power machinery, non-electrical (711)	2	13	2	8
Agricultural machinery (712)	2	4	7	1
Office machinery (714)	1	15	2	13
Metalworking machinery (715)	3	7	9	2
Electrical power machinery, switchgear (722)	2	9	8	1
Electrical distributing machinery (723)	1	13	5	3
Telecommunications equipment (724)	1	13	6	1
Electrical machinery n.e.s. (729)	1	15	4	6
Road motor vehicles (732)	1	9	6	2
Aircraft (734)	1	7	1	12
Miscellaneous manufactured goods (8)				
Clothing not of fur (841)	1	11	1	17
Instruments, apparatus (861)	1	13	3	8

*1974 Figures.

**South Africa's ranking among all other major country markets for each commodity group.

***Not elsewhere specified.

Sources: Commodity Matrix Tables in <u>The United Nations International Trade Statistics Yearbook</u>, 1975, vol. II.

countries. In these days of resource diplomacy and resource nationalism, it is easy to exaggerate the importance of any one country or region's "independence" on another for any particularly primary product. In particular, the effect on European economies of a restriction in trade in primary products with South Africa cannot be measured as simply the "gap" that would appear were European imports from South Africa to cease overnight. Alternative sources exist in the case of virtually all EEC imports from South Africa, and substitute commodities exist in others. Table 5 summarizes the place of South African minerals production in world totals compared to the production of other leading alternative suppliers.

Nonetheless, although alternative sources are available to Europe—and to Japan, which also imports raw materials from South Africa—the magnitude of some of the readjustments that would be required, were such imports to be foregone on account of sanctions or civil disturbance, would be considerable in some cases. In 1973, EEC Europe obtained 50 percent of its uranium from South Africa.[9] In 1975, South Africa was the source of 19 percent of Europe's platinum, 30 percent of its gold, 35 percent of its ferrochrome, 23 percent of its asbestos, 38 percent of its manganese, and 38 percent of its vermiculite.[10]

A greater cause of worry to some Europeans is the fact that in several of the commodities currently purchased from South Africa, the alternative sources are relatively concentrated in a few countries—countries that are in several cases political adversaries or economic competitors, including in some cases the United States (see Table 5). For a wide range of minerals, black Africa is not significant as an alternative source for European needs (see Table 6). In the case of materials such as asbestos, vermiculite, chrome, manganese, and antimony, EEC imports from Africa basically signify imports from South Africa. A Europe and Japan without the kinds of strategic stockpiles held by the United States cannot be wholly sanguine about the possibility of relying on the USSR for nearly all its chrome, platinum, or gold (a commodity that has industrial as well as monetary uses); nor are they entirely sure that the United States would share its strategic stockpile with them in the event of a disruption in South African supply. Nor do many Euopeans and Japanese feel wholly at ease with the prospect that in commodities such as nickel, uranium, asbestos, or vermiculite cutting South Africa out might mean large windfall profits to Canadian, Australian, and sometimes American producers—assuming that these last could in any case both readily augment production in the face of currently formidable environmentalist resistance to

TABLE 5

GEOGRAPHICAL DISTRIBUTION OF PRODUCTIVE CAPACITY, SELECTED MINERALS PRODUCED BY SOUTH AFRICA:

ESTIMATE FOR 1980 (% OF WORLD TOTAL)

Mineral	S. Africa	EEC	U.S.	Canada & Australia	U.S.S.R	Other	Total World Production
Asbestos	2%	3%	1%	47%	34%	13%	5,661,000 short tons
Platinum	48	**	*	7	44	*	9,065,000 troy ounces
Chromium	24	0	0	0	26	50	3,490,000 short tons
Manganese	15	**	1	10a	43	31	15,095,00 short tons
Industrial Diamonds[b]	13	**	6	**	26	55	31,000,000 carats
Vermiculite[c]	32	**	63	**	n.a.	5	800,000 short tons
Fluorspar[b]	5	15	4	1	11	64	4,890,000 short tons
Antimony	21	1	6	8	6	58	125,500 short tons
Uranium[c]	13	4	40	25	n.a.	18	59,400[d] short tons
Gold	56	**	5	7	16	16	53,250,000 short ounces
Vanadium	29	0	17	*	40	12	48,200 short tons

*Less than 1%
**Figures, if they exist, too insignificant to be detailed separately

a Only Australia
b 1976 actual production estimate
c Excluding centrally controlled economies

Source: Mineral Facts and Problems, 1975 Edition, Bureau of Mines, U.S. Department of the Interior.

TABLE 6

EUROPEAN COMMUNITY IMPORTS OF SELECTED RAW MATERIALS FROM

AFRICA AND SOUTH AFRICA AS A PERCENTAGE OF TOTAL IMPORTS

(1974-1975 Average)

UNPROCESSED RAW MATERIALS

Item	From Africa	of Which, South Africa
Asbestos	25%	80%
Lithium minerals	49	55
Vermiculite	37	97
Iron ore, less than 42% iron content	25	4
Manganese ore, all grades	80	45
Lead ore	15	20
Zinc ore	5	40
Copper ore	11	64
Chrome ore	26	64
Antimony ore	11	82
Zirconium ore	4	100
Anthracite coal	8	100

PROCESSED AND SEMI-PROCESSED MATERIALS

	From Africa	of Which, South Africa
Diamonds, for non-industrial use	9	89
Gold and alloys	62	100
Platinum and alloys	17	100
Platinum group metals and alloys	14	100
Ferro-manganese	8	100
Ferro-chrome	27	93
Ferro-silico-chrome	36	100
Copper: refined, non-alloyed	39	20
Nickel	8	100
Aluminum	4	0
Lead	11	45
Cobalt	34	6
Manganese metal	53	94

SOURCE: NIMEXE Tables for 1974, 1975 the European Community.

mining activities and resist the temptation to use their enhanced market power to form economic or political cartels. Indeed, were supplies from alternative sources not readily forthcoming, the possibility exists that the consequent higher prices paid by European and Japanese customers could end up making sanctions on South Africa even profitable to the United States, Canada, and Australia—a somewhat galling, if not fatal, prospect for the raw material importing countries of Europe that fear that they would end up paying the bill.

From the European and Japanese point of view, South Africa has played an extraordinarily useful, if somewhat embarrassing, role in primary product markets of having been the residual "free market" country in the system. South Africa has never, or at least not yet, halted any exports to Europe or elsewhere—unlike the Arab oil exporters, or for that matter the United States, which has refused to export soybeans, steel scrap, and oil to Japan in recent memory. Expansion of mineral production in South Africa, often by European companies, has been unhindered by environmentalist pressures—or strikes—unlike production in Australia, Canada, or the United States.

Uranium

South Africa's role as residual supplier of uranium has been, and appears likely to be, of particular consequence to EEC Europe. South Africa has been rapidly expanding its mining capacity at a time when other suppliers have been unresponsive to European desires. Australia has delayed exploiting its reserves (20 percent of world totals) on account of internal environmentalist disputes and of arguments over what nuclear nonproliferation safeguards to require of customers. Simultaneously, Canada embargoed uranium exports to Europe and Japan for more than a year in order to extract new safeguard agreements. South Africa—inclusive of Namibia—possesses one quarter of world uranium reserves; within a decade, it is expected to surpass Canada, the non-Communist world's current largest exporter in both production and exports, and to achieve some 16 percent of the world market. What is more, "South Africa remains the single major uranium supplier prepared to sell freely on the international market."[11]

South Africa (including Namibia) is likely to provide some half of the uranium supplies of the EEC, for the foreseeable future, even if Canadian shipments of natural uranium proceed unimpeded to Europe, and if Australia is allowed by its environmentalists to develop its deposits. Since free European access to Canadian and Australian uranium ore appears less than totally certain, it is conceivable that Europe—or some European countries—could come to rely even more heavily on South Africa. The United States has become a net importer of uranium, despite the recent slowdown in U.S. nuclear power plant construction and is unlikely to be able to provide Europe with any assured alternative source.

Namibian uranium could, in theory, become "decoupled" from South African events should a settlement or other political change take place in that territory. Indeed, the United Kingdom (though not France or Germany) has a decoupling policy in effect: the United Kingdom has refused to purchase uranium ore from South Africa proper but does purchase ore from the Rossing mine in Namibia, the world's largest and one in which the United Kingdom's Rio Tinto Zinc shares ownership with French and South African capital.[12] Britain has agreed to purchase Rossing ore in spite of an earlier pledge by the Labour party not to do so, and in spite of a UN resolution outlawing the exploitation of Namibia's mineral wealth. Namibian uranium reserves are roughly equal to those in South Africa proper, and, since Namibian ore is not mainly a by-product of gold mining, as it is in South Africa, output can be expanded (or contracted) more readily than can that of South Africa proper.

Whether such decoupling of Namibian uranium supply is in any way a practical eventuality is doubtful, however. Events in Namibia are hardly likely to be totally independent of events in South Africa proper (unless, perhaps, to be more disrupted in the case of instability), particularly as long as South Africa insists on maintaining control over the port of Walvis Bay through which Rossing uranium must transit.

European Interests and European Behavior

There is no surprise in the fact that the magnitude and diversity of European economic interests in South Africa have led to some European countries taking positions on South Africa that appear a good deal more conservative than do the moves of the Carter administration in fanning the winds of change. These interests are compounded and strengthened by the approximately 350,000 holders of European, principally British, passports in South Africa,[13] and the over 30,000 persons holding or eligible to hold German passports in Namibia.[14]

There is also little reason to be surprised that among European countries, there is a strong correlation between the degree of economic interest in South Africa and the degree to which European governments and industries have been either perturbed by the U.S. moves or have been seen to respond to them in "conservative" ways. Governments of countries in Europe with minimal interests in South Africa, have had few compunctions about economic measures against South African policies, compared to the United Kingdom, Germany, and France. In the UN General Assembly, Denmark, the Netherlands, Ireland, Italy, Norway, and Sweden actually voted against their larger fellow European countries (and the United States) in favor of a resolution urging the Security Council to consider moves to end foreign investment in South Africa. The same group also refused to oppose a resolution calling for an end to all "economic collaboration" with South Africa.[15]

At a March 1978 meeting, the foreign ministers of Denmark, Finland, Iceland, Norway, and Sweden approved in principle an "action program for national implementation to (1) try to ban all new investment in South Africa; (2) negotiate with Nordic companies to get them to limit the production of their South African subsidiaries; (3) require visas for South African visitors; and (4) end all sporting and cultural contacts with South Africa."[16]

The correlation between political positions and economic interests has been less than perfect: Britain cut off arms sales to South Africa (if not sales of licenses for the technology of arms production) long before France—despite the fact that Britain has export and investment stakes, although not raw materials and uranium, in South Africa greatly superior to those of France. But the correlation has existed and would doubtless increase were the relatively pro-South African Conservative party to come to power in Great Britain.

There is more reason to be surprised, and even to be made hopeful for multilateral, U.S.-European cooperation, by some of the things European governments and private economic actors have done with respect to South Africa. Multilateral diplomacy with respect to the Namibian problem in the form of the UN Security Council "contact group" of five exists. (Members are the United States, United Kingdom, Germany, France and Canada.) This group provides a forum for thrashing out

U.S. and European differences of interests over negotiating positions to take with partisans of Namibian independence before U.S.-European conflicts become public, open sores. To be sure, European interests in Namibia, important as they may be, are minor compared to those in South Africa itself.

To implement the Security Council–mandated arms embargo, France cut off delivery of two escort vessels and two submarines under construction in French yards for South Africa. Both France and England subsequently curtailed further transfers of weapons technology and paramilitary material. Still, unlike the United States, they stopped short of precluding exports of so-called grey-area equipment: items not necessarily designed for military use, but which could be so employed (such as Land Rovers and computers). Instead, they retain case-by-case discretion over most such decisions.[17]

A corporate code of conduct was adopted by the Confederation of British Industries in 1974. It served as a model for the subsequent EEC Code of Conduct, approved in September 1977.[18] Apart from gaining official government backing, both demand rather more than the unofficial code of the so-called Sullivan principles (named after the Rev. Leon Sullivan, a member of General Motors' Board of Directors) voluntarily adopted by many U.S. firms. All three codes require equal pay for equal work, equal employment practices, desegregation of the work place, training programs, skilled positions for nonwhites, and a commitment to improve employees' lives outside work in areas such as housing, health, and transportation. But the European codes go several steps further, requiring periodic progress reports, movement toward a minimum wage, and encouragement of the unofficial black labor-union movement.

In November, West Germany limited government financial guarantees on exports to South Africa to a term not to exceed five years and an amount not to exceed $25 million, citing the sharply increased political risks involved. In addition, the German government made guarantee applications dependent upon corporate pledges to follow the EEC code in their South African operations.[19] At present, the U.S. Export-Import Bank limits the term of export guarantees to South Africa to three and one-half years, but neither sets official limits to their size nor conditions on corporate conduct.

This European behavior toward the current regime in South Africa permits a number of possible interpretations. The least charitable of these could treat codes of conduct and limited (and, in the case of France, belated) prohibitions on exports of military equipment, narrowly defined, as a response consisting mostly of statements of good intentions rather than of serious efforts to put European stakes at risk to provoke real social change in South Africa. But by these standards, U.S. rhetoric has also outpaced U.S. action. A more charitable interpretation might note that in some ways, notably the injunction for European companies to recognize black labor unions in South Africa, the European governmental response to the South African problem has been *more* "progressive" than that of the United States; this in spite of the quickly and loudly voiced protests against this aspect of the EEC code by the German and Dutch (British?) employers federations.

To be sure, one way of walking a tightrope is to carry a pole that reaches far out over both sides of the rope; the EEC, British, French, and German combinations of resisting any official interruption of commerce and investment with South Africa, while urging progressive social behavior on the part of their firms, bear comparison with the metaphor. The tightrope is one stretched by the fact that Europe, of course, has interests not only in South, but also in black Africa, and thus cannot afford to tip too much to either side. Were it not for the disproportionate role South Africa plays as purveyor of minerals to Europe (see Table 6), those interests in black Africa could be considered equal or superior to the European interests in South Africa (see Table 7). Some Britons have argued that their "balance of interest" has shifted toward black Africa since exports to, and oil imports from, Nigeria alone now exceed British trade with South Africa. Investment stakes are, however, hardly comparable.

But perhaps the most plausible interpretation of European behavior is that it underlines Europe's great interest in peaceful and—if such can be imagined—stable change in South Africa. European action on South Africa demonstrates a consensus that Europe can afford change: interests do not equal inertia. But

TABLE 7

PROPORTION OF U.S. AND EUROPEAN NATIONAL INCOME DERIVING FROM

ECONOMIC RELATIONS WITH BLACK AFRICA

($ MILLIONS)

Item	U.S.	France	Germany	U.K.
Exports to Black Africa, 1975	1665	3221	1710	2367
Investments	2458*	n.a.	208	1480
Est. returns on investment (@ 15% p.a.)	369	n.a.	30	222
Subtotal	2034	—	1740	2589
GNP, 1975	1,508,680	304,600	408,250	214,940
Resulting percentages Trade only	.11%	1.05	.41	1.10
Including investment income	.13	n.a.	.43	1.20
Including probable indirect and multiplier effects	.26	2.10	.86	2.40

*Includes all of Africa except Libya and South Africa.

Europeans almost certainly cannot afford uncertainty, especially the kind of uncertainty promised by a U.S. policy that hides both carrots and sticks from view of the Afrikaners—and from U.S. allies. They equally fear the sequence of events propounded by the authors of "South Africa: What Is to Be Done": a gradual deterioration of economic relations culminating in the disruption and eventual suspension of commercial link. Even more disquieting is the possibility that the United States may already have started a chain of events that it may at some point no longer be able to control; it may not see the limits to what even a superpower can do on its own and may thus provoke conflict beyond the limits of what our allies can accept. If the United States were, by some chain of circumstances, forced into accepting economic sanctions against South Africa in the Security Council, the large European countries would be faced with an excruciating dilemma: should they accept the costs of disruption of economic relations with South Africa—at a time when Europe's unemployment and economic growth prospects appear mediocre at best—or break ranks with the United States and much of the third world at no small political cost.

Yet, precisely because the Europeans have more to lose than does the United States on both sides of the racial divide in Africa, they have more to gain from a peaceful resolution of conflict. Without the Europeans it is not clear that the United States can do much of anything to bring either sticks--or carrots —really to bear on transforming Afrikaner domination. The presence or absence of commercial links with the United States is important to South Africa: the United States accounts for one-tenth of South Africa's exports and supplies, one-fifth of its imports, and a similar proportion of its foreign investment. But the European connection is much more critical: in exports, imports, and investment developed, Europe provides South Africa with a majority of all its commercial links to the rest of the world.[20] Since the United States has such little direct "leverage," unilateral U.S. policies toward South Africa risk producing Afrikaner obstinacy followed by the nonpeaceful "settlement" Europeans fear. But South Africa could simply not ignore multilateral U.S. and European or U.S.-European-Japanese initiatives.

Working with allies on matters in which their interests are so much at stake might prove a novel experience for a United States accustomed to assuming that—to quote former Secretary Kissinger—only it has global interests. But ignoring one's allies raises questions as to whether they are such.[21] Ignoring them is also all too likely to result in unilateral measures having little useful or predictable effect on South Africa. If the United States wants to implement a South African policy, multilateral diplomacy is how to do it.

Notes

1. Clyde Ferguson and William R. Cotter, "South Africa: What Is to Be Done?" *Foreign Affairs* 56 (January 1978):253-74.

2. Sundqvist, Sven-Ivan, *Syd Afrikas Guld Alder* (Stockholm: Askild & Karnekull, 1974), Chapter 13. Since 1964 the South African authorities have grouped foreign investment by region, rather than by country, thus obscuring precise country comparisons.

3. U.K. Ministry of Trade and Industry, *Trade and Industry*, February 25, 1977, p. 532.

4. U.S., Department of Commerce, *Survey of Current Business*, August 1977, p. 45.

5. These last percentages are almost certainly underestimates. Calculations of the national economic benefit of foreign trade and investment require one to estimate rates of return on foreign investments. Our estimates used the average return on South African investments reported by U.S. manufacturing firms to the U.S. commerce department between 1960 and 1975 of 15 percent. Such figures are only the most approximate indicator of the total returns from foreign investments, especially direct foreign investments, because they do not include contributions to profits that show up in home countries, such as royalties, management fees, and interest on intercompany debt. As already noted, the British figures do not include (probably considerable) service income. And the German investment figures do not include retained earnings; if they did, the contribution to German GNP might reach 1.8, instead of 1.6 billion dollars.

6. "Activities of Transnational Corporations in Southern Africa and the Extent of Their Collaboration with the Illegal Regimes in the Area," U.N. Commission on International Corporations, April 6, 1977, pp. 15, 16.

7. Ibid., p. 15.

8. Ibid., Table 5, p. 14.

9. *Europe, Raw Materials and the Third World* (Brussels: Directorate General for Information Commission of the European Communities, May 1974).

10. NIMEXE Tables, the European Community, Brussels.

11. "Uranium and Africa's Future," *Africa Confidential* 18, no. 14 (July 8, 1977):6.

12. "Namibian Uranium," *Economist*, October 8, 1977, p. 97.

13. Jeffrey Butler, "The Significance of Recent Changes within the White Ruling Caste," in Leonard Thompson and Jeffrey Butler, eds., *Change in Contemporary South Africa* (Berkeley: University of California, 1975), p. 92.

14. Franz Fegeler, "Washington Counts on Bonn in Southern Africa Issue," *Nordwest Zeitung*, September 8, 1976, reproduced in *German Tribune*, September 19, 1976, p. 1.

15. "Resolutions on *apartheid* adopted by the United Nations General Assembly in 1977," U.N. Centre against Apartheid, Notes and Documents, February 1978.

16. "Nordic Ban Expected on South African Investment," *Financial Times*, March 2, 1978.

17. "France Stops Delivery of Vorster Warships," *Financial Times*, November 9, 1977; "U.K. Move on South African Arms," *Financial Times*, March 4, 1978; "South Africans Troubled by Carter Ban on Strategic Equipment," *Financial Times*, March 10, 1978.

18. Commission of the European Communities, "The European Community and Southern Africa," *Information: Cooperation/Development*, *166/77E* (Brussels, November 1977), Annex.

19. "West Germany Limits Its Exports to South Africa," *Financial Times*, December 1, 1977.

20. United Nations, Dept. of Economic and Social Affairs, *U.N. Commodity Trade Statistics*, 1976; and Table 2 above.

21. See Eugene McCarthy, "Look, No Allies," *Foreign Policy*, Spring 1978.

9
How Strategic Is South Africa?

Richard E. Bissell

A plain question deserves a plain answer: South Africa is of great strategic importance, whatever one's point of view. With that point made, however, all consensus dissolves. South Africa is just one battle in everybody's different war, as various strategic visions come to bear upon one place and moment in history. Whether South Africa represents the major source of chrome or it represents a hated racial policy, the future of that country has an importance that suggests Western policymakers will have to develop clear options for dealing with present and future challenges to Western interests. Our purpose here, then, will be to avoid answering the question of this chapter according to unstated assumptions—for it is those assumptions that cause Western societies to divide over the issue of South Africa. Its problems are seen as being important enough to justify emotional debate, but the views of Western strategy that underlie that debate are so nonnegotiable as to cause the debaters to exclude them from discussion of the South African future. At some point in time, however, the West will have to face up to such divisions in its societies, either at a time of crisis and violence, or now when there is some flexibility left in formulating options toward South Africa.

This essay will thus cover three main areas: the conceptual frameworks of "strategy," particularly as they have evolved in

The author would like to express his appreciation to Scott Snedden for his help in locating diverse evidence for the views that exist on this topic.

American thinking over time, the specific issues of prime importance that are disputed as a result of such different strategic perspectives, and the attempted institutionalization of those strategies. Finally, the conclusion will assess the possibility of these strategic perspectives resolving their conflicts for the formation of a coherent Western policy toward South Africa.

Conceptual Frameworks for "Strategy"

The twentieth century has witnessed the evolution of strategy in Western thinking to a point where Clausewitz would not recognize the concept. Although there are a multitude of statements on strategy, this essay will have to take three perspectives as representative of the spectrum, particularly in that they represent the strongest current of thought today. They will be called the military, political, and socioeconomic perspectives.

The "military" perspective is based in large part on the traditional precepts of Admiral Alfred Mahan, Carl von Clausewitz, and Halford J. Mackinder. There are several essential points learned from such writings about the formation of a strategy involving South Africa. The first point, of course, involves the utility of military power, its likely use, and, even in the case of abstinence from use of force, its utility in influencing the political environment. This view is often described as "traditional," because the history of man as recorded has generally involved the use of force for the solution of disputes as a last resort. The psychological quest for security and survival has led societies wishing to plan for their futures to pursue more comprehensive plans for their military survival against likely aggressors. As societies have found it desirable to project their influence too, they have found military power useful in subduing possible opposition. The West has been an active participant in this tradition, although by no means monopolizing it; note the contribution of the Chinese strategist, Sun Tzu, to the field. During the last few centuries, however, it is clear that such military strategy has had an important role to play in Western societal organization.

The military strategy is based also on geographical factors: the importance of contiguous territories for a more effective defense, the role played by sea-lanes and reinforced choke points on those sea-lanes, and the availability of physical resources needed to wage the conflicts that will inevitably arise. In effect, this perspective assumes that a strategy must service the needs of the territorial state first, and that certain land and physical resources, as well as military positions abroad, may be necessary to achieve that purpose. The writings of John Herz notwithstanding, there remains a debate about the value of basing a foreign policy on the territorial state.[1] That debate is not resolved, and for those still committed to the security of the state, through military means if necessary, South Africa has a specific role to play, as we shall identify later.[2]

Critics of the military perspective essentially maintain that security cannot be achieved in the 1980s through military force. To them, a nuclear conflict is, by definition, a failure—for destruction of our civilization as we know it is said to be the result. The waging of conventional war has been deprecated essentially on the basis of experience: the Korean and Vietnamese experiences should have persuaded the United States, as the Boer War and the Vietnamese War persuaded the British and French publics, that war achieves nothing except expenditure of resources needed at home. And perhaps most importantly, the creation of a credible military force is seen as a diversion of resources from meeting domestic reform needs, thus ultimately weakening a society at home faster than an attack from outside would. They argue that the commitment to peace, made by the United States at the United Nations and elsewhere, means that the United States should not prepare for war or for the use of force unless a clear aggressor has emerged. For them, the fact that the United States was the largest military power in the world in 1945 and for much of the period since then, suggests that the United States is able to lead the world toward disarmament and restraint in the use of force. That force is still a prominent theme of international relations is not in dispute;[3] the proper American strategy in a time of the American loss of military hegemony is still open to debate.

The "political" perspective endows strategy with a much more complex set of factors to consider. Although military preparedness may be one of the factors to consider, the political perspective suggests that the conflict will be all but settled before it ever arrives at the stage of military warfare. Military power exists primarily as a psychological factor in international relations, amidst a host of other influences on the resolution of global conflicts. For most, the strategy remains oriented toward the preservation and growth of a global "democratic" consensus in political affairs. American observers debate the shape of the political order to be created as well as the historical forces that play a large part in implementing such a strategy.

Thus, one genre of this perspective would be the speeches of Andrew Young since he took office in 1977. His themes have been clear: (1) Africa would gradually become more like American society, and the natural interactions in the economic area would continue; (2) force would not be decisive in determining the future of South Africa; and (3) South Africa would be engulfed by the historical wave of decolonization and black rule seen in Africa since the late 1950s. Young appears to be opposed to the spread of Soviet influence (aside from his view on Cuban troops in Angola as being a "stabilizing force") and has concluded that the best way to avoid the increase of that influence is by following the lead of the black African states on southern African issues.

At the same time, another political perspective would call for the reinforcement of ties with South Africa. The view that the political-psychological battle with the Soviet Union will probably involve the use of some force, particularly through proxy forces in third world areas, suggests the utility of close ties with South Africa. But of equal or greater importance to such a perspective is the steadfastness of American purpose, as expressed through political, economic, psychological, and diplomatic methods.[4] The interplay between domestic and international developments becomes quite intense through this approach. Western diplomacy becomes weakened by a loss of will among its publics, which can be induced by a dramatic rise in the price of gasoline and a corresponding drop in the standard of living in the West. The interplay of sectors of life creates a demand for comprehensive relations with those we support. Strictly military alliances are seen as opportunistic; the ties to allies must also express economic and political solidarity for them to be valid. But in the inclusion of those other factors comes the complication: are human rights or economic stability more important? Is the world order of the future going to be dominated by private enterprise or public initiatives? In the dispute over Western strategy toward Africa, one can see mirrored the domestic disputes that complicate life in each of the Western countries.

The third perspective, the socioeconomic approach, is based upon the vision of the social scientist. War and conflicts are mere expressions of frustration derived from the struggles of peoples attempting to meet their basic needs. Much in the rhetoric of the United Nations' agencies supports this view that world peace would be achieved by ignoring conflict and meeting the root causes of social and economic unrest. From this perspective, there is no global conflict, except perhaps the temporary one between rich and poor, and all conflicts can be solved with sufficient understanding.[5] The African roots of this view go deep; there is an Ashanti saying that "the ruin of a nation begins in the homes of its people." The perspective of the socioeconomic strategy argues for the long-term irrelevance of global conflicts—the importance of South Africa is only in terms of its own future. This approach is very nearly an "anti-strategy," except that there is a strong internationalist push in the West to implement such an understanding of strategy. The socioeconomic status of every society becomes important, quite logically, because if any one state chooses to develop its power for purposes of projection, other states might be tempted to arm in response. Objections to such an approach include the fact that force does still exist in the world as a potent influence, that there are still enormous differentials between countries in the degree of control over their own futures and those of others, and the spirit of the Western masses is still too selfish to warrant any faith in the future of self-denying socioeconomic perspectives.

The disputes over these perspectives on Western strategy are rarely addressed directly. In large part, they boil down to one's sense of historical momentum, the ability of man to control his destiny, or a general sense of optimism or pessimism with regard to human nature. Can a strategy, for instance, be based upon rationalism? Should a strategy be based upon man's sense of greed? People who address the question of South Africa's strategic importance rarely answer such queries, for they make clear the degree to which the West, and the United States in particular, is not a coherent community. Instead, we only sense such divisions, insofar as we arrive at different answers in specific aspects of American strategy toward South Africa. It is in the evaluation of such critical issues that we understand the divisions over the strategic importance of South Africa.

The Issues in Dispute

The question of American and Western strategic interests in South Africa must be considered in specific terms. Many of the specific issues impinge upon one another, since Western foreign policies rarely have singular objectives. Where these strategic points are interrelated, therefore, the issue becomes more complicated. In an arbitrary fashion, however, this essay will attempt to deal with six issues of strategy: the role of the sea-lanes around the Cape of Good Hope, the production of strategic minerals in South Africa, Soviet goals in southern Africa, the responses of South African political groups to Marxist-Soviet projection of influence and power, the record of South African government in responding to American human rights standards, and South Africa's utility to the West as a proxy.

The Cape Connection: Sea-Lanes and Western Strategy

The sea-lanes around the Cape of Good Hope constitute a choke point in terms of traditional sea control. The ability of any government in South Africa to restrict waterborne traffic is clear; the hazards of navigation that would result from ships attempting to sail further south closer to the Antarctic have been demonstrated. The Cape route itself is sufficiently dangerous for it to have been named originally the Cape of Storms.

The military perspective on the Cape sea-lanes has thus involved two elements. On the one hand, the growth of Western imports of energy has made the Cape route far more important:

over 2,300 ships transit the Cape each month, including 600 tankers. In terms of NATO planning, 57 percent of Western Europe's oil needs and 20 percent of American oil needs pass by the Cape.[6] Yet the military perspective does not place high emphasis on the oil transit needs: there is sufficient oil stockpiled in the United States and Western Europe to meet the military tasks laid out for NATO forces. The military importance of oil transitted by the Cape lies in the continuing functioning of Western economies in case of a protracted conflict. At the same time, the Western states have deliberately withdrawn the scope of their missions in the Indian Ocean theater to conform to the limitations of possible instability in southern Africa. In 1969, for instance, Henry Kissinger's task force on NSSM 39 looked at the sea-lanes and commented not on the oil traffic, but that "this geographically important area has major ship repair and logistics facilities which can be useful to our defense forces."[7] In addition, the study cited the fact that South Africa had the only facilities in the region capable of repairing a ship as large as an aircraft carrier. The strategic assumptions have thus gone through a significant revolution.

It is the political perspective that is most concerned about the sea-lanes. The ability of the West to wage an extended conflict in the face of a cutoff of a large percentage of energy supplies is doubted. The weakness of the supply chain indicates that American security, in its democratic reliance upon the support of its citizenry for foreign policy efforts, will find its foreign options restricted by the vulnerability of the supply of oil.

Two arguments are posed against the importance of the sea-lanes. First, "it would not be necessary to control the stormy Cape seas in order to cut off the West's supply line; there are more likely spots for interdiction, for example, the Strait of Hormuz at the mouth of the gulf instead." Secondly, "for the long term, however, this argument [on the importance of the sea-lanes] could be taken as favoring a policy of friendship toward the future, rather than the present, rulers of the region."[8] Both arguments reflect curious perspectives on Western strategy. Security of sea-lanes is a relative proposition; yet the first argument suggests that if the entire transportation link is not secure, there is no reason to protect any part of the route. If the strategy of security were based on the assumption of any effort requiring a certain outcome, the West would probably abandon any effort to project its influence abroad. In part, the assumption may reflect a view that the threat to American interests can be of only one variety: total war. The same author went on to say that "any attempt to interrupt shipping anywhere along that route could be taken as an act of war. Such a grave action is not likely except in extreme circumstances."[9] Yet did the United States take the oil embargo of 1973-1974 as an "act of war"? A likely threat to the sea-lanes, for instance, comes from a nonofficial group, such as the Palestinian Liberation Organization. In case of an attack from such a group, and the possibility always exists, the strategy for security can only be an effort to maximize, not a guarantee that it can be obtained. On the second argument, regarding the need to take a future-oriented policy, the West needs to know what the future will be. If the West makes assumptions about a future that is not yet certain, the West will simply be making history—and that is the nub of the argument among Western observers of South Africa: what kind of a future does the West want to make in that country, and by what means?

The perspective of the socioeconomic school of thought is important on this issue, even though its adherents dismiss it as having little relevance. Much of that perspective is devoted to the cutback in the use of nonrenewable resources and the transition in the West to environmentally sensitive economies. In that case, the potential for cutting of Western oil supplies is not a hazard, but a possibility that is implicitly welcomed as facilitating more important goals.

Strategic Minerals from South Africa

The military security of Western societies is not threatened by a potential cutoff of access to South African minerals, but the economic and political stability of the West would certainly be threatened. The minerals in question are chrome, platinum, manganese, gold, diamonds, and lithium. Each plays or has the potential to play a key role in Western economies. The political manipulation of price or access to the minerals would create serious problems.

South Africa's influence is certain to be felt in mineral markets in the future. Its share of global reserves were estimated by the Organization for Economic Cooperation and Development (OECD) as 74 percent of chrome, 45 percent of manganese, 19 percent of vanadium, 71 percent of platinum, as well as small percentages of other minerals. South Africa's output in these key minerals is directed almost entirely to the OECD states, and possible interruptions in that output would have extraordinarily detrimental effects on the Western economies, and particularly space and military programs.

In part, the essence of the issues is the question of alternative access to such minerals. In nearly all the instances, the major alternative source is the Soviet Union.[10] The West is thus reassured at the present time that the hostility of the Soviet Union and South Africa will ensure some degree of competition in the international marketplace in those minerals. The emergence of a South African government having mutual interests with the Soviet Union would present a situation similar to OAPEC (Organization of Arab Petroleum Exporting Countries). This possibility haunts those attempting to project a stable economic future for the West. The growth of American dependence on the importation of such resources, to a degree that makes the Americans and Europeans almost parallel in some situations, has eliminated the cushion for Western planning that existed when the United States was a net exporter of resources.

The objection to considering resources a serious problem arises from the perspective that sees all people as "economic man." In other words, the primary motivation of people everywhere to earn a living will ensure that South Africa, whatever the shade of its government, will sell its minerals to the Western consumers, i.e., our confidence in man's greed will obviate the need for a strategy. This peculiar Western perspective may or may not be valid, but it misses the point. One possible scenario for a threat to Western economic planning would be the cutoff of access to the minerals, affordable by both importer and exporter only in the short term. The West has stockpiles to survive the short term, and South Africa presumably has monetary reserves to survive the shortfall in revenue. The more important scenario of long-term significance is the steady escalation of price in minerals that would simply bleed the West of its economic vitality and raise defense costs prohibitively. The impact of an OAPEC in ten different mineral commodities would force the West to export its capital stock to pay for the imports, and force the Western economies into negative growth patterns. The West has no strategy for dealing with such a long-term problem, whereas it can deal with the short-term problem (albeit at some considerable expense).

The perspective that does have a strategy for the long-term problem is the socioeconomic school. The development of an economy that avoids dependence upon nonrenewable resources, and particularly imported resources, is seen as the highest goal for revitalizing the American sense of mission and community. The structural adaptations required by such a perspective have appeared to be so overwhelming as to daunt the desire of a politician to move in that direction. The South African instability, then, becomes an ideal tool in the strategy of the socioeconomic perspective to educate the West with regard to the foolishness of relying upon imported, nonrenewable resources. South Africa as an issue, if it did not exist, would have to be created in order to provide the "shock" necessary to develop a new political will in the West. South Africa thus becomes important for domestic purposes.

The issue of strategic resources is valuable in illustrating the various time frames that preoccupy those with different perspectives. Some see a short-term need to maintain the flow of resources at a reasonable price for as long as we can. Others see the world going through a transition, in which the short term will be unpleasant, perhaps even a necessary shock to our economic system in order to push the West through that transition. Others simply wish the West didn't have to deal with present contradictions and hope for a future in which the West's political and economic goals can be pursued simultaneously in South Africa. Clearly, none of the strategies have found a formulation in South Africa that would provide reasonable assurance of being successful in the short and long term.

Soviet Goals in South Africa

The varied interpretations of Soviet behavior in southern

Africa do much to create disagreement among the strategic perspectives on South Africa. Some are quite explicit about the relationship of South Africa and Soviet goals: "Any appraisal of Western interests in Africa should begin with an analysis of Soviet activity in the region and in the southern hemisphere generally."[11] From that perspective, Soviet activities are seen as having a variety of purposes, to which a proper American strategy must respond. The interpretation of Soviet purposes, ranging from imperial designs to the benign view of Ambassador Young, is essential, for if Western goals are in fact identical to Soviet goals, South Africa would have no strategic meaning in terms of meeting the Soviet challenge.

Most observers do find the Soviet Union to be working at cross-purposes to American interests in South Africa. Moscow is seen as working to "erode U.S. power and influence."[12] It is seen as seeking to mobilize use of the "raw materials weapon."[13] The ultimate goal, in this scheme, would be for increased incorporation of third world countries into the Council for Mutual Economic Assistance (COMECON), on the model of Cuba.[14] In that way, the West would easily be denied the resources essential for the running of the developed economies. Finally, the Soviets seek in the long run to break the "imperialist" ties between the West and the third world, a struggle "the Soviets insist they mean to wage against us to the point of either complete triumph or defeat."[15] The agenda for an American strategy, in effect, is defined by the purposes of the Soviet Union.

There are those observers who accept the above thesis in large part, but argue that there is little that can be done about it. "The Soviet Union's immediate objective—to support the military struggle against white minority rule—is simple, and enjoys virtually universal African approval. Nor have the Western powers been in a good position to cavil at Soviet military aid as long as no other form of pressure appeared effective. Given this major advantage, Soviet activity in southern Africa will probably continue to grow."[16] The word "immediate" is important, for there is little effort in that interpretation to deal with the long-term advantage seen in becoming involved militarily: "Soviet military aid will help to change the face of southern Africa, but whether the Russians will have attained a secure foothold there when the long crisis over majority rule finally ends must be highly questionable."[17] Again, we see raised the need for a policy to yield *certain* results, an unlikely possibility in an era of changing politics and in a region of instability. In effect, no strategy is the best answer, and requires the least effort.

The actions of the Soviet Union in recent years in southern Africa have done little to assuage its critics. Its active role in the Angola civil war, as well as its contributions to the liberation movements in the region, bespeaks an investment in some future ill defined. In the currently shifting balance of international power, the Soviet Union has been in the role of the aggressor, taking up power positions in areas vacated by the West. The outcome has invariably been detrimental to the West, sometimes in an inconsequential fashion (the time spent by Guinea under Soviet tutelage), or sometimes quite tragically (the bloody anarchy in Ethiopia since 1975). The costs sometimes have to be measured in terms of military disadvantage, economic losses, or loss of freedom and human rights. To the extent, then, that South Africa is seen as a deterrent to more extensive Soviet influence in Africa, it has a strategic importance; this question is treated at greater length below.

Given the different time frames utilized by observers with different perspectives, one has to fall back upon the question of the tone of Soviet-Western relations on South Africa. Cooperation has been nonexistent. Both in the short and the long term, we are engaged in a competition, with no ground rules existing even when there is agreement on the goals. The episode in August 1977 over the alleged plans of South Africa to test a nuclear device clearly illustrates this.[18]

It has been known for some years that South Africa not only had the capability to produce all the materials for nuclear weapons, but was also probably fabricating crude nuclear devices with no apparent practical use. Nobody expected the South Africans to "bring their bomb out of the closet." Thus it was something of a shock when, in early August 1977, Brezhnev sent a personal message to President Carter, reporting that Soviet spy satellites had revealed a nuclear testing platform in South Africa's Kalahari Desert. The Soviet Union, in its self-anointed role as the arbiter of peace in South Africa, also notified France, Britain, and Germany of the threat to the peace. Part of the Soviet concern appeared to derive from anxieties about facing a nuclear opponent in southern Africa at a future date.

Brezhnev also indicated that the Soviet Union would let loose a verbal barrage against South Africa two days later in *Pravda*, and did the United States wish to join the condemnation? The Soviet Union not only wished to pursue its own unilateral tack, but it was clear that such a public trumpeting of South Africa's nuclear intentions would do grievous damage to the American diplomatic initiatives on Rhodesia and Namibia, where South African participation was essential. It was not in the Soviet interest for such negotiations to reach fruition. Such a Soviet attitude appeared merely to add one more layer to the game of competitive power politics, rather than introducing cooperation on a long-term basis.[19] Apologists for Soviet behavior often suggest that the Soviet Union is only reacting to South Africa's "racism." As good a case could be made that many in the West have become sympathetic to the South African viewpoint in reaction to Soviet aggressive actions in the region.

The Responses of South African Political Groups to Soviet Purposes

Given the nature of long-term tangible interests of the West in South Africa itself, any coherent strategy attempts to take into account the state of opinion among politically involved people in South Africa, in particular the emerging black activists. It is of great significance, for instance, that the questions of "communism" or "Soviet influence" are virtually unmentioned in the entire treason trial transcript of Steve Biko.[20] At the same time, there are those who see Soviet influence, particularly in its ideological sense, at the center of dispute: "Washington is showing signs of seeing the strategic issue completely the other way around: that South Africa, because of its racial policies, is a liability instead of an asset in the struggle against the growth of communist influence in southern Africa."[21] What one witnesses in these differences of opinion is a split between the political and the socioeconomic perspectives.

The overarching issue is the creation of a democratic system embracing all races in the South African environment. Some argue that such an evolution can be manipulated through a variety of developmental pressures from the West. In effect, the lesson learned from the international antiapartheid movement of the last decades is that the movement resulted in some loosening of the apartheid system, and that South Africa is shifting away from the rigid implementation of the separate development plans. Whatever the evidence cited, there is no clear link of causation between whatever liberalization has occurred and the international movement that has developed. The faith, whether blind or not, does exist that South Africa can find a "middle way" out of the present dilemma. As John de St. Jorre said in conclusion to one constitutional proposal, "It would also give hope to those struggling to hold the middle ground,"[22] as though that were the greatest attribute a proposal could possess. Keeping South Africa on a middle course of reform and progress is widely considered in the Western interest, the effort being worthwhile because the West is engaged in a zero-sum game with the Soviet political system: "Any political bonus for the West in Africa is an automatic political deduction for the Soviet Union."[23] In this way, the variable political views of the emerging black groups in South Africa (treated in Chapter 2 of this volume) are essential to a strategy.

As mentioned above, however, many of the powerful groups in South Africa have no interest in international ideologies, capitalist or socialist. It may be that there is no link between the efforts of the West to develop a democratic system in South Africa and the eventual results. The West may be in the position of the proverbial Ethiopian cow: "A cow gave birth to a fire: she wanted to lick it, but it burned; she wanted to leave it, but she could not because it was her own child." That colony of whites in South Africa is no longer a colony, and it is a certain source of danger for the West. Yet the West will remain to be hurt.

Thus those with a socioeconomic perspective advocate doing nothing about South Africa's political future, except perhaps to spur change by cutting South Africa off from the world. There is a desire to provide South Africans with an education on a just and democratic life, but without any illusions that it can be instrumentally implemented. The American strategy must be to liberate as many South Africans as possible from the existing fetters of political and economic life, in order to allow their "social fundamentals" be expressed in a reorganization of life. Thus a withdrawal of investments is called for, a termination of external props for the South African government, and an insistence that South Africa arrive at an internal equilibrium without outside interference. For such observers, it is unlikely that South African political groups will have much interest in either Soviet Marxism or Western capitalism. If dissident political groups do decide to accept outside instrumentalities, such as Soviet arms shipments, to obtain their independence, that decision is consistent with the long-term strategy of developing an internally valid social structure.

The evidence for such a radical approach to strategy can be seen partly in some of the black South African political groups. Biko's interest was not only absent with regard to communism, but was quite engaged in the African efforts to articulate an indigenously based social order: the writings of Frantz Fanon, the political organizations of Julius Nyerere and Samora Machel. Some of the most dramatic confrontations between Biko's black consciousness movement and the government came over demonstrations in support of FRELIMO's coming to power in Mozambique. In effect, one sees here the "localization" of strategy—that the only valid strategy for the West is one preoccupied by the local conditions; for in the very long run, the local political realities will predominate.

The South African Response to American Human Rights Standards

An American strategy to get at the roots of international conflict in recent years has been to press for an international consensus on the observance of individual human rights. It is primarily a political campaign, one that has been aimed with particular pointedness not only at South Africa, but also at the

Soviet Union. Much of the effort in this area derived from the initiatives of the Carter administration after its entering office in 1977, when it perceived the need to find a positive element to project American influence abroad at a time when Americans were generally moving in an isolationist direction. The emphasis on a human rights strategy conformed well to the need for an approach that would embrace as wide a spectrum as possible of internationally minded people in the United States and the West. The campaign was softened only when it became apparent that the damage done to military interests and other political interests of the West was dividing American consensus more than the emphasis on human rights was pulling it together. For some, however, it remains the core of American strategy.

Those most committed to a human rights strategy see a clear connection between the domestic and international manifestations of a given problem. In effect, they see no boundaries, and a threat abroad to a human rights standard is seen as a challenge to the domestic order. "This latent polarization of American politics on southern Africa is potentially explosive. A major U.S. policy decision taking sides between blacks and whites in southern Africa, or violent conflict between blacks and whites there, could stir up significant political friction in this country, with open racial overtones."[24] The active intervention of black groups in the United States in African affairs, as in the formation of Africare in Washington as a lobbying group on African policy, has increased with the encouragement of Ambassador Young and President Carter. This universalization of the American commitment can be seen as a demonstration of the depth of American feelings on racial discrimination; it can also mean that the future of domestic stability is held hostile to only partially tractable events abroad. In other words, the connection between domestic and international developments on human rights is not only descriptive—it is also prescriptive. Those who argue the relationship between domestic and international standards are engaging in a form of tacit blackmail over the makers of foreign policy of this country: if we do not press for human rights standards in South Africa, it is implied, the cities of America will go up in smoke. South Africa thus becomes a strategic instrument for those who wish to flex their muscles in the American domestic environment. In that sense, the South African "crisis" in American policymaking is an invented situation. The moderate reforms taking place will never be sufficient to defuse the protest from some groups, for South Africa is only one part of a larger strategy.

South Africa is playing an additional key role in the movement for sensitizing business corporations to the need for greater social responsibility. In both Western Europe and the United States, the last half-decade has witnessed the growth of powerful waves of public sentiment and social strategists attempting to restructure the private sectors of Western economic life. There have been a variety of issues seized upon to mobilize the political forces necessary for such change, and one has been the impact of Western investments in South Africa. The ethical implications of doing business in an overseas society where wages are based, either formally or informally, upon racial criteria have created a crisis in Western boardrooms to an extent not seen before. The militance applied to the issue, such that for a long time there were only two solutions, has created a polarization based upon very fundamentally different views of the role business should play in judging the noneconomic impact of its activities. A compromise formula for American businesses was not found until 1976, when the Reverend Leon Sullivan of Philadelphia established a set of guidelines for integrating the races in South African operations. The acceptance of those guidelines by virtually all American corporations operating in South Africa has represented a basic compromise of principle by those companies, in that they accept a responsibility for the social welfare of their employees abroad. However, Reverend Sullivan's approach has not been positively acknowledged by the most military groups demanding change in South Africa, and that includes the most vocal black groups in the United States. In effect, the Sullivan guidelines do not fit into their strategy, because their strategy (even though enunciated in terms of human rights) is not fundamentally focused on human rights issues.

The human rights campaign of the Carter administration has a totally different meaning when transmitted abroad. The concept of human rights, particularly when given the cast of "natural law," is seen as being quite different in the South African environment. For those South African blacks who live on two bowls of maize each day, their sense of expectations will be radically different from two-car American families. The transmittal of American human rights standards abroad rarely includes the needed emphasis on the human will and organization required to maintain a high standard of living. Thus, human rights become reinterpreted to mean redistribution of rights (particularly economic rights), and in the zero-sum game that results, coercion and violence necessarily result. The Americans light a match with human rights campaigns, but do not remain to control the fire.

The issue of conformity to human rights standards by the South African authorities is muddied by the confusing rhetoric within the West. Much of the verbiage on human rights emanates from those who are only using it as a weapon to gain power within the United States and presumably in the South African political system. Others who take the human rights stand more on its own merits, such as the Sullivan proposals or the reports of Freedom House,[25] have found much to be grateful for in the South African response, while continuing to press responsibly for the continuing integration of South African society.

South Africa's Utility as a Proxy

The coincidence of many of South Africa's interests with those of the West make it tempting for South Africa to be assessed in terms of its ability to fulfill certain regional tasks for Western powers without the West becoming directly involved. Speculation along this line takes place with regard to both military matters and political or economic issues.

There is tremendous ambiguity with regard to the military relationship between South Africa and the West. The organic ties are virtually nonexistent at the present time, after having been virtual allies in past decades. Even the ties between intelligence services have been cut to a large extent, thereby reducing the quality of knowledge of current developments in southern Africa among Western governments. At the same time, South

Africa independently pursues a number of policy courses that the West would wish it to pursue if it were an ally: monitoring Soviet traffic around the Cape of Good Hope, building the armed forces to deter the spread of conventional Soviet forces into the southern African region, and cooperating with a number of American allies around the world (Israel, Iran, Taiwan, etc.). The limited nature of Western military interests in the southern Africa region, however, indicates that the political liabilities of a South African link will continue to outweigh for some time the slight military gains of enlisting South Africa as an active proxy.

In the economic realm, however, South Africa means much more. It is an outpost of orderliness and well-managed enterprises in a region of disorder and highly uncertain political futures. Western businessmen, when faced with the choice of investing in a mismanaged situation such as Zambia, or an orderly economy (with a long-term risk) such as South Africa, tend to pick South Africa. The ability of South Africa to continue to fulfill key economic functions in the region, despite the intense ideological hostility towards it, can be seen in the South African management of Maputo harbor in neighboring Mozambique, in the reopening of the railway between South Africa and Zambia to transport critical goods, and in the continuing violation of the proclaimed OAU economic embargo on South Africa by most of the black-ruled African states. South Africa's role as an economic partner to the West is, naturally, replete with political implications. The rapidly increasing trade deals between Israel and South Africa mean far more than the coal, steel, electronics, and chemicals traded back and forth;[26] the relationship between their respective pariah status and their traditional ties to the West make their association both natural and a net advantage to the Western strategy of maintaining maximum influence abroad.[27] In the wake of the American diplomatic break with Taiwan, one will probably witness a corresponding increase of intensity in relations between Taiwan and South Africa.

Those who have been most hostile toward South Africa among Western government leaders, however, have been those attempting to construct an "Africa policy." Much of the hostility derives from the need for an African policy to meet the perceived needs of the clients—and for that reason, there has been a major effort on the part of the Carter administration to replace South Africa as an American proxy with Nigeria. There is a need in the West to identify those African states that can "lead" the continent, and in that strategy, South Africa clearly does not qualify and will not qualify until it is admitted to the Organization of African Unity. The dictates of an Africa policy imply more than the South African capacity to wage war or raise the gross national product. South Africa will have to meet a criteria for legitimacy, rational or irrational, established by other African states if the United States and other Western states wish to formulate a policy to the region. In the past, the West has thus generally failed to develop an "Africa policy," and it is not clear that present attempts to do so are being successful in furthering Western interests.

The Institutionalization of Strategy

The emergence of debate in the West over the strategic value of South Africa is most vividly illustrated in the attempts to create permanent arrangements that involve South Africa. At one time, the associations with South Africa were clear-cut: South Africa was a member of the Commonwealth, and in that spirit was considered a British client for all intents and purposes. The resignation of South Africa from the Commonwealth in 1960-1961, however, and the interest of the United States in formulating an independent foreign policy in Africa have resulted in a wide range of possibilities being created to express the importance of South Africa.

On the military level, there were in the past expressions of interest in including South Africa in the North Atlantic Treaty Organization, or in the creation of open arrangements between NATO and South Africa regarding the sea lines of communication through the South Atlantic Ocean. They have not come to pass, as other strategies have come to predominate Western thinking.

A more integrated strategy has emerged that centers on the economic ties between South Africa and the West. The importance of South Africa as a producer of important minerals, originally gold and diamonds and now uranium, vanadium, chrome, lithium, and others, has been the spur to the creation of a diffuse strategy that attempts to cover both the present relationship as well as the possible evolution of South African internal politics. The inclusion of South Africa in international gatherings is sought in those areas where it could be a destabilizing force, e.g., the International Atomic Energy Agency, the International Monetary Fund, and the London Nuclear Suppliers' Group. The maintenance of investment and commercial ties with the South African economy is facilitated, through the use of bank loans and links between South African entrepreneurs and Western groups. At the same time, there is a deliberate disassociation from the political goals of the South African government, through such tools as the Sullivan principles, speeches at the United Nations, and public rebukes of South African racial policies made in the media. The strategy, in other words, involves a separation of politics and economics that is difficult to execute. The American political system is better suited than most Western governments to carry out such a strategy: the different executive departments frequently engage in contradictory policies toward foreign countries, with the State Department African Bureau attacking South Africa, the Treasury Department arranging gold sales with South Africa, and the Commerce Department pressing for Ex-Im Bank credits for South Africa. Other Western governments do not have the same degree of internal dissonance, although it still exists. The strategy can be maintained, however, only so long as those internal contradictions are tolerated at the top political levels and by the public.

The other formal strategy is that of total ostracism of South Africa: a consistent, neat, possibly impractical strategy that would have unknown consequences. It embraces all the issues cited in the previous section by simply arguing for a withdrawal from South Africa—certain to precipitate a total collapse—so as to allow the inhabitants of the region to reconstruct a social and political order as they wish, most likely with Soviet-assisted law and order. If South Africa is an unmitigated "evil," so goes this view, the West should have no association with it at all; and the sooner South Africa as we know it perishes, the better for mankind. It is a strategy that sacrifices the present needs of South Africans, and also the material needs of the citizens of Western countries, for the possible emergence of better social order from the ashes.

This last approach illustrates as well the impatience with which many Westerners approach the issue of strategy: take up the sword and slash the Gordian knot that is South Africa. The more patient strategy that urges Westerners to untie the knot, to find the healthy strands of the rope to be saved, is the most difficult process. But South Africa may be, in that fashion, important to Western strategy in the most fundamental way—it may teach Westerners once again that strategy is a long-term process involving consistency of purpose. South Africa could be a lesson for the West that would force it to come to grips with the most difficult issue in foreign policy—for without a strategy, the West will cease to project its influence and become a drifting victim of the turbulent winds of change in southern Africa.

Notes

1. John H. Herz, *The Nation-State and the Crisis of World Politics* (New York: David McKay, 1976).

2. In general, see Daniel O. Graham, *The Crisis in Africa: U.S. Strategy at a Crossroads?* (Washington: University of Miami Center for Advanced International Studies, 1976); and the text of National Security Study Memorandum 39, in Mohamed A. El-Khawas and Barry Cohen, eds., *The Kissinger Study of Southern Africa (Secret)* (Westport, Connecticut: Lawrence Hill, 1976).

3. See Klaus Knorr, "On the International Uses of Military Force in the Contemporary World," *ORBIS* 21 (Spring 1977):5-28.

4. See Robert Strausz-Hupe et al., *A Forward Strategy for America* (New York: Harper and Brothers, 1961).

5. See Saul Mendlovitz, ed., *On the Creation of a Just World Order* (New York: Free Press, 1975). A fine critique of this perspective, described as "radical," exists in James P. O'Leary, "Envisioning Interdependence: Perspectives on Future World Orders," *ORBIS* 22 (Fall 1978): 503-38.

6. Daan Prinsloo, *United States Foreign Policy and the Republic of South Africa* (Pretoria: Foreign Affairs Association, 1978), p. 57.

7. El-Khawas and Cohen, *The Kissinger Study*, p. 81.

8. Jennifer Seymour Whitaker, *Conflict in Southern Africa*, Foreign Policy Association, Headline Series 240 (New York, August 1978), p. 55.

9. Ibid.

10. Allan E. Goodman, "The Threat to the Third World: Mounting Challenge to US and Western Economic Superiority?" Proceedings of the Fifth National Security Affairs Conference (Washington, D.C.: 1978), p. 185.

11. James E. Dornan, "The Strategic Importance of South Africa," in *South Africa—the Vital Link* (Washington, D.C.: Council on American Affairs, 1976), p. 28.

12. Graham, *The Crisis in Africa*, p. 13.

13. Ibid., p. 14.

14. Ibid., p. 15.

15. Ibid., p. 19.

16. Whitaker, *Conflict in Southern Africa*, p. 59.

17. Ibid., p. 62.

18. The details of this episode were leaked to the *Washington Post* by National Security adviser Brzezinski and are drawn from the article for purposes here.

19. For a more extended analysis of this instance, see my "Southern Africa: Testing Détente," in Grayson Kirk and Nils H. Wessell, eds., *The Soviet Threat: Myth and Reality* (New York: Praeger, 1978), pp. 88-98.

20. See Millard Arnold, ed., *Steve Biko: Black Consciousness in South Africa* (New York: Random House, 1978).

21. John de St. Jorre, *A House Divided: South Africa's Uncertain Future* (New York: Carnegie Endowment for International Peace, 1977), p. 130.

22. Ibid.

23. Ibid.

24. Whitaker, *Conflict in Southern Africa*, p. 82.

25. See Raymond D. Gastil, ed., *Freedom in the World: Political Rights and Civil Liberties, 1978* (New York: Freedom House, 1978).

26. St. Jorre, *A House Divided*, pp. 106-08.

27. See my "Africa and the Nations of the Middle East," *Current History* 71 (November 1976):158-60.

10
Conclusion

Richard E. Bissell
Chester A. Crocker

In late 1978, a key American policymaker spoke before an American audience on the subject of South Africa. He asserted there were three "facts" with regard to that troubled country: (1) the problem of racial polarization in South Africa is serious and is growing; (2) change *will* come in South Africa. The welfare of the people there, and American interests, will be profoundly affected by the *way* in which it comes; the question is whether it will be peaceful or not. (3) Our efforts to promote constructive and peaceful change have involved both cooperation and strong differences with South Africa.[1] Because these "facts" have been the litany of American policy for several years, we have not accepted them without question in this volume. The unhappiness of the relationship between South Africa and the world and the very diversity of South African views that are not included in such a trinity formulation suggest that it is necessary to examine other facts of the South Africa political equation for a useful view of the future.

This slim volume, then, has attempted to establish facts of power and political influence from both domestic and international sources, without pretending that they are two discrete categories. The strength of labor unions within South Africa, for instance, has some relationship with the commitment of international unions to having influence in South Africa. Likewise, the role of corporations in the process of integrating South African work places will be, in large part, a result of international pressures placed on those corporations, combined with a testing of South African tolerance for change in the domestic environment. At the same time, many of the domestic political groupings in South Africa are pursuing their own courses, only intermittently drawing upon external sources of power to augment their own influence; many of the black groups, for instance, have followed the example of Mozambique in pursuing essentially self-reliant political power.

The permeability of the domestic-international barrier is important to recognize, particularly as it casts doubt upon the reliability of the "facts" repeated like dogma by external observers. Consider, for instance, the issue of historical inevitability. Change will come in South Africa, of course, just as change permeates the human condition. We know that South Africa will be changing as it moves into the 1980s. But this does not tell us much about how South Africa's complex power equations will actually unfold. Nor does the "fact" of inevitable change establish a clear-cut set of choices for the internal parties most directly concerned—no matter how tempting it may be for outsiders to pose choices in the starkest and most abstract form. To examine another form of inevitability, we also know that change in Africa has been increasingly violent during the 1970s. The trend line, ranging from the quiet, nonviolent decolonization movement of 1960 to guerrilla wars that characterized change in Angola, Mozambique, and Rhodesia, suggests that the prediction of nonviolent change is at best naive; at worst, it is a prelude to abdicating responsibility for the situation in the 1980s.

Is it not naive to assume, as the official Western litany appears to do, that the governing authorities in South Africa are as weary of exercising power as the French, British, and Belgian decolonizers of 1960-1964? Is it not equally naive to assume that the mass of white South Africans are as politically secure—and, hence, fundamentally law-abiding—as the majority of white southerners in the United States in the 1950s and 1960s? The naiveté even extends to the role played by external forces in southern Africa during the 1970s, during which the theme of the OAU Liberation Committee and the Soviet-Cuban forces has been the bankruptcy of peaceful, political change. To establish the basic question as to whether change will "be peaceful or not" is to create an unreal dichotomy. Rapid redistribution of power has rarely occurred peacefully (except where one side simply quit), and force will be necessary in South Africa—whether force exercised by blacks or force exercised by a white government committed to change and to keeping change within restricted bounds "for the welfare of the people there, and American interests." For that reason, the deployment of forces in southern Africa, whether through arms sales, advisers, buildup of military units, or security guarantees through "treaties of friendship," is an indicator of a fundamental historical trend whose implications seem to be ignored by Western observers groping for a cost-free road to acceptable change.

The reasons for the possibly bloody transition to postapartheid society, let alone to an ultimate "solution," are many as we have seen. Not least of these are the potential staying power of the whites in the face of growing pressures and the difficulty of identifying political alternatives that begin to address the fears and demands of the major population groups that must live under any new deal. Looking into the 1980s, the situational pressures behind white political behavior will become increasingly clear. All forms of change, including the current incremental evolution taking place behind the rigid façade of apartheid, will have an impact on white living conditions and standards. The timing and degree of change will hinge on the economic possibilities of accelerating black (i.e., African, Coloured, and Asian) participation while also addressing the threat faced by whites unable to compete in an egalitarian job market or to emigrate.

At first glance, this calculation suggests the inevitability of protracted bloodshed. Yet it must also be recognized that whites are not the only people trapped in this situation. Relatively few South Africans of any race have the option to emigrate or the ability to forego involvement in the day-to-day operation of the socioeconomic system. External economic pressures (including possible capital or trade sanctions) may destroy the traditional liberal dream of resolving black aspirations peacefully through economic growth. But the majorities of all races will have to live, eat, and work in what remains of the society whether it is relatively peaceful or relatively violent. Before the black population groups are able to bargain effectively, it may first be necessary for them to gain a far greater stake in the economy, the political system, and the bureaucracies now so clearly dominated by whites.

The perceived prelude to disaster in South Africa is based upon the first "fact" mentioned above, causing many outsiders to prepare mentally for abdicating responsibility. The "degree" of racial polarization in South Africa cannot be documented, as demonstrated in essays in this volume on both white and black opinion in South Africa. It may be that an assessment of South Africa as increasingly polarized is a projection of the observer's own experiences elsewhere; it may be an attempt to simplify the South African situation for outsiders in terms that make sense to a European or American audience. The essays here indicate that political power and activity in South Africa has certainly become increasingly *fragmented*, which is an entirely different condition than being polarized.

White politics are fragmented along several lines, both within and outside the National party, as whites consider a variety of avenues for controlled change. Afrikaner tribal solidarity and the interplay of contending bureaucratic interests postpone a significant white political realignment that is built into the white social structure. The vision of an inevitable and growing polarization depends on the continuation of the political stalemate within Afrikanerdom. We see no reason to assume its indefinite continuation.

Politically, the Coloured and Asian communities include activist radicals who seek to develop a bargaining position simultaneously on their black and white flanks, using whatever levers are available. This explains the growth of a black orientation that rejects participation in established institutions prior to the holding of a national convention to negotiate a new order. But there is an equal, if not greater, number of ambivalent fence sitters in both communities, to say nothing of a bitter but still apathetic mass of people who do not yet appear to believe in the political kingdom. The African population offers similar evidence of fragmentation. However radicalized the exiles and the young urban leadership—and however pervasive the leftward momentum of their thinking—these trends reflect the stalemated political conditions and socioeconomic structures of a

South Africa still governed on Verwoerdian principles. Active and latent divisions among Africans rival those seen in the Rhodesian conflict, and they are no longer simply ethnic in character.

The sophistication of political thinking among the increasingly educated elites in both white and nonwhite populations has caused them to consider the fundamental questions of political change and the importance of that process of change for the shape of South Africa's future. Realignment based on individual and group interests and power, complicated by ethnicity and language issues and the republic's vast geography, could overturn the truisms of polarization as events push political elites into a postapartheid future.

If outsiders suggest to South Africans, however, that the only political division that makes sense is a racial one, those South Africans who wish to draw upon external resources will cast their commitment in racial terms. There are many political leaders in South Africa ready to examine the divisions of their society in nonracial terms; if they are abandoned by those outside South Africa, they will surely be destroyed by internal war. Those who predicted a cataclysmic race war will have their satisfaction surely as they helped to bring it about. The fundamental process occurring in South Africa, however, is not that racial division so frequently discussed, but rather the emergence of that natural spectrum of political forces that occurs in any society with a degree of liberty of expression. Just as human nature varies widely, so there will be a spread of opinion in South Africa in both white and black groups with regard to the use of force, the need for self-reliance, the degree of trust in people from different linguistic or cultural backgrounds, and the manner of governing the common wealth. Each of these viewpoints is being expressed today, whether at home or in exile; the fact that they are being reported and communicated is a healthy sign. A parallel could be drawn to the reporting of crime rates: an increase can mean an increase in crime, but more commonly it means an increase in the willingness of people to speak out and report the crimes. The increasingly outspoken involvement of all races in political debate can be seen as constructive or destructive. Much depends upon the listener and his capacity to interpret the significance of what is said in its local political context.

Thus we have chosen to spend much space in this volume on the nature of the listener abroad. The interstices of power between domestic and international actors are becoming more prominent all the time, particularly as the opening of South African society has increased. The uncertainty of the white community and the restlessness of the black community have caused them to look abroad for political formulations. To the extent that outsiders agree to suggest or recommend blueprints, they thereby acquire responsibility in an internationalized bargaining situation, whether they realize it or not. Thus, external decision makers and opinion molders are coming ever closer to the day when they must choose whether they wish to carry the responsibility of involvement in South African affairs. It is clear that some external sources of power are not particularly interested in the resolution of South African domestic problems. Their main concern is with the Soviet-American rivalry, with their own domestic political survival, with smoothing diplomatic relations with black-ruled African states, with protecting their economic interests via the instruments of trade and investment, or with any other abstraction that tends to ignore the realities in South Africa. Those whose real concern is elsewhere, however, have the ability to transfer influence to certain parties in the South African environment and thereby decisively alter the outcome in that country. Such is a natural process of international politics; most international actors exploit foreign situations for their own needs or interests. If, however, the historical momentum in southern Africa suggests that force will be needed to resolve South Africa's future, it is clear that some political groups will have greater influence than others. Likewise, the acceptance of a racial division as the basis of South African politics will have implications both for the influence of predominantly white societies abroad and for various disputes within societies abroad over the allocation of power and social welfare.

The implications for the republic of the rapidly moving situations in Namibia and Rhodesia/Zambabwe must also be factored into the equation. The range of possibilities is awesome but the likelihood of a profound impact appears certain. The eventual advent of more or less legitimate black governments in Windhoek and Salisbury will further erode the political and strategic position Pretoria has faced since the loss of its Portuguese buffers in 1974-1975. The loss of geopolitical maneuvering room will occur when there is an end to distracting crises beyond the republic's own borders; isolation will increase and timetables will be foreshortened. However adept Pretoria's leaders may become at influencing neighboring African political and economic forces—through aid, investment, diplomacy, intervention, and subversion—the probability of hostile regimes developing on its borders is obvious. Sooner or later, some or all adjacent states may be prepared to pay the price of outright hostility toward the republic in terms of conventional, guerrilla, or economic warfare. Since that price will be high for them, the likelihood of competitive outside involvement will remain high as well. Consequently, both South and southern Africa appear destined to become an internationalized battleground. No local or external party is likely to monopolize the direction of conflict in the region or to shield itself effectively from the interconnectedness of South and southern Africa. But this view may overlook certain benefits flowing to South African decision makers from a clear-cut resolution of neighboring conflicts over the transition to African rule. In military terms, lines of defense will be shorter, threats clarified, and doctrinal coherence more likely. The focus of effort need no longer be dissipated among a range of hypothetical scenarios. The advantages of geographically finite defense will replace the uncertainties of Pretoria's current exposure to the risk of distant engagements—explicit or implicit—on behalf of minorities and transitional regimes beyond its borders. The purely defensive stance of a sovereign state maintaining internal order and territorial integrity offers diplomatic and legal advantages, as well as military and economic ones, over the current exposed position. Although outsiders will now be free to turn their attention toward South Africa itself, Pretoria will no longer have to live with the responsibility for fragile transitions in two other territories.

Of course, if matters were so simple, Pretoria might already have moved to cut its entanglements in nearby transition struggles. But South Africa continues to face complex trade-offs in these conflicts: domestic political reasons produce an inability to act, or to be seen to act, in ways that undercut the position of Namibian or Rhodesian whites; the need to avoid future political debacles along Angolan lines; the desire to forestall the emergence of hostile regimes or regimes dependent for their survival on the Communist powers; the wish for continued lines of influence and dependency with neighboring territories after Africans take over; the desire to avoid a rupture with the West and, if possible, to obtain Western involvement in stabilizing the region; and the necessity of demonstrating resolve and strength without incurring open-ended military responsibilities for the maintenance of a new order. The republic did not "cause" the transition conflicts to which it is now a party; but it is inescapably a decisive factor in their evolution. At the same time, Western action (or inaction) will also be of critical importance, not least for the lessons South Africans draw from the experience.

The governing whites will reflect upon the Namibian and Rhodesian transition episodes for evidence of Western interest in minority rights, Western readiness to compete with Moscow and Havana for influence in adjacent black states, and Western willingness to stand by commitments made even when it produces domestic strain or African displeasure. If Western actions confirm white South African suspicions of perfidy—the main lesson apparently derived from the Angolan fiasco—one can expect a reduced readiness in Pretoria to tolerate Western involvement in its internal affairs and a less reasoned approach in handling domestic issues. If outsiders are written off by the whites, in other words, it may be in part because outsiders failed to listen to all South Africans in the preceding period. Similarly, a failure by the United States and Europe to sustain fragile, moderate forces in such places as Botswana, Zambia, Rhodesia, and Namibia may undermine military restraint in Pretoria. A converse set of lessons may be drawn by the black communities of South Africa, fostering indigenous support for moderate or radicalized goals and tactics. There are organic connections between the conflicts of southern Africa and these

derive ultimately from the uncertain relationship of South
Africa with the West.

Finally, this volume has implicitly sought to analyze the implications of countries such as the United States, Nigeria, the
Soviet Union, and others attempting to universalize their ideals
in an environment as distant as South Africa. Many political
leaders attempt to pursue their humanistic goals in a foreign
envrionment when the political costs of doing so at home would
be too great. No country is exempt from this practice, making
South Africa one of the great battlegrounds (ideologically, and
perhaps militarily) of the 1980s. In that process of universalization, the greatest risk is not "losing" South Africa—for geographic, strategic, and material interests do change over time—
but that we shall have ignored more than we have heard. South
Africans, black and white, have a future to negotiate in the
1980s, and the external world could all too easily rob them of
the opportunity to control their own future.

Note

1. Anthony Lake, director of the Policy Planning Staff, U.S. State
Department, "American Policy toward South Africa" (Speech before the
Africa Conference, San Francisco, October 31, 1978).

Further Readings

Adam, Heribert. *Modernizing Racial Domination: South Africa's Political Dynamics.* Berkeley: University of California Press, 1971.

——. *South Africa: Sociological Perspectives.* London: Oxford University Press, 1971.

Barber, James. *South Africa's Foreign Policy: 1945-1970.* London: Oxford University Press, 1973.

Barratt, John; Brand, Simon; Collier, David S.; and Glaser, Kurt; eds. *Accelerated Developments in Southern Africa.* London: Macmillan Press, 1974.

Bell, Trevor. *Industrial Decentralization in South Africa.* Cape Town: Oxford University Press, 1975.

Bissell, Richard E. *Apartheid and International Organizations.* Boulder, Colo.: Westview Press, 1977.

Breitenbach, J. J., ed. *South Africa in the Modern World (1910-1970).* Pietermaritzburg: Shuter and Shooter, 1971.

Buthelezi, M. G. *White and Black Nationalism, Ethnicity, and the Future of the Homelands.* Johannesburg: South African Institute of Race Relations, 1974.

Butler, Jeffrey; Rotberg, Robert I.; and Adams, John. *The Black Homelands of South Africa: The Political and Economic Development of Bophuthatswana and Kwa Zulu.* Berkeley: University of California Press, 1977.

Carter, G. M., and O'Meara, Patrick, eds. *Southern Africa: The Continuing Crisis.* Bloomington: Indiana University Press, 1979.

Cervenka, Zdenek, and Rogers, Barbara. *The Nuclear Axis:*

Secret Collaboration between West Germany and South Africa. New York: Time Books, 1978.

Christie, M. J., *The Simonstown Agreements: Britain's Defense and the Sale of Arms to South Africa.* London: Africa Bureau, 1970.

Clifford-Vaughan, F. McA., ed. *International Pressures and Political Change in South Africa.* New York: Oxford University Press, 1978.

Cockram, Gail. *Vorster's Foreign Policy.* Pretoria: Academica, 1970.

Davidson, Basil; Slovo, Joe; and Wilkinson, Anthony R. *Southern Africa: The New Politics of Revolution.* London: Penguin, 1976.

De Villers, Andre, ed. *English-speaking South Africa Today: Proceeding of the National Conference, July 1974.* Cape Town: Oxford University Press, 1976.

Dugard, John. *Human Rights and the South African Legal Order.* Princeton, N.J.: Princeton University Press, 1978.

Duggan, William Redman. *A Socioeconomic Profile of South Africa.* New York: Praeger, 1973.

Du Toit, Andre. *Federalism and Political Change in South Africa.* Durban, 1974.

El-Khawas, Mohamed A., and Cohen, Barry, eds. *The Kissinger Study of Southern Africa: National Security Study Memorandum 39.* Westport, Conn.: Lawrence Hill, 1976.

El-Khawas, Mohamed A., and Kornegay, Frances A., Jr. *American-Southern African Relations: Bibliographical Essays.* Westport, Conn.: Greenwood Press, 1975.

First, Ruth; Steele, Jonathan; and Gurney, Christabel. *The South African Connection: Western Investment in Apartheid.* New York: Barnes and Noble, 1973.

Gerhart, Gail M. *Black Power in South Africa.* Berkeley: University of California Press, 1978.

Gervasi, Sean. *Industrialization, Foreign Capital and Forced Labour in South Africa.* New York: U.N. Unit on Apartheid, 1970.

Gibson, R. *African Liberation Movements: Contemporary Struggles against White Minority Rule.* London: Oxford University Press, 1972.

Grundy, Kenneth W. *Confrontation and Accommodation in Southern Africa: The Limits of Independence.* Berkeley: University of California Press, 1973.

——. *Guerilla Struggle in Africa—An Analysis and Preview.* New York: World Law Fund, 1971.

Hall, Richard. *The High Price of Principles: Kaunda and the White South.* New York: Africana Publishing, 1970.

Hoagland, Jim. *South Africa: Civilizations in Conflict.* Boston: Houghton Mifflin, 1972.

Horrell, Muriel. *The African Homelands of South Africa.* Johannesburg: South African Institute of Race Relations, 1973.

Houghton, D. Hobart. *The South African Economy.* 5th ed. New York: Oxford University Press, 1976.

Houser, George M. *United States Policy and Southern Africa.* New York: Africa Fund, 1974.

Karis, Thomas. "South African Black Organizations and Their Demands and Aims." Paper delivered at the Conference on Urban Conflict and Change in South Africa, Department of State, Washington, D.C., April 28-29, 1977.

Kitchen, Helen, ed. *A Symposium on Where Is South Africa Headed? Options for Americans.* Mount Kisco, New York: Seven Springs Center, 1979.

Klare, Michael T. *U.S. Arms Deliveries to South Africa: The Italian Connection.* TNI Special Report. Washington, D.C.: Transnational Institute, 1977.

Klerk, W. A. de. *The Puritans in Africa: A Story of Afrikanerdom.* London: Rex Collings, 1975.

Kortzé, D. A. *African Politics in South Africa, 1964-1974.* London: St. Martin's Press, 1975.

Legum, Colin. *Vorster's Gamble for Africa: How the Search for Peace Failed.* New York: Africana Publishing, 1976.

Leistner, G. M. E. *South Africa's Development Aid to African States.* Occasional Paper no. 28. Pretoria: Africa Institute of South Africa, 1970.

Lever, Henry. *South African Society.* Johannesburg: Jonathan Ball, 1978.

Liff, David M. *U.S. Business in South Africa: Pressures from the Home Front.* Washington, D.C.: Investor Responsibility

Research Center, 1978.

Mackler, I. *Pattern for Profit in Southern Africa*. New York: Atheneum, 1975.

Mayer, Philip. *Urban Africans and the Bantustans*. Johannesburg: Oxford University Press, 1972.

Mazrui, A., and Patel, H., eds. *Africa in World Affairs: The Next Thirty Years*. New York: Third Press, 1973.

Minty, Abdul. *South Africa's Defense Strategy*. London: Anti-Apartheid Movement, 1973.

Molteno, R. *Africa and South Africa: The Implications of South Africa's "Outward Looking" Policy*. London: Africa Bureau, 1971.

Moody, T. Dunbar. *The Rise of Afrikanerdom*. Berkeley: University of California Press, 1975.

Morrel, James, and Gisselquist, David. *How the IMF Slipped $464 Million to South Africa*. Special Report. Washington, D.C.: Center for International Policy, 1978.

Motlhabi, Mokgethi, ed. *Essays on Black Theology*. Johannesburg: University Christian Movement, 1972.

Mugomba, Agrippah T. *The Foreign Policy of Despair: Africa and the Sale of Arms to South Africa*. Nairobi: East African Literature Bureau, 1977.

Nedbank Group. *South Africa: An Appraisal—The Sovereign Risk Criteria*. Johannesburg: Nedbank Group Economic Unit, 1977.

Ngubane, Jordan K. *An African Explains Apartheid*. London: Pall Mall, 1963.

Nolutshungu, Sam C. *South Africa: A Study of Ideology and Foreign Policy*. New York: Africana, Publishing 1975.

Nyathi, R. *South African Imperialism in Southern Africa*. Dakar: ECA Institute for Planning and Economic Development, 1974.

Oudes, Bruce. *A Symposium on South Africa: Issues and Policy Implications for the United States*. Mount Kisco, N.Y.: Seven Springs Center, 1978.

Potholm, P., and Dale, R., eds. *Southern Africa in Perspective*. New York: Free Press, 1972.

Randall, Peter, ed. *Directions of Change in South African Politics*. Johannesburg: SPROCAS, 1971.

Rhoodie, N. J., ed. *Southern African Dialogue: Contrasts in South African Thinking on Basic Race Issues.* Johannesburg: McGraw-Hill, 1972.

Rogers, Barbara. *Divide and Rule, South Africa's Bantustans.* London: International Defense and Aid Fund, 1976.

———. *South Africa's Stake in Britain.* London: Africa Bureau, 1971.

———. *White Wealth and Black Poverty: American Investments in Southern Africa.* Westport, Conn.: Greenwood Press, 1976.

Royal United Services Institute. *The Security of the Southern Oceans—Southern Africa the Key.* London: RUSI, 1972.

Sachs, Albie. *Justice in South Africa.* Berkeley: University of California Press, 1973.

St. Jorre, John de. *A House Divided: South Africa's Uncertain Future.* New York: Carnegie Endowment for International Peace, 1977.

Schlemmer, Lawrence. "Theories of the Plural Society and Change in South Africa." *Social Dynamics* (University of Cape Town) 3, no. 1 (June 1977).

Schuettinger, Robert L., ed. *South Africa—The Vital Link.* Washington, D.C.: Council on American Affairs, 1976.

Seidman, Ann, and Seidman, Neva. *South African and U.S. Multinational Corporations.* Westport, Conn.: Lawrence Hill, 1978.

Seiler, John. *U.S. Foreign Policy toward Southern Africa: Continuity and Change.* Johannesburg: South African Institute of International Affairs, 1973.

Seymour, S. M. *Bantu Law in South Africa.* Capetown: Juta and Co., 1970.

SIPRI. *Southern Africa: The Escalation of a Conflict, A Political-Military Study.* New York: Praeger, 1976.

South African Institute of Race Relations. *A Survey of Race Relations in South Africa 1977.* Johannesburg: SAIRR, 1978.

Spence, J. E., *The Strategic Significance of Southern Africa.* London: Royal United Services Institutions, 1970.

Starcke, Anna. *Survival: Taped Interviews with South Africa's Power Elite.* Cape Town: Tafelberg, 1978.

Steward, Alexander. *The World, the West and Pretoria.* New

York: David McKay, 1977.

Thompson, Leonard, and Butler, Jeffrey, eds. *Change in Contemporary South Africa*. Berkeley: University of California Press, 1975.

Vandenbosch, A. *South Africa and the World: The Foreign Policy of Apartheid*. Lexington: University of Kentucky Press, 1970.

van Rensburg, W. C. J., and Pretorius, D. A. *South Africa's Strategic Minerals: Pieces on a Continental Chess Board*. Johannesburg: Valiant Publishers, 1977.

Walshe, A. P. *The Rise of African Nationalism in South Africa: The African National Congress, 1912-1952*. Berkeley: Univeristy of California Press, 1971.

Weyl, Nathaniel. *Traitors End: The Rise and Fall of the Communist Movement in Southern Africa*. New York, 1971.

Wilson, Monica, and Thompson, Leonard. *Oxford History of South Africa*. Vol. 2 (1870-1966). New York: Oxford University Press, 1971.

Worrall, Denis, ed. *South Africa: Government and Politics*. Pretoria: J. L. van Schaik, 1971.

Index

DUE DATE

	DEC 1 0 REC'D		
FEB 18 2013			
	201-6503		Printed in USA